PUBLIC SECRETS AND JUSTICE

GM

FRIENDS
BOOK
EXCHANGE

Illustration by Sonja Lamut

Pima Monthly Meeting

ABOUT THE AUTHOR

Laura Melvin was appointed as Circuit Judge by the Governor of Florida to fill the unexpired term of a judge who was killed in an accident; she was then re-elected twice to that position. She served as a judge for 10 years sitting in each of the divisions of Circuit Court: Criminal (felonies that include serious drug crimes, burglary, rape, and murder), Juvenile (children who have been abused or neglected and those charged with a crime), Family (divorce, custody, child support), Civil (personal injury and wrongful death, contract, business, etc.), and Probate (wills and trusts). She taught in the Florida Advanced Judicial College and the New Judges' College and wrote a bench book for judges on Juvenile Law. A graduate of Florida State College of Law, she practiced law for 10 years before going on the Bench.

In her retirement she enjoys traveling extensively in her RV. While on the Bench, Laura began skydiving, completing 600 jumps. More recently she has become an avid motorcyclist. She is an instructor with the Motorcycle Safety Foundation and has published several articles with *Rider Magazine*, including "4 Corners 4 Kids" in the June 2013 issue that describes her 13,000 mile solo ride on a Goldwing around the four geographic corners of the United States to raise awareness of and money for four child-focused charities.

See her Facebook page for that ride at 4 Corners 4 Kids.
Your comments are welcomed on her blog
www.gypsyjudge.com
For more information and to order autographed copies
visit the author's website
www. LauraMelvin.net

PUBLIC SECRETS AND JUSTICE

Journal of a Circuit Court Judge

Laura Melvin, Circuit Judge - Retired

"What doth the Lord require of thee, but to do justly, and to love mercy, and to walk humbly with thy God?" Micah 6:8

Shayna Publishing, Inc

Shayna Publishing, Inc
6223 Highway 90 #200
Milton, FL 32570
www.GypsyJudge.com
ShaynaPublishing@Gmail.com
www.lauramelvin.com

Cover Design: Ballinger Publishing, Pensacola, FL
Interior Design: Ballinger Publishing, Pensacola, FL
Cover photos: Documented Modern Photography,
Hara Gabrielle, Pensacola, FL

ISBN-10 0989497305
ISBN-13 978-0-9894973-0-5
LCCN 201390992

ACKNOWLEDGMENTS

I am grateful for the support and encouragement of many people who prodded me until I completed this work. A special thank you to Michael McMillan, a blunt and honest friend with a great eye and enough patience to read multiple rewrites. I received invaluable help from Ellen Goldstein and Judith Geary, as well as other editing comments from Maria Krenz, Molly Baker, and Bob Niemela. Bob Ray and Jack Remick have variously lead, pushed, and taunted me to continue. Jentel Artist Residency Program in Banner, Wyoming, provided beautiful, quiet space so that I could begin. At Jentel I became friends with Elizabeth Gilbert, who insisted I get it done, or as she says, "Just put the kid on the bus, Laura!" A special thank you to Pierre A. Lehu for believing in me and offering wide-ranging assistance.

This is not a compilation of newspaper articles or an analysis of the Law, nor is it a report of my genealogy. I write through the lens of my memories, personal thoughts, and feelings. Yet I know that memory can be an unreliable shape-shifter. In telling my stories, I do not pretend to have the only version or interpretation of yesteryear; my lens may not produce the same picture or story as yours. In Alcoholics Anonymous they say, "Take what you like and leave the rest."

Walt Whitman, in his introduction to the 1855 edition of *Leaves of Grass*, said, "... reexamine all you have been told at school or church or in any book, dismiss whatever insults your own soul..."

Contents

PUBLIC SECRETS AND JUSTICE

"In spite of everything, I still believe that people are really good at heart." Anne Frank 1929 - 1945

PREFACE

This book is dedicated to Autumn, a little girl who at age four was kicked to death by her stepfather. A little girl whom I came to know because I was the Judge for her murder trial. A little girl who, after all these years, continues to prod me with her memory and her lessons.

I write to share glimpses of humanity and lessons learned from Autumn and other amazing people I met through the legal system. There are no composites, no fictionalized personas here. I've changed names, but their stories are so strong, I dare not alter them. I also tell you something of my life as a female in the Deep South and my professional struggles "to do justly." There are many interpretations of "justice," and I hope to challenge the certainty of your own definition.

Over time I saw more and more of the underbelly of humanity and our legal system, and it became more challenging to focus on the positive. Though I became more efficient in the "administration of justice," it became harder to hide behind the robe and more difficult to ignore the cataclysmic impact of my orders on the fundamental lives of others. I learned to protect myself from the sea of humanity by acting hardened and cynical, but found I didn't like the person I had become. I also experienced a growing and irreverent desire to travel now, not later–a yearning that sunk deep, past all my rational goals and ambitions to land on a tiny patch of rebellious, fun-loving, adventuresome, freedom-seeking soil deep in my soul. And there it began to grow.

Finally I came to know that I simply could not stay on the Bench; I had to leave though I didn't really know what that meant. No one walks away from such a position of power and prestige–not early–not without secure financial footing. But I did, anyway. In these pages, I describe only my experience. My stories may or may not ring true for others, particularly other judges and lawyers.

Children's books of puzzles and games often include a page of "Find the hidden objects." The child is to find the rainbow, lollipop, ball glove, fireman, train, and horse hidden in plain view by a couple of hundred other objects, people, and animals.

I invite you to read as though this book were a page of "Find the hidden objects." Can you find the courage, hope, love, forgiveness, kindness, and commitment? They are each there, hidden in plain view among pain, violence, control, deceit, betrayal, mean-spiritedness, and aggression. I confess that as I worked in this kaleidoscope of humanity, at times I just couldn't see those hidden virtues and the darkness seem to win. Yet those characteristics which make us a better people are there. To find them, we need to remember what we're looking for.

CHAPTER 1.
MORE THAN ONE THING CAN BE TRUE:
Appearances, secrets, and ceremony

After Mother's funeral in 1999, we added her date of death to their double headstone–the one that marks the spot where neither of my parents is buried. A monument to paradox. Soon we had two boxes of ashes and another family secret.

Five years earlier a large crowd had come to the same small cemetery to pay their last respects to my father, Judge Woodrow Melvin, a man known for his wisdom and kindness. People parked close to the graves of friends or strangers, beside cedar trees, live oaks, magnolias, or azaleas; they walked across the sand to the Melvin family plot where Dad's parents and grandparents, as well as several brothers, aunts, and uncles are buried.

I couldn't breathe as I watched the pallbearers carefully remove Dad's coffin from the hearse and place it on a wheeled gurney at the center of a small semi-circle of chairs set up for the family. I was on emotional autopilot, hoping to make it through this very public ceremony of my private grief. Under the coffin was the familiar blanket of green artificial turf. As I moved to join the family, I looked around discretely. There was no mound of dirt nearby. A small smile brushed across my face, and I took a deep breath.

In the Baptist tradition, the casket was not lowered into the ground as part of the graveside ceremony. When the preacher concluded, the crowd left. The men from the funeral home waited. Only the immediate family knew what would happen next.

Dad wanted to be cremated, but in this northwest Florida community people were buried because–well, because it's always been done that way. End of discussion. The rural church Mom and Dad occasionally attended echoed their Baptist upbringings, and they particularly enjoyed the old hymns. Being where you've been before can be comforting. My parents also held a broad view of a loving God, one not so tightly confined by tradition and ceremony. Yet Mom didn't want to try to explain Dad's decision. Nor did she want to create a stir or diminish Dad's image in the eyes of those securely bound to the church and not comfortable outside the confines of the familiar box.

So the men from the funeral home waited until the coast was clear; then they put Dad back in the hearse and returned him to the funeral home to be cremated. The preacher didn't know. No one knew except the immediate family and the funeral home. And we're good at keeping family secrets.

Later Kim, one of the adult grandchildren, said, "Grandma, I want to go to the cemetery and put flowers on Granddaddy's grave." Mom responded carefully, "You know, honey, he's not really there." Kim answered, "I know, Grandma, but I still want to leave some flowers."

Five years later, at the age of 85, Mom died at home looking out across Blackwater Bay; she had just finished sampling chicken wings my brother Jim was cooking for a party. Jim explained, "Mom said she wants a funeral just like Dad's." I sputtered, "Just like Dad's?" "Yes," he repeated, "just like Dad's." And so we did. Back at the Melvin plot in the Milton Cemetery, I watched as the pallbearers unloaded Mom's casket and placed it on the wheeled gurney at the base of the large double headstone. I ducked my head and let out a quiet sigh of loss, pain, love, memories, and hope. Below the casket was green artifical turf. I furtively scanned the area; there was no mound of dirt nearby. After the graveside service, Butch, a close family friend, stood quietly beside Mom's casket. Butch had worked with Dad for years and was known for her high energy, quick laugh, and unshakeable loyalty to him. She was close to my mom and good friends with my sisters and me. She had obviously heard the story of Dad's funeral, for she caught my eye with a raised eyebrow that seemed to ask, "Did you do it again?" I smiled ever so slightly and nodded, yes. She lowered her head, as though in prayerful remembrance;

then she slowly moved her right foot under the casket and patted the astro turf. It was firm ground; Mom's grave had not been dug. Butch looked back at me, her eyes twinkling. I shrugged with a small grin and quickly turned my head.

After the services, the men from the funeral home waited until the coast was clear. Then they put Mom back in the hearse and whisked her away to the funeral home to be cremated. Again, the preacher didn't know. No one knew except the immediate family and the funeral home. Then we added her date of death to their double headstone, together with the Dag Hammarskjold quote she requested. Engraved in black letters across the back of the otherwise traditional pillar, the gravestone that marks the place where neither of my parents are buried, are the words: "For all that has been, thanks. For all that is to come, yes."

Mom wanted their ashes mixed together and then spread over their property on Blackwater Bay. We decided to have the ashes ceremony on Valentine's Day because everyone was not available January 1, our parents' wedding anniversary.

I took the two boxes of ashes out on my back porch and returned to get a five-gallon bucket from the garage and a long-handled spoon from the kitchen. Cremation produces a silvery gray powder peppered with white particles of bone and teeth. A human body generates a surprising amount of volume; much of that volume is fine, like cake flour. The ashes blew around easily. They were not dirty, slimy, or otherwise repulsive, but it was hard to get my head around the reality that this was the incinerated remains of my parents. Though it was a little disorienting, I had work to do, so I began by alternately dumping some of Mom, some of Dad, some of Mom, some of Dad into the five-gallon bucket. Then I used the long-handled spoon and stirred them together as best I could.

When I finished mixing the ashes, I looked like Pig Pen in the Peanuts cartoon; a layer of fine powder covered me and everything around me. I sneezed several times as I brushed Mom and Dad off my jeans and sweatshirt, then I swept some of them through the boards on my patio. They didn't seem to mind. Next I turned on the hose at the edge of the house and washed Mom and Dad off my face and hands. There were still lots of ashes left to spread at the Bay.

Mom had pasted an eight-by-ten-foot color map of the world to a wall in their bedroom with pins marking who had traveled where. She loved to study maps. She loved to travel, though she'd done very little. She was curious about almost everything. And there were so many ashes. I knew she'd like my idea.

My sister-in-law Jackie was helping, and we put a dollop of ashes in the center of a couple dozen square pieces of purple cloth and tied them closed with a ribbon—something like the small bag of rice passed out at weddings. Then we carefully arranged the purple bags on two serving trays. We had a large volume of ashes to spread at the ceremony and small bags for whoever wanted to take Mom and Dad with them, to scatter in multiple beautiful places.

Cooking has never fascinated me. I cook because I'm hungry and am grateful to clean up the kitchen when someone else prepares the meal. But I decided to fix a family tradition—crab gumbo (blue crab, shrimp, chicken and dark roux, over white rice)—and serve it after the ashes ceremony. My silent memorial. I'd often watched Mom prepare gumbo, but I'd never tried it. She didn't use a recipe; she just dumped, and it always turned out right. My impression was it was time-consuming, and the roux seemed mysterious.

Mom cooked for a large family, and I don't think she knew how to cook a little bit of anything. She always cooked gumbo by the gallons. She had a special pot for gumbo that was so deep she had to stand on a stool to stir. But now it was my turn. Standing on her stool in my kitchen, I added all the ingredients into her pot. The roux wasn't as complicated as I thought, and somehow everything blended to taste just like Mom's. Jackie was stirring the pot when I came in from the patio. The devil got the best of me, or was it Mom and Dad egging me on? Mom, Dad, and I had lived a life of structure and propriety, carefully weighing and considering each move and word. Yet without giving it a second thought, I took the spoon from Jackie and plopped a tablespoon of ash into the gumbo. It seemed like an inside joke from Mom and Dad, "There! Lighten up, Laura. You don't have to take this so seriously." Then I stirred and swore Jackie to secrecy.

The cremation remained a secret, so only the family gathered at the Bay to spread their ashes. I brought rose petals to drop with the ashes and several readings to insure everyone was included in the ceremony. It was a respectful time of remembering, one also marked with laughter. Afterwards we ate gumbo and rice, with pulled pork my brother made. When they left, everyone took some of Mom and Dad with them.

I was born in 1947 in Milton, Florida, in the same bedroom my father was born in, in the house his father built. I lived in that home until age 12 when we moved to the house on Blackwater Bay. I didn't leave Milton until I went to law school in Tallahassee at the age of 30. I was raised in the Deep South on Southern Baptist religiosity, fried mullet, grits, raw oysters, and fresh field peas. I was assigned the role of female, which meant I was supposed to be soft-spoken, subservient, and acquiescent. I could be a tomboy but I was to be responsible. I could be intelligent but not smart-mouthed. As I matured, my ambitions were to remain tapped down into the box of traditional roles: dutiful daughter, wife, mother, responsible one. If I worked outside the home, my choices would be as a helpmate; I could be a secretary, teacher, or nurse. Education was encouraged, curiosity rewarded.

But this world of assigned roles, paradox, and family secrets keeps changing.

"When your ship, long moored in harbour, gives you the illusion of being a house... put out to sea! Save your boat's journeying soul, and your own pilgrim soul, cost what it may."
Dom Helder Camara, former Archbishop of Brazil

LEAVING

After 10 years as a Circuit Judge[1], 10 years as a lawyer, and 53 years as a dutiful daughter–I resigned. I sent that easy-to-imagine-but-difficult-to-send letter to the boss, the Governor of Florida, telling him not to send me any more of those big pay checks. There were many reasons to stay–the prestige, power, money, and security; and then there's the opportunity to listen deeply to ordinary people and stay up late at night struggling to earn their trust and balance justice with mercy. I had two years left on my second six-year term on the Bench, so there was nothing pushing. There was no reason to leave, except that I had to, really. I had to find out if there is life after law. I had to know if this legal world is all that I am.

For a number of years, my work as a Judge went well. It was intellectually challenging and personally rewarding, though at times difficult. Then I started skydiving, and this unconventional and experiential pastime on the weekends began to mess with all my expectations and beliefs–several hundred times I proved it wasn't true that I cannot jump out of a perfectly good airplane. As I repeatedly launched my smiling self into open air two miles above the earth, it felt like I was jumping over a jumble of rigid rules. And I began to wonder, what else isn't true?

Then I bought a 5th wheel–an RV trailer that attaches to a large hitch in the bed of the pickup rather than hooking onto the bumper. I took some solo trips, hoping that would assuage a

---

[1]A Circuit Judge handles Criminal cases involving crimes punishable by state prison (from grand theft auto as a less menacing crime and moving up through serious drug offenses, robbery, rape, and murder); Civil cases involving more than $15,000 in dispute (serious personal injury, medical malpractice, contract disputes, etc.); Probate (wills, trusts, guardianships, competency issues); Family law (divorces, custody, child support, visitation, alimony); and Juvenile (Dependency – children who have been abused or neglected, and Delinquency – children accused or convicted of crimes.)

growing compulsion to hit the road. It didn't.

In my own way, I had become the rhinestone cowboy in Glenn Campbell's song. I'd worked long and hard; I'd paid my dues. Instead of being in his "star spangled rodeo," I was in the legal spotlight doing complex work. Yet I also felt like Wile E. Coyote in the Roadrunner, for I'd run off a high ledge in pursuit of success. And though I'd accomplished more than I could have imagined at age 20, in my early 50's I'd become restless and unhappy; rather than feeling content, I was challenging the importance of pretty much everything in my life. And as crazy as it sounded, it felt more and more like the only way to find out if I belonged in the legal world was to leave. Leave it all.

One day, I bought a four-place setting of dishes for the RV and thought, "Four is enough of anything." So I made up a new rule to live by–The Rule of Fours. It didn't matter what the question was, the answer was "Four or less." How many pairs of shoes or jeans did I need? Four or less. What about sheets, glasses, forks, coffee cups, or towels? Four or less. Applying this new Rule, I rented a garage apartment, sold my 2,000 square foot house on 20 acres and began to give away everything I owned that violated My Rule. My only child, Clay, was married, gainfully employed, and owned a nice house. When I told him my new rule, he rolled his eyes and declined my offer to give him everything I owned. My niece Kim, at age 30, had her master's degree in engineering, her first home and mortgage, a good job, and no husband. Therefore, unlike my son and daughter-in-law, she'd never had a wedding shower to accumulate silver, china, crystal, etc. I wondered, "Where is it written that a young woman has to get married to have nice things?" So, I loaded up a U-Haul–filled with gifts from weddings gone by, piled in family antiques, garden tools, furniture–and my niece had Instant Home.

Why four, instead of three or six? For me, it spoke of the four seasons, the four directions; it spoke of nature. But really, I couldn't explain the reason behind "four," any more than I could explain what was compelling me away from everything I'd ever worked for and known.

In May of 1990, in a crowded courtroom in DeFuniak Springs, Florida, my dad, Judge Woodrow Melvin, swore me in as a Circuit Judge. It was hard to know who was more proud or hopeful, he or I. With my back to the audience, I put my left hand on his Bible, well read and worn by years of seeking; it was opened to Micah 6:8 "What doth the Lord require of you but to do justice, love mercy, and walk humbly before thy God." He'd opened the same Bible to the same verse ten years earlier to swear me in as an attorney.

Dad was short of stature, barrel-chested, and overweight. He described himself as portly. His sparse silver hair lay like a horseshoe on his shiny head. He was the timeless image of a judge in his robe, standing on hardwood floors in an old courthouse. I was the 43-year-old female brunette, dressed in a business suit, wearing pantyhose and heels.

I remember many details of the day and particularly his clear, resolute voice as he gave me the Oath of Office. I looked into his eyes with a small smile, but he was focused over my right shoulder. He was Judge Melvin, administering the oath to yet another young judge. He didn't look at me and his voice didn't quiver. I was puzzled but not dismayed. I understood that I was stepping into his world of the judiciary and that I had many lessons to learn from this master teacher. Dad and I each had a hand on his Bible; we spoke to one another clearly. When I turned to face the audience, I was surprised to see several people crying.

After the oath of office, the local Bar association gave me a robe and my son Clay helped me put it on. Then I was invited to join the several male judges who were seated behind the Bench for the ceremony. The other judges were seated in the jury box where chairs had been added to accommodate the large number. Everyone in this elite club wore a black robe.

As the years went by, I realized that Dad simply could not look me in the eye and give me the oath, for his emotions were too close to the surface. I've learned through experience what he showed me that day—that sharing eye space is an act of shared humanity, a risky communication that may prick our humanness and cause it to leak out across our faces and robes.

Nine years after Dad swore me in, I had begun to seriously consider leaving the Bench and was asking myself questions that could not be spoken in polite, professional company. There was no place in my work-a-day world as a Circuit Judge for internal turmoil, reminiscing, challenging, or assessing my life. I tucked deeper into what felt like a turtle shell, but looked like a black robe, and hid my confusion and soul-searching as I continued my everyday life of hearing contested divorces, difficult custody cases, and long criminal trials. To complicate matters, if I left, I would trigger an income loss that could not be rationally justified, and I didn't have assets to even begin to offset such a reduction. At night I wrote the stories of people I had met at work, but I also wrote to plumb the depths of many a dark hole in my psyche. During the day I continued to act and look professional, appropriate … and judicious.

And one night I wrote a letter to a retired judge—my dad—four years after his death.

❖ ❖ ❖

Dear Dad,

Can I explain this need to leave? Can I find the words to express the fire and confusion in my chest?

Over the years you often quoted Micah 6:8 "What doth the Lord require of you but to do justice, love mercy, and walk humbly before thy God." Dad, I've tried to deeply live those instructions, and I continue to wrestle with issues of justice and mercy. But, I'm tired. It seems that most of my days, most of my life is spent searching for justice while looking into the face of mean spiritedness and unbridled revenge, while encircled by aggression-for-hire aimed at winning at any cost.

It wounds my soul to listen to those professional wrestlers with greasy tricks who seek revenge in the name of justice. No, all attorneys and litigants are not so motivated, but as the years go by, it's harder to get beyond the distracters to the truth. And what am I to do? Much of the legal system is geared toward "Head 'em up, move 'em out," geared to efficiently move more and more widgets down a conveyor belt, cash-register justice with computerized predictability. The problem is, humanity and its needs won't fit safely or efficiently into one pat solution, but it seems few notice.

So much has changed, Dad. People seem to want a lawyer who is aggressively obnoxious—like those on reality TV. In Family Law, husbands and wives who once lived and loved and raised children together brag that their attorney bullied their spouse and beat up the other lawyer. Legal preparation, ethics, and professionalism are not valued by the many litigants who demand that their attorney exact, at a minimum, a pound of flesh. Unfortunately, there are legions of lawyers willing to provide such drama—for a hefty price, of course. And if the litigant would feel well-served with preparation, ethics, and professionalism, many attorneys push right past such an ideal, as though rudeness, aggression, and posturing are required, as though the attorney is entitled to pitch childish tantrums in order to represent his client. Among this growing population of attorneys, civility and professional courtesy are viewed as a sign of weakness. Dad, we know the Law is greater than the tarnish being thrown on it. But it's tough, trying to be the referee of such a brawl.

Being a judge was your love and your life. Yet the role to which you were so faithful has become my tar baby after only nine years. I fight, hit, and kick, yet get more and more stuck. My heart races; I don't know what's going to happen.

Let me tell you about this fire in my chest. It's like a sea of flames inside of me. Remember when you had pleurisy? Well, imagine pleurisy, bronchitis, and reflux holding hands to line dance on your solar plexus. The physical pain is real and is being treated by several doctors with a variety of meds for shifting diagnoses. But my heart knows it's not as simple as taking medicine. It's a soul issue. To prove its dominion, the fire spreads as I write, and it seems to feed on the rational, on rules, and boundaries. Will the inferno stop once it has destroyed all that I *have relied upon as well as my relationship with the institution in which I've lived my life? Or will it burn me at the stake and then blow past my insignificant pile of cinders?*

So Dad, I'm unlike you—you who were always rock solid in your commitment to the Law and to Mom. Unlike you, I'm single by choice, and I'm turning, twisting with questions that you never asked. And my questions suggest answers that are very anti-everything-I've-ever-known.

Dad, if I leave, if I give up your way of life, will you still love me? I've spent my life doing anything to get you to love me. Now, I'm looking at leaving your way of life. Are your ashes smoldering, rumbling in your bucket?

"What doth the Lord require of thee?" I have no clue. Today the question is—what does my birth father require of me? I've given my focus, my career, even my life to you, and it wasn't a bad deal. I lived in your town, worked as your secretary, went to law school, discussed legal issues with you, and joined you on the Bench. We shared a deep relationship; I learned many life lessons from you and acquired the education and training to earn a good living. But now, at 52 the fire in my chest rumbles, "Move on. It's OK to leave now." Am I wrong to leave; were you right to stay? Maybe. And I'll probably have to leave to know.

❧ ❧ ❧

Finally I had to admit to myself that the robe had become too heavy and being a rhinestone cowboy wasn't fun anymore. And so after ten years on the Bench, I left work early on a journey to find what really matters. I needed to listen to the open road and the lessons of people I'd met in Court: children, grownups who believed the children, grownups who didn't, and miscellaneous colorful characters, good and bad. I needed open space to see who I was. Did I even exist without my role and robe?

✦ ✦ ✦

At the Milton Cemetery

A few days after retiring and before leaving Northwest Florida, I drove over to the Milton Cemetery—a quiet resting place where generations lie under ancient magnolias in bloom and live oak trees wear skeins of Spanish moss that blow in the wind like feather boas. I sat alone in the truck, pensive, wishing I could tell my parents about my big trip. Wishing they could see me off. Remembering them as they'd stood together and waved goodbye. They'd wave at whoever left—family, friends, and professional colleagues. They'd wave goodbye for short trips or long ones. I'd never gone very far before, not really. I'd gone to Tallahassee to law school; there was a move to Central Florida for a few years and a couple of other trips. Now that I'd left my job, sold my home and given away everything that didn't comply with my Rule of Fours, I wanted them to see me off—I wanted them to stand on the steps at the back of their home, holding hands, smiling, waving at me— I wanted them to always be there in my rearview mirror.

But reality touched ground again. They were no longer there. Both of my parents were gone, dead. Smiles, warts, grace, and all. Most of what I'd worked for, lived for and loved, most of what I'd owned—it was all gone, too. By my choice, but still very gone. I ached for my parents' approval in my rearview mirror. I sat in the cemetery, totally alone.

I got out of the truck and looked up through tears at the thick clouds—just the right gray for cemetery atmosphere. I read the quote from Dag Hammarskjold carved in black letters on the backside of their otherwise-proper headstone, "For all that has been, Thanks. For all that will be, Yes." And we talked without words. Dad was a bit worried; Mom was mostly excited.

Mom laughed, "You'll be fine. Be sure to take my good-looking eyes with you."

Dad said, "Promise me, baby, that you won't drive at night. And be sure to take Bruin every time you get out of the truck."

I swallowed a lump in my throat and the moss swayed.

"Go on, honey, you'll be fine. The answer is Yes."

✦ ✦ ✦

"I am always doing that which I cannot do, in order that I may learn how to do it."
Pablo Picasso

CHAPTER 2. ON THE ROAD: GEORGIA, NORTH CAROLINA, AND KENTUCKY:
Dinosaurs, mountains, and bartenders

It's time to go. There are no more excuses, no more details to work out. I've quit my day job; the RV is ready. But leaving is not as much fun as I'd hoped.

Pat, the next-door neighbor, comes over to visit but I can't, so I mumble and turn away. I can barely breathe, much less chitchat about the trivia of my leaving everything and everyone I know. Finally when there's nothing left to do but go, the tears come in shoulder-jerking sobs. My friend, whom I'll call Al, holds me and says, "You'll be fine. Now get going before you make me cry, too."

As I drive away with the 5th wheel following faithfully, Al stands in the roadway and waves. Waves a flood of memories and impossible wishes. An impossible wish–to have my parents stand holding hands, smiling as they waved goodbye to me. But now that I was finally leaving home at the ripe old age of 53, they were already gone. I look in the side mirror, and Al waves again. I make the first turn, and he's gone, too.

Gone with most of what is known and comfortable in my life. Things like the routine of my workday, the security of a big paycheck, the comfort of being with friends in familiar places. Gone, like "Judge," the first name that came with my robe. There would be no more voices commanding, "All rise!" No chorus to coo, "Yes, Your Honor," to everything I say. No black robe to deflect humanity, mine or others. No label to hide behind. I turn onto the highway and reach across the seat to bury my hand in the deep fur of my German

Shepherd. He looks up at me as I explain, "This is it, Bruin. We're gone. Riding down the road. The bird flying from her cage. I bet every cage feels comfortable and claustrophobic; especially those furnished as well as mine. What do you think, old boy?" He looks out his window and doesn't answer. Weighing 95 pounds, Bruin has a head the size of a soccer ball, feet the size of coffee cups, and a boundless heart–all covered in perpetually shedding black and tan hair. I'd been on the Bench for three years when Bruin came to live with me; Suzie, the head canine officer for the Sheriff's Department, put us together. Bruin flunked out of police training because he was not quite hyper or aggressive enough but he's the perfect companion for me. Bruin had learned commands in German–sit = sitz, down = platz, stay = blibe, etc.–so he was way ahead of me. He understood German and I didn't, and he knew many commands he wasn't interested in me learning. It wasn't long before he had me trained. I much prefer his company to that of the cold steel revolver I'm encouraged to carry.

The week before, my well-furnished office on the sixth floor of the courthouse morphed into empty space that echoed. I stood in my chambers, after two long, hard days of signing last orders, boxing up personal things, and throwing away years of work. It felt like I was painting the floor, painting myself out the door. I quietly said a final goodbye to the office, to the prestige, the power, and the security. That wasn't so hard; those things were fancy trappings– comfortable and convenient, but not important. The hard part was saying goodbye to the sea of faces I'd seen over the years, ordinary people who came in search of justice and mercy. Through the windows of my 6th floor office, I looked over the crowns of massive live oak trees, beyond the flat roof tops of adjoining office buildings and ribbons of asphalt roadways to the wide expanse of Pensacola Bay, where the crinkled water had begun to pick up shades of orange as the sun slid to the west. It was a comforting view, one that had often helped center me when struggling with what was required to do justice as I presided over a human firestorm. I prayed that the new judge who would soon occupy this space would acquire the wisdom to apply our Rules of Law, the compassion needed to listen deeply to these real people with real problems, and the courage to flavor justice with mercy. The treetops waved, and it was simply time to go. I locked the office door behind me and walked down the secured maze of private halls that connect the judges' offices to the courtrooms and private elevators–space designed to keep judges safe from angry litigants.

When a Judge retires, all of the judges, court reporters, clerks, many attorneys and law enforcement officers stand around for a while in one of the courtrooms eating cookies and drinking punch. My reception would be in Courtroom 101, the one in which I sat so many times for Domestic Violence Hearings. The reception, scheduled for 10:00 a.m, came and went, an obligatory experience soon forgotten.

The courtroom emptied as everyone returned to his or her office. I had no office, but I had to go to the Milton courthouse for another reception at 2:00 p.m. My parachute was in my truck; I'd made a beach jump the weekend before, and I hadn't repacked it. I could feel the Devil's nudge, and I thought, "Why not? I'm outta here–and a little incongruence may be good for this stoic place. I've followed all the rules all my life; on my way out the door, I'll take a different tack." So I went to my truck and returned to Courtroom 101 with the parachute rig hung over my shoulder. The Domestic Violence Courtroom is not a place that sees lightheartedness or bright colors, but I laid the neon rainbow parachute out in front of the bench, ran the lines down the center aisle, dropped to my knees, and began packing, still dressed in my black silk Ann Taylor suit. I'd packed that chute several hundred times before; it was my proof that letting go can be freeing and fun; it was my reminder that sloppy choices can be painful and even fatal. Before I finished, Andy, one of the security officers, came into the empty courtroom. I looked up at him and laughed, "Who told you what I was doing?"

"No one had to, Judge," he responded, "I saw you on the courtroom monitor."

I retorted, "I figured either someone would catch me, or I'd give you guys grief for failing to monitor a courtroom scheduled as empty."

"Judge, as soon as you dropped that thing, I called, 'Hey everybody! Come look at what Judge Melvin's doing in 101.' They're still watching!"

I looked over my shoulder at the monitor. The Security Officers had always watched over me–herding me into and out of courtrooms and responding without question or delay each time life in court began to unravel too close to violence. For me, it was hard enough to defend myself legally, intellectually, and emotionally; because of Security, I didn't have to also defend myself physically. These guys always had my back; I trusted and respected them. I smiled and waved good-bye at the camera, "Thank you!"

After the reception, I turned in my keys and security card. Andy went with me on my last sequestered elevator ride down to the judges' parking lot, a space cordoned off by brick walls and a card-activated garage door. As I drove out under the huge metal rolling door, Andy stepped onto the sidewalk and waved good-bye. I understood what I was leaving. Ahead, I couldn't get a glimpse of much more than darkness.

Without the keys to that inner sanctum of secured halls, gated parking, and private elevators, without my title or robe, those specially guarded tunnels were off limits to me. The next time I went to the courthouse, I would walk in off the street, use the front door, pass through the metal detector, and ride the public elevator. Yet I understood I still had an ace in the hole for I had a standing invitation to return as a Senior

Judge, which is something like a substitute teacher, handling whatever you find on the docket of judges who may be sick, on vacation, or just need help. I had to leave and that meant shutting the door on my office, my docket, and on the security of the big paycheck; yet I also knew I could come back in an abbreviated form. It felt something like when I got married and moved out of my parent's house into a single-wide trailer parked in their yard.

I spend my first night on the road at a campground in North Georgia miles from that empty office in the courthouse. I sit alone at the picnic table to write and soon the tears come–not tears of regret or fear, but sad, missing-you-Mom-and-Dad tears–tears that value the friends I left behind. OK, some of the tears may be a fear of what's out there wherever I'm going, an abstract booger-man fear, but that's a fear hard to flesh out while pleasantly distracted by the hoot of an owl. With hot tea in my mother's china cup, I ponder the phrase, "at home." In theory I'm at home; my stuff is all here. This 30-foot RV has everything you could ask for–a full kitchen with a refrigerator, stove, and microwave; of course, there's a queen size bed, entertainment center with a large TV, CD player and radio, furnace, AC, full bath, couch, dining room table and chairs. It even has a ceiling fan, a reclining rocker, and dark purple throw pillows. But it's hard to convert stuff jammed into a 30-foot tin can attached to the bed of a four-wheel drive diesel truck into a feeling of "home," at least today, my first day on the road.

I've always had a role–daughter of my father, wife of my husband, mother of my child, attorney of my clients, and then Judge of my community. I've always had a home, an office, and a face that was recognized. All of that is left behind as I drive north with the 5th wheel in tow, but I still carry tiny footprints on my soul, left there by children I've met through those roles. Big lessons imprinted by little people. And it's these little people who have more to say to me, popping in and out of my consciousness as I drive. My first night on the road alone, as I ruminate on my loves and losses, I remember an important lesson. Jewel and her foster mother taught me of true love, one that grew in a crucible of tragedy, a love not known by the faint-hearted.

❖ ❖ ❖

"Children are the hands by which we take hold of heaven"
Henry Ward Beecher

Jewel

Jewel died at the age of thirteen after serving a life sentence for a crime she didn't commit. Jewel did her time without a sound and without resistance in a body the neurologists described as unable to respond to any stimuli.

A few years before Jewel's birth, her parents left the four older children unattended twice for at least six hours, long enough to get the System involved. The oldest was not yet five and the youngest was 18 months old. With a focus on reunification of the family, the System assumed people would change and that all children were better off with their parents. So, though the children were briefly removed from their parents, they were soon returned to a home where nothing had changed. And then Jewel was born.

Before Jewel's second birthday, she fell headfirst from a mattress into a bucket of water and floundered there long enough to suffer serious brain damage. No one explained why there was a bucket of water beside the bed or why she was unattended. As a tribute to science, if not her birth mother's love and attention, Jewel lived but she could no longer eat, walk, talk, swallow or move any part of her body. She had a feeding tube in her stomach and a trachea tube in her throat. The System, bolstered by the law and eternal optimism, returned Jewel to her parents as it had done her older brothers and sisters. She stayed with her parents and four siblings a few more months. When she was removed from her parents the last time, her diagnosis included "non-organic failure to thrive"; she was slowly starving because she was not being properly fed.

A few months after Jewel's second birthday, Maria got a call, "I don't think this one will live through the week. Can you take her?"

Maria could be the icon for foster parents. She was in her mid-forties, tall but otherwise non-descript until you got a glimpse of her patience and love. Maria invariably had someone else's child woven into the fabric of her own family; there was always room at her table and in her heart for another child who needed unconditional love and structure.

Under the impeccable care and persistence of her foster parents, Jewel lived through that week and another eleven years. Maria dressed her up like a china doll and included her in all the normal things going on in their crowded home. Maria also fed Jewel through a stomach tube, kept the trachea tube clean, changed her diapers, and propped her up in a special wheel-chair. And there were days and weeks in the hospital for a variety of complex medical emergencies.

Maria kept a cotton handkerchief tucked beside Jewel's lifeless hand because Jewel couldn't control her saliva. Wiping Jewel's drooping mouth was part of what Maria's hand did, without a thought, an automatic response, a hand that was always there.

Though Jewel never walked, talked, moved a finger, or swallowed, her foster parents did not question her worth, nor did they doubt that Jewel was conscious and aware. Given the extent of Jewel's brain damage, the doctors said she was totally unresponsive to stimuli. But her foster parents knew better; when her foster dad came into the room whistling softly, Jewel would turn her head toward him.

I was the Judge assigned to Jewel's case for six years, and the case came up for Judicial Review at least twice a year. During those routine if not perfunctory Judicial Review hearings, I'd review paper-work, listen to brief summaries, sign an order, and call the next case. It wasn't necessary that Jewel come to Court, but Maria and I enjoyed it so she was always there. Because of the number of cases on my docket, I often held court straight through lunch to be able to start the afternoon calendar on time. Ignoring the pressure of people waiting and too many cases left to be heard, I would take off my robe and come down from the bench to visit with Maria, to speak to Jewel and to see her always perfectly coordinated outfit. I remember a small Dalmatian purse tucked beside Jewel's motionless hand—a fashion statement to accessorize black patent leather shoes and Dalmatian socks with white lace at the top. Her feet didn't point in the right direction, but they were styling! She wore a black jumper with a large Dalmatian on the pocket, and a white blouse with Dalmatians on the collar. And there was the omnipresent cotton handkerchief. I felt like part of the family; Maria sent me photos of Jewel; my favorite is one of Jewel and Santa.

The funeral home was a one-story building with a weather-beaten roof, located in an industrial district next to an electrical contractor and across the street from a plant nursery. Maria walked quickly across the tiny chapel; she came to me with a strong laugh, a big hug, and tears brimming in her eyes. She held me close and said "I knew you'd come. Are you OK?"

Jewel's birth mother was in the Chapel—the woman no one had been able to find for eleven years. I knew that Jewel had lived at the same address for eleven years and that her siblings had contact with her but not her birth mother. The woman sat on the opposite side of the small room talking to relatives who had also chosen to reject Jewel. It felt like them against us, and I chose not to introduce myself. I watched from the corner of my eye—the woman gesturing and talking across the room—she's the one who left Jewel eleven years ago and never made contact again. Until now, now that Jewel was dead. Perhaps leaving was the birth mom's greatest gift, for then Jewel was loved and cared for by true parents—parents who don't give up on a child when there's a problem—true parents whom the birth mother doesn't know by choice.

Maria talked freely, "We had her 11 years! And they said she wouldn't live a week. There were a couple of times the Department tried to make us give her up 'cause they wanted her in a nursing home. I know it would've been cheaper for them, but we fought *'em. Jewel needed us, needed family. If they'd have stored her in a nursing home, she'd have died a long time ago."*

I asked, "Did you see this coming?"

"Oh, yes. She was having problems, but she felt good enough to go to Chuck E Cheese's with us Friday night! But then her kidneys began to fail. We knew it couldn't be long. By Sunday, Jewel was struggling to die; it was time, but she wouldn't let go. Jewel has a 20-year-old sister, Teresa, who lives here in town."

I interrupted, "I didn't realize she had a sister here!"

"Oh, yes, Teresa lives in Pensacola. She's very close to Jewel and has always stayed in touch with us. So I called Teresa about 11:30 Sunday night and asked her to come over because Jewel needed her. When Teresa got to the house, I asked her to tell Jewel it was OK for her to leave now, OK to go to heaven. Teresa leaned over, kissed Jewel on the forehead and said, 'It's OK—go now.' Jewel took one breath and died. Jewel waited for Teresa; she knew she was there. And Jewel got to die at home, with us."

❦ ❦ ❦

As Jewel's memory settles quietly back into my soul, I realize I'm a little tired and hungry, sitting here on the apron of the Smoky Mountains. It's hard to believe that I don't have to go back to work,–that I can choose for me now. I can write all morning or take a nap, I drive long hours or sit still, I can choose where to go and then change my mind.

From Gainesville, Georgia, I'll drive to North Carolina to enjoy the cool of the mountains and visit Lee, a close friend for 20+ years. And then I'm going to Iowa to a writing workshop.

I'm tense as I drive steep, winding back roads in the Smokies, pulling my 13 foot-high RV that weighs 11,000 pounds and is 30 feet long. I'll unhook and leave the 5th wheel at the RV park before I go see Lee, but I have to get it there first. I make another tight turn with an eye on the extended mirror on the passenger side and long for my little Nissan 300X.

The next morning Bruin and I leave the RV at the park and

ride two hours across the mountains.

Lee, a folk singer and naturalist, is a wealth of information. As we hike some of his paths less traveled, he points out wild-flowers, trees, and plants with the enthusiasm of a kid in a forest of Christmas trees. One of my favorites is a low-growing plant with puffy-soft leaves the size of a soup bowl used by the Cherokees as baby diapers. It comes equipped with gentle green fuzz for tender baby butts.

The afternoon before we leave for Iowa, Bruin and I drive back over the mountains to hear Lee in concert. I park the truck in a secluded spot with plenty of shade for Bruin. I have an early supper with Lee and then enjoy the music, though increasingly aware this night will mean yet another leaving, and that my driving will take me further and further from all I've known. It's raining hard as the concert ends. In a tired voice, Lee asks, "Do you want me to walk you down to the truck?" Not meaning a word of it, I reply, "You don't have to. I have my raincoat." To my surprise, he gives me a big hug and says good-bye. I walk off into the pitch-dark rain, my bravado leaking out of my wet shoes as I fuss at myself for having left my flashlight in the truck. I can't see my feet much less the heaves, cracks, or turns in the black road that meanders down the steep incline. I walk slowly, shuffling to feel the road. Several times I realize I'm off the asphalt as my feet sink into grass, stumble in soft dirt, or crunch loose rock. It's no more than a half of a mile down to my truck, but it feels like ten times that. The rain falls in heavy, wind-blown sheets. If there were light–and there isn't–this would have been a difficult, stormy walk. With time, my eyes somewhat adjust to the almost total darkness as I grope my way to Bruin. Things don't lighten up when I finally get to the truck; I fumble as I try to get the key into the black hole on the black door of the truck parked under a black tree. Bruin's head pops up in the window and he waits patiently as I bumble around. "This isn't what I had in mind, Old Boy. He could've been a little worried. He could've asked us to stay over. But we can do this, can't we." Finally the key finds the hole, and I join Bruin inside the dry cab. I begin the long drive back to my RV, and the rain continues its horizontal dance with the black wind. The hair-pin turns that earlier had been scenic are now hair-raising. As I work my way up and down several mountains, the world is pitch black; there are no street lights and the asphalt roads are hooded by tall trees. The head lights from the few cars I meet appear as blinding balls in a fog-diffused tunnel. I feel increasingly vulnerable and lonely. I turn off the radio, grip the steering wheel with both hands, and sit up straight. "Nobody knows where we are, Bruin. If we slide off this mountain, no one would miss us. And when someone finally noticed we're not calling in, they'd have no idea where to look for us." Three hours later I pull into the dark RV park with Bruin and a migraine. Safe at home and bolstered by a cup of hot tea, I think of Melissa Fox, a 16 year-old runaway who knew much more than I about scary places, dark rainy nights, and times when no one knows where you are. Melissa also knew how to balance freedom and schedules, so she showed up in court, on time, and uninvited.

❖ ❖ ❖

A fox in the courthouse

Melissa Fox's case was one of too many on an already crowded docket; her file was scheduled for routine review. Melissa's mother had a lot of problems—just couldn't seem to get herself together— couldn't hold a job—couldn't keep her head above water. So she'd left Florida, moving to the promise of a better life in New York City. Melissa stayed behind with her grandmother. Her grandmother lived in a cinder-block house, and her son, Melissa's uncle, was a back-door neighbor. Melissa, age 16, was under supervision of the Court, so a case worker was required to check in on her—the law said at least once a month. I was to review her case at least once a year. I always read reports the night before the hearings; the volume of paperwork was too much to focus on during the push and pull of Court, and sometimes important facts were brushed over.

Reading Melissa's report over supper the night before, I made notes in the margins as questions began to pop up in my mind. The Department said that the mother reported having a job and an apartment in New York City for more than six months, but that because of funding cuts their counterpart in New York couldn't provide supervision at this time, and the mother had only one bed in the apartment. The Department determined that Melissa could not be allowed to live with her mother. At the beginning of the report the caseworker concluded that Melissa was doing well with her grandmother, yet buried in a long paragraph several pages later, were statements that Melissa had begun to run away and had not been seen for the last couple of weeks. And so over my supper of honey-nut Cheerios with a glass of white wine, I wondered, "What's going on here?"

The next morning when the case was called, I was surprised to see Melissa there. After taking testimony from the Department caseworker, I asked Melissa "Is there anything you'd like to say to me—here in the courtroom or in private?"

She answered, "Could I talk with you in private?"

I called a recess and asked Melissa to come with me to my office. I took off my robe, and we sat down on the couch.

Her eyes began to fill with tears and she said, "Please let me go live with my mom!"

"Tell me what's going on, Melissa. Why do you think you need to go to New York?"

She began haltingly, "You know my uncle. He was messing with me. A lot."

"What do you mean, messing with you?"

"Well, he made me go down on him, and he made me have sex with him."

(I was trying hard to keep my judge face in place, to listen without judgment, conclusions, or surprise. But I was not doing so well. The report said she had been a runaway. It made no reference to

34

sexual abuse. But, one and one often equal two.) "Did you tell your grandma or case worker about this?"

"Yes ma'am, I did. But they wouldn't believe me. My caseworker just told my grandma he couldn't come over any more. But he lives right there."

"Did your grandma stop him from coming?"

"Well, not really. He still eats with us every night. But now he's not supposed to come over when I'm there alone. But, he keeps messing with my stuff."

"Tell me what you mean."

"Well, he comes in my room when I'm at school, and he goes through my underwear and stuff. He leaves my panties out on my bed. One time he tore up my favorite ones. He took some of my jewelry and pawned it. It wasn't really worth anything, but he pawned it. Then he bragged about it. He messes with my stuff, just to mess with me."

"OK, Melissa, but I can't just put you on a bus by yourself and send you to New York."

"You don't have to, Judge. My mom's here."

"What?!"

"Yes ma'am, she came down on a bus last night. I finally told her what was going on."

"Has she talked with your case worker?"

"Yes ma'am, they talked outside this morning."

"Where is your mom?"

"She's in the courtroom."

My mind was at full tilt. Why didn't the mother stand up when the case was called? Why didn't the Department attorney or caseworker tell me they had seen the mother and that she was in the crowded courtroom? Don't get distracted by your anger, Laura, just keep moving.

"How long has it been since you slept at your grandma's?"

"Oh, a couple of weeks."

I didn't ask where she'd been sleeping. What would I do with her answer?

"Melissa, how did you know about this hearing?" *(My mind dashes. The kid is sleeping God-knows-where, yet manages to get down here to Juvenile Court and on time?)*

"My mom told me. She's been ready for me to go back with her. But they won't let me!"

By now I'm losing the battle to keep my judge face in place, and my anger is barely contained. I put my robe back on—it's easier to hide my emotions behind that black armor—and I went back into the courtroom with Melissa. I began to question the caseworker in a somewhat civil voice about Melissa's report of sexual abuse by the uncle, no mention of which was in their report.

The caseworker responded, "Melissa told me of her problems with her uncle, but I have been unable to verify the abuse because Melissa also admitted to being sexually active."

(Another real test of my ability to remain inscrutable! I listen but I'm thinking sarcastically, "Oh, so that's how you justify leaving the sexual abuse out of your report. Yeah, I remember now. When you have a 16-year-old sexual battery victim who is later involved in consensual sex with a minor, you don't have to believe a word she says because she's 'sexually active.' Since you've found an excuse to disbelieve everything she says, she could not be raped, by anyone, in the past or in the future. And better yet, you don't have to do all of that messy, time-consuming work!! Right...") The worker went on to assure me that she had insisted that the grandmother prohibit or supervise all contact with the uncle; I was not assured.

"Did you know that the mother is in court this morning?"

"Yes, Your Honor, I talked with her this morning. She's here."

By this time most of the thoughts running through my head were in the form of four-letter words. I managed to keep my thoughts away from my tongue and called the mother's name. A woman stood up toward the back of the courtroom. I asked her to come down to the podium, and from there I talked with her briefly. She told me about her job, her hours, and her apartment. She explained that she lived only three blocks from the school Melissa would attend, and that she had met with the teachers there. She briefly explained the school's curriculum.

I looked at the Department attorney and asked in my best Judge

Voice, "Why should the Court not send Melissa home with her mother today?"

The attorney gasped and replied, "Your Honor, we cannot verify that there is a separate bed for Melissa at her mom's!"

I looked at her mother and asked, "Where would Melissa sleep?"

Mom replied through tears, "She can sleep in my bed; I'll sleep on the couch."

And I thought, "If she had to sleep on the floor, at least she wouldn't have to share the space or her underwear with her uncle."

The attorney squeaked, "But Your Honor, because of budget cuts New York won't be able to provide services for at least three months. You can't send her now!"

I managed to avoid saying, "Oh, how well we provide services to the frightened and vulnerable." I took a deep breath and simply said, "Effective immediately, the Court returns custody of Melissa to her mother, subject to protective services supervision when such is available. Court is in recess!"And I bolted out of the courtroom, trying to look judicious when all I really wanted to do was to yell and tear faces off. Then I stared at a blank wall in my office as I tried to rein in my anger at a bureaucracy that focused on the fine print and ignored the very real child.

That night I sat with my still smoldering anger and a glass of wine, pushing my pen across a blank piece of paper, and then staring out across the dark pasture. A movement caught my eye, and I sat very still. The shadow moved again; it was a fox feeding on my compost pile. I laughed, feeling my tension break. What choice did I have? Like Melissa Fox, this little four-legged beauty showed up uninvited, alert, inquisitive, and hungry. A survivor. The fox slid back into the shadows of the pasture; Melissa boarded the Greyhound bus with her mom, heading to New York.

✢ ✢ ✢

The next morning, I hook up and head toward Iowa for the writing workshop. Determined to avoid schedules and reservations, my plan is simple–drive until I'm almost too tired, and then find a place for the night. So I pull off the road just south of Cincinnati at Big Bone Lick State Park, in north central Kentucky near the Ohio River at a quiet campground where dinosaurs once roamed.

I stop my truck near my assigned spot and walk over to check out the angle required to back in, the camber of the lot, and the location of the utility hookups. Two men sitting on the adjoining lot with their wives are obviously curious. Soon one calls out.

"Are ya gonna back that thing all by yourself?" he asks.

I laugh, "Sure."

Both men are on their feet, and I become their entertainment. They give me directions, "Come on back–hard left–straighten up." After they have my 5th wheel perfectly aligned with my cement patio, they pull up a chair and include me easily in their banter. Both men are retired truckers, traveling with their wives full-time in RV's. Half an hour later one of the wives laughs, "We gotta get home, honey. It's time for you to dye my hair." She explains, "There's always some left over, but he won't let me dye his–yet."

This will be a one-night stand, so I leave the 5th wheel connected to the truck. After I've lowered the stabilizing jacks, put the slide out, and hooked up the utilities, Bruin and I take a long hike. On the way back to the RV, we're waylaid by a small covey of kids. Bruin, a German Shepherd who outweighs even the largest, romps with them like a gentle giant. As we're leaving, a petite girl maybe four years old wraps her arms around his neck. She buries her head in his massive chest and peeks out at me. "I really love him!" I know how she feels.

Bruin is easy-going, affectionate, and loyal; he loves children. He also has his own radar system and a deep growl that makes the ground shake. I never worry about waking up in the middle of the night with the booger man standing over me. No matter where we are, I know Bruin has my back. He also has my heart.

Heading back to the 5th wheel, we have to ford a mountain creek, one that I could have crossed with some dignity by simply taking off my shoes and rolling up my jeans to the knee. But, no, Bruin didn't even consider crossing it like a grown-up; instead he flops down in the creek and starts rolling. He looks at me curiously, then stands up and begins flinging curtains of cold water. I'm standing in a dinosaur graveyard, leashed to a 100-pound carwash.

With cold creek water dripping from my face, hair, and clothes, I have to laugh. Bruin's aim was better than the bartender's.

✦ ✦ ✦

The bartender's revenge

As an Assistant Public Defender in central Florida, I worked with a specific judge, and cases were assigned to the judge by a blind, random system. I represented those criminal defendants in my judge's division who could not afford to hire a private attorney. The defendants did not get to pick their judge or court-appointed attorney, and the court-appointed attorneys did not get to pick their clients.

In this case, I was representing a man charged with a particularly violent rape. He was accused of kidnapping a young waitress/bartender at knifepoint and forcing her to drive to an isolated parking lot. The police report said he then spent hours brutalizing and terrorizing her. As I read the report, the only thing I could think of that he had not done was to kill her. The State was understandably insisting on a long prison sentence, and my client wouldn't talk to me. So my only choice was to get ready for trial, which meant I had to talk to the victim. I scheduled her deposition—the time at which I could ask her questions with the prosecutor and court reporter present. My client would not attend.

I learned during the deposition that the victim worked at a local yuppie watering hole. I knew the place; I had been there a number of times with friends. As the attorney for her rapist, I was as gentle as one can be when asking for the graphic, horrific details of her worst nightmare. And in my defense, I accepted her answers without a series of follow-up questions, covering only the basics I would need for trial. In her defense, she had never been raped before or deposed afterwards, so she failed to see or appreciate the deference I gave her. My tone was polite and professional as I asked the essential questions, but my hands were shaking so I kept them below the table. I looked everywhere except into the eyes of the victim. Listening to this ordinary woman who was my age as she described a nightmare I could not have made up—well, sometimes maintaining the intellectual detachment required by my job is hard. Serving as defense counsel is an important, rewarding profession, but it was particularly difficult that day. If she were to read this, I'm sure she'd bristle at my whining. "So you think you were uncomfortable! Let me tell you about uncomfortable!"

Anyway, armed with my factual assessment of her as a very strong witness, I had a prayer meeting with my client. I told him everything she had said and explained that the judge would give him the max after hearing this sordid story straight from the victim. His only response was, "Huh. Well, see what you can get me." I talked with the prosecutor, who talked with the victim, and they agreed that if the Defendant pled guilty, he'd receive a sentence slightly less than the maximum; their motivation was to avoid the necessity of the victim reliving her nightmare in public. Then without giving me his version of the facts or otherwise acknowledging that he was in any way involved, he waived his right to a jury trial, plead no contest to the rape charge and was sentenced to prison.

A few weeks later, I went with Mike and Bob to the restaurant where the victim worked. All three of us were lawyers and we looked it, dressed in our yuppie blue and gray suits. We were talking at a small round table when a hand slid a cocktail napkin in front of me. I turned my head and there she was; she stared for a quiet moment. *It was clear she remembered me, with a vengeance. She jerked my napkin back, stiffened, and walked away from me to stand beside the two men. She took our drink orders and left.*

Bob asked, "What's wrong with her? What was that all about?"

I briefly explained, adding that I doubted she would serve us. In a few minutes I watched as she stopped at the far end of the bar and picked up a large tray filled with drinks for several tables. Then she walked a few feet and paused; she spoke quietly to a male waiter and nodded in our direction. He took the heavy tray from her and walked to our table, positioning himself farthest from me and between the two men. Then with Olympic grace, speed and dexterity, he dumped the entire tray of drinks across the guys' shoulders, backs, and onto the table. What aim! But not a drop or ice cube hit me. Mike and Bob jumped up, scooping ice out of their laps and pulling off their coats. I began laughing; the more I thought about it, the harder I laughed until tears were running down my face. When she saw the mess, who had taken the hit, and perhaps my unexpected response, she joined her friend in cleaning up. I caught her eye and nodded "Yes!" still laughing tears, as I helped wiped ice and drinks from the table. She chuckled and left without a word.

The manager came to our table, full of apologies. He paid for dry cleaning the guys' suits and bought drinks. But even after the round of free drinks and my full explanation, Bob never saw the humor or the justice. He was mad and stayed that way.

My best guess is, after she picked up the tray, she said to her friend, "Remember the defense attorney I told you about? The one representing that animal. Well, over at table number three. I don't want to go back over there. Would you deliver their drinks?" Her buddy took the tray, and assuming the defense attorney was one of the two men in suits and ties, dropped revenge for his comrade.

A true friend, willing to lift his leg on the devil's agent, in the name of Justice.

✦ ✦ ✦

Bedraggled and cold, I follow Bruin across the creek and back to the RV.

The next morning we leave Kentucky and drive through Ohio, Indiana, and into Illinois. In Bloomington, Illinois, I spend my first night sleeping at a Wal-Mart. As a marketing strategy, Wal-Mart welcomes self-contained RVs of all sizes to spend the night in their lighted, security-patrolled parking lots. Well-heeled, Americanized gypsies stay the night, shop, and move on down the road, often to another Wal-Mart. I'm one of five RV rigs in the lot at Bloomington. This isn't roughing it; everything I own is in my rig, from my winter coat to my bathing suit. My neighbors, in their 40-foot $400,000 Prevost aren't suffering either. It's an interesting experience–standing butt-naked in the hot shower of an RV while shoppers push their buggies past in the Wal-Mart parking lot.

Early the next day I leave Bruin in the truck and walk to a gourmet coffee shop. The guy behind me in line, dressed in a dark blue suit, shockingly white shirt, and shiny Italian loafers, is obviously on his way to court. I return to my truck, put my latte in the cup holder on the dash, crank up the diesel, and head west with my dog and a big smile on my face.

As I pull onto the Interstate, I pass a guy holding a cardboard sign with "Iowa" scrawled at an angle. He's dressed in dirty jeans and T-shirt; his hair is long and unkempt; at his feet are a black garbage bag and a rolled blanket tied with a rope. I wave and smile; he nods. I know better than to make any assumptions of that man, for good or bad. I was an Assistant Public Defender Office for four years and learned much about life from people I would otherwise have never met. Some of my clients were hard-working; some were not. Some would tell me the truth; some would not. Most had family and friends whom they loved. In so many ways, they were ordinary people with hopes, frustrations, fears, strengths, and weaknesses. Some had let opportunity slip through their hand; some had never been able to break even, much less get ahead in life. Very few had a good education. All of them were poor, frequently of a minority race, and each was charged with a crime, sometimes a violent one. Some of my clients were guilty; some were not. Many were guilty of something but not the exaggerated charge initially filed. They were each entitled to the full benefit of our laws; each had the right to be treated with dignity and respect. So it was my job to stand with them through the legal process and help ensure they were not punished for more than what they did or that they were not punished at all if the State could not prove its case. Though I'm certainly not naïve after years as defense counsel, I developed a life-long affinity for those guys. In so many ways, they are just like you and me. As a Judge, I always called the defendant by his name, looked him in the eye, said "yes sir" or "no sir," and asked if he had anything he wanted to say. As defense counsel or judge, I seldom had a problem with the defendant's behavior.

❧ ❧ ❧

Spending time in jail

I was born in Milton, a small town in Northwest Florida, and was raised Southern Baptist in a white, well-educated middle class society. I lived sheltered in my hometown until at the age of 30 I moved 180 miles east to go to law school.

After law school, I moved to Central Florida where, to my father's horror, I went to work as an Assistant Public Defender. One of my job requirements as defense counsel was to spend a great deal of time in jails and prisons, interviewing clients. Jail is not a place you really want to get used to. My on-the-job training began immediately as the secretary handed me a stack of files and said, "These are in jail." I didn't even know where the jail was, and it was clear no one was going with me. I swallowed hard, and headed to the door. I knew better than to call home, "Hey, Mom, Dad! Guess what! I get to go to jail today!"

So I went to jail for the first time—a two story, drab brick building with tiny windows and sunlight glinting off the razor wire. I went to the front desk and introduced myself. The Corrections Officer (or CO) barely acknowledged my presence though I was far from routine; I was the only female Public Defender in the four-county Circuit. The CO pointed to a ledger on a long counter. After I signed in, a buzzer sounded and the CO jerked his head toward a solid green door to my left. I pushed on the metal door, it opened, I went through, and it slammed behind me with a steely echo. I was alone. I walked down the hall to a barred door and pushed a doorbell on the side. I heard the locks shift; when the sounds stopped, I pushed but nothing happened. I pulled, and the door opened. Now I was looking up a flight of grungy stairs. As I walked up the steps, careful to avoid touching the railing, I could feel my maternal grandmother, a pious and haughty Hard Shell Baptist, sneer from her grave with ladylike disdain for how far I'd fallen.

At the top of the stairs was another buzzer and another green metal door. Now I was on the second floor with the inmate cells. There are interview rooms on the ground floor but those are only used by the "real lawyers." The Public Defenders saw so many people that the Correction Officers figured it would take too long to move our clients up and down the stairs. So we came upstairs to talk with our clients in a tiny room adjacent to the cells. When I pushed the buzzer at the top of the stairs, steel tumblers began to move. When the sounds stopped, I opened the heavy door and stepped into a long hallway of dirty gray steel doors opening onto a beehive of individual cells. I could hear the inmates stirring around; there were a couple of catcalls, and a TV blared. The whole place had that tangy antiseptic smell that is designed to mask other odors, but doesn't. I inhaled the smell of many men with not much hope and with few reasons to give a damn about keeping their rooms clean.

Standing outside the maze of cells, I gave the CO the name of my first client. He moved a short distance, stuck a ridiculously large key into a hole, pushed the door open, and yelled out my client's name. A stranger in jailhouse-issue green coveralls walked out, and I introduced myself. This guy, like the others, shuffled in plastic shower shoes. His face was blank as he looked at me; he stretched, yawned, and rubbed his eyes. He didn't have body odor, but his breath would peel paint off metal. His teeth were velvety, like they hadn't been brushed this week. He followed me the few feet into the cinder block room perhaps six by eight feet with no windows. In the room were a small metal picnic table and two benches, all bolted to the cement floor. I wondered if the Establishment was afraid the residents would toss them around, or perhaps try to collect a matched set from other jails. As I shut the door to the tiny dungeon, I saw the practical question, one I'd failed to ask of my colleagues. Where and how do I sit? On my first trip to the jail, I began a career-long habit. The "where" was obvious—closest to the door. And for the "how"—do I want to climb in over the bolted bench and put my feet under the table? No, because I didn't want to take the time to climb out if a client got really pissed at the Messenger, me; a quick retreat when my legs were under the table was also complicated by the fact that I wore straight skirts. So I always sat closest to the door with my feet on the outside of the bench, swiveling at the waist to use the tabletop.

I interviewed the clients and left. On my first trip to a jail, I heard every click of every lock, flinched with each door that slammed, felt the coldness of the steel, saw the dull institutional colors, noted the bland detached faces, and smelled the antiseptic floor wash that couldn't flush out the fear, the anger, or the despair.

Months later I had been deep in the bowels of the jail for hours talking with clients, when suddenly I realized I had not heard the locks click or the doors slam, had not stopped at the bottom or top of those grungy stairs, had not felt the cold clammy steel, or smelled the antiseptic and the fear. I don't know which day bothered me the most— experiencing the cage of humans, or becoming accustomed to it.

✳ ✳ ✳

When a child walks down the road, a company of angels go before him, proclaiming "Make way for the image of the Holy One." Hasidic proverb

CHAPTER 3.
IOWA:
Monks, parents, and other authority figures.

I cross the Mississippi River at the Illinois/Iowa border. I'm to attend writing classes at the University of Iowa in Iowa City but I'm here several days early, so I head north along the river. Though intellectually I know the geography, it still surprises me to find the Mississippi River, alive and well, so far north for I've only associated it with the Deep South in general and Louisiana in particular. Though my anchor is shifting, these muddy waters roiling past a northern shore pull my thoughts back home and to time spent with Al in New Orleans. I slide back to another world, one best described in a Southern drawl–a world of street vendors hawking their art next to jugglers and mimes, beignets at Café DuMonde where the floor is splotched with white confectionary sugar, horses with bows in their manes and bags under their tails that plod down cobbled streets and across trolley rails, and a lone saxophonist who plays for tips from his perch on a river piling. In Iowa, the world that surrounds Old Man River feels more civilized, with interesting but less exotic food, spices, coffee, accents, rhythms, and music. But the Mississippi River issues the same churning call from around the next bend.

Al and I met skydiving. I fell deeply in love and moved in with him. Al travelled with his job, but that was not a problem for we had our times alone and then together. The glue of the relationship was that we played well together. We laughed and romped like little kids. Al clowned around with words, making up new phrases; he loved to dance; he was bright and optimistic.

Al is a big man, and he has a gift for mechanical things. Part of our relationship was how he used those traits, though not always with a great deal of patience, to encourage my adventuresome spirit.

While we were living together, we made a skydive from the Cessna, and I hit my foot on the step of the plane as I jumped. Back on the ground as we were packing our parachutes, without comment I pulled up the leg of my jump suit to show him the red welts.

"How did you do that!!?"

"I hit the step on exit."

"How could you hit the step!?!" he retorted. Then he grabbed me by the hand, "Come see!" We walked out to the plane, and Al climbed inside. "Look, if you just position yourself like this, there's no way you can hit the step!"

By now both my ankle and my feelings were hurt. I finished packing my chute, and we went up for another jump. I changed my position in the door and didn't whack the step as I fell from the plane.

Al and I had been together for about a year when I realized that getting drunk from time to time was part of his life plan. The ground shifted under me. With my family history of alcoholism, I'm like a young child who was badly bitten by a snarling dog; it just doesn't work to tell me the growling dog isn't going to bite this time. Al was sure that his drinking was just a good-old-boy thing, and I was sure I couldn't live with it. I saw nothing endearing about drunkenness–the stumbling, falling, slurping, slurring, and passing out. I offered several unilateral treaties: "Don't drink around me." When that didn't work, "OK, drink but just don't get drunk." Of course, nothing I did made Al change. I should have known better, for I'd tried all that and more a few years earlier with Frank, another person I loved who drank too much. After several years in a downward emotional spiral with Frank, I began going to Al-Anon meetings, a 12-step program that became an important part of my life, helping me to see that I didn't have to continue the dance of alcoholism and codependency. I learned, through experience, that living in a world saturated in alcohol is not healthy for me, the person I am and want to become. When the relationship with Frank finally ended, I promised me I'd never again live with someone who abused alcohol. I assured myself that living alone was better than not knowing when the next drunken shoe would fall. I promised myself that abuse of alcohol was a deal-breaker in a relationship–no matter what. With Al, the "no matter what" was that I deeply love him. I moved out of his home but left my heart behind. He continues to drink; I continue to hope he'll stop getting drunk. And I've kept various and generally ineffective boundaries up around my heart. For several years we've shared a rapport and deep caring.

Before leaving on my trip, Al and I agreed we were not in an exclusive relationship. There are too many open miles and months before us, and too much history behind us. Al plans to fly out to meet me at some point. I want the comfort and security of his presence, but I also have to learn to do this world–all by myself.

Bruin and I stop at a campground in the rolling farmland south of Dubuque. Looking at the map, I realize I'm only five miles from the New Melleray Abbey, a Trappist Monastery. Now I have plans for tomorrow.

I enjoy the irony that I am a non-Catholic, recovering Southern Baptist, and not a member of any structured religion, yet I'm making plans to go to a Trappist Monastery in the rolling hills of Iowa. I was raised in a Southern Baptist church that taught a hell-fire-and-brimstone god who gleefully struck blows of revenge. Gratefully, my Baptist parents, though steeped in that tradition, showed their children a God of love and respect. As a young adult, I revolted from the Baptist church, and for years avoided all structured religions. My parents never mentioned my wayward ways; they just kept on loving me. While on the Bench, I read Frank Bianco's *Voices of Silence, Lives of the Trappists Today,* and Kathleen Norris' The Cloister Walk, and decided I wanted to know more about the world of the silent Catholic. I found another book, *Sanctuaries of the West Coast and Southwest,* by Marcia and Jack Kelly, and made plans to go to New Camaldoli Hermitage in Big Sur, California, one of the sanctuaries they summarized. I am an introvert who loves to travel and enjoys nature, so going to California to spend a week of my vacation at Big Sur without talking sounded like fun. At the Hermitage I stayed alone in a "cell," which was a small trailer with everything anyone could want or need: a comfortable bed with a good reading light, a bathroom, kitchen, a chair with a good light, and a tiny dinette. The kitchen was stocked daily with fresh fruit, bread, nut butters, and cereals; we walked down to pick up one vegetarian meal each day. I think the completeness I found in that little trailer is what spurred me to live in an RV. Perched on a cliff overlooking the Pacific, my "cell" even had a garden with a resident hummingbird. Day after quiet day, I walked down to the Chapel to hear the monks chant the Psalms at Mass. They were dressed in ageless brown tunics but on their feet Crocs and Tevas peeked from behind the long hems. One afternoon as I walked far from the compound, I met a monk dressed in blue jeans. He was hiking with his dog. We sat on a bench and talked for a long time. I respected what I heard and saw at the Hermitage in California. And so I'm curious about New Melleray Abbey here in Iowa. I don't expect to find THE answer to life's great questions, but a glimpse would be nice.

There's a herd of Boy Scouts at this campground south of Dubuque. Their noise ricochets through the park–their laughter, their loud voices, their busyness as they set up tents and haul water–good kid-sounds, little guys playing outside without the artificial distractions of boom boxes or video games. They use my faucet to fill up their water buckets, leaving each time with a "Thank you, ma'am." I smile watching them–a large group of noisy kids chaperoned by parents and other adults who care, who notice, who listen. Kids unlike so many of those I worked with over the years. How I wish Earl and Bobby could have the adult attention that these guys enjoy.

❈ ❈ ❈

Failure to parent

Phillip was charged with Aggravated Stalking of his ex-girlfriend, Kathy. At Phillip's Pretrial Conference, the Prosecutor explained that he didn't have much of a case–no one had seen the Defendant on the ex-girlfriend's property–but that Kathy and her ex-husband, Bob, were furious and pushing hard because their children, Bobby, Earl, and Patricia, were home alone at the time.

The two boys, Earl, age 12 and Bobby, age 9, were the prime witnesses. They came into the courtroom dressed in unkempt play clothes. Earl's jeans were about an inch too short and had permanent stains on both knees. The neck on his faded T-shirt was stretched out of shape. The heels of his dingy tennis shoes were worn. Bobby had on a T-shirt that may have been white in an earlier life, and his jeans stopped considerably short of his scuffed tennis shoes tied with frayed shoestrings. Both boys needed a haircut, and it looked as though neither had brushed their scruffy manes since at least the first of the week.

The State called Earl as the first witness. Earl testified in a voice that was at times as deep as a man's; then suddenly, his voice would crack and sound like a seven year-old's. Earl testified, "Mom works nights. She has to leave the house by seven and comes home ... well...it depends on if she has to close. And sometimes she goes out or eats with friends first. Our big sister, Patricia, baby-sits us. Patricia is 14. Daddy lives close to us; we get to see him pretty often."

"We use to could call Mama at work. But she said we was calling

too much. *She made a new rule. We can't call her. We have to call our dad."*

"Sometimes we get really scared. One time Shadow, that's our dog, was barking and barking. Bobby said he bet it was Phillip hiding out there in the backyard. We was scared. We called daddy and he came right over. He couldn't find Phillip, but he stayed with us 'cause we was really scared and couldn't go to sleep by ourselves. So Daddy slept on the couch. That happened some more times."

"Patricia won't ever come out of her room. She just stays in there watching TV. She don't believe us when we say we're really, really scared."

"Anyway, Daddy got mad at us for calling 'cause we was bothering his sleep. So when we called him the last time we was too scared to call the cops. Patricia wouldn't come out. She just yelled through the door, "Leave me alone!" So a long time later–we knowed we'd be in trouble–but Bobby called Daddy again anyway. He came over, but he was really mad at us 'cause we got him up. As soon as he got to our house, he called the cops. Patricia wouldn't even open her door when the cops were there. I think she pretended to sleep through everything. And she didn't even have to come to court today."

The mom testified next. *Kathy wore tight jeans and a pale yellow shirt with yellow fringe at the neck. She had on yellow sandals, and her toenails were a bright red. Her bleached-blonde hair was pulled back into a neat ponytail. She was in her mid-thirties, medium height, and of small build. She was the supervisor of the night shift as a bartender. She admitted that she'd had an on-again, off-again relationship with Phillip, the Defendant, and that they each had a restraining order issued against the other. "Well, yes, we continued to see each other some after the restraining orders were issued, but I'm through with him for good now. And I won't put up with him scaring my kids! They have a right to be safe in their own home! And he's scaring them to get at me. No, I don't have to work nights. But I make more money at night. Have you tried to find a really good daytime job?!! I want to be able to buy extra things for my kids. They deserve that. I don't want 'em to have to wear clothes from Wal-Mart! No, I don't worry about the kids being at home. Not really. Patricia is a great babysitter. She's very responsible, and she knows the rules."*

"Yeah, I told the boys they couldn't call me at work anymore. No matter what. And they knew I meant business! No, I wasn't getting in trouble at work from them calling me. But—you know—they've got a dad, too! Let 'em call him!"

Next Bob, the dad, was called to the stand. He was wearing brown polyester pants and a short-sleeve dress shirt. The outline of a pack of cigarettes showed through his shirt pocket. Bob testified he'd gone over to the house several nights but he never found Phillip there. He had stayed with his boys and slept on the couch. Then he got tired of it.

"I need my sleep! When they called me that last time, I told them if they really thought Phillip was out there, call 911! But they waited and called back, still crying. Sure I was getting mad. Wouldn't you, with two little boys calling you at all times of the night? This time it was midnight, and I had to get up and go to work the next morning. But I got dressed and went over. Then I called 911. I figured we'd put a stop to this one way or the other. No, I didn't see Phillip. But I saw how scared my boys were! And I won't put up with him scaring my kids in their own house!"

The jury found Phillip not guilty of Aggravated Stalking. I wondered what the verdict would have been if the mom and dad had been charged with failure to parent.

✦ ✦ ✦

The following day the first herd of Boy Scouts moves out, only to be replaced by a larger herd and more kid-sounds reverberating through the park.

Mid-morning I drive into Dubuque where I spend most of my time lost, unable to find landmarks and frequently backtracking. I guess I'm doing on the outside what I feel on the inside—lost without a robe or role, with no sense of direction in this all-but paralyzing freedom to choose anything I want, and no idea what to do next. I'm exactly where I said I wanted to be–on the road alone, homeless, jobless, and able to drift. But somehow, it's not much fun after all. Soon I feel totally overwhelmed by choices. Do I turn left or right? Walk along the waterfront? Eat downtown? Find the library and send out emails? Where is that park? Where am I? Finally I pull into a small, nondescript restaurant that I've passed several times today to choke down a late and not very good lunch. I have to be in a good space to enjoy eating alone in a restaurant; otherwise it's lonely and depressing. This was not one of my good-space days. I drive back to my RV and take a nap. When I wake up, the world looks less intimidating.

The next day I drive over to the Monastery, a huge rock building on a green bluff in Swiss Valley. A very quiet, peaceful place. I decide to wait around for the 6:30 p.m. service. I go looking for a bathroom in the deserted building. My steps echo on wooden floors as I walk down a long corridor with high ceilings and rows of closed doors on each side of me. I feel like a child who doesn't belong in this empty hallway. I pass a room with the door ajar–inside are caskets. I check the hall to be sure no one is looking and then slip in, curious and silly scared, like an eight-year-old enjoying ghost stories around a bonfire. My skin prickles. This is crazy–an empty hallway in a deserted monastery–me sneaking into a room filled with caskets. I go to each casket, my grownup-self scoffing but the eight-year-old-self insisting I double check, just to be sure. Yes, of course, the half a dozen coffins are empty. Then I realize I've been holding my breath and laugh. The caskets, made of various woods, are shaped like those in the old cowboy movies—angling out in a straight line from the head to the shoulders, then straight down to the feet. The literature on the corner table explains that the monks build these coffins as part of their cottage industry. If what they have in stock doesn't fit your frame or your fancy, you can special order through their web site–modern marketing that seems incongruent with the grey stone building erected at the close of the Civil War in 13th century Gothic architecture style.

I check the hallway and sneak out the door, as though I might be in trouble if caught. Then I sit outside on the lawn for an hour, waiting for the service. I watch the wind play in the tall grass, listen to the voices in my head pinging and whining, and feel the wind blow through my hair. Several years ago I began to meditate daily, and I've learned to value this deep listening and the intention required to even briefly quiet the committee of critics in my head. I hold my breath and smile as a butterfly lands two times on the knee of my then twice-blessed jeans.

As an adult, I pushed far from the traditional structure of religion to slip in and out of various institutions and belief patterns. At times I paused briefly, like this butterfly; when it felt comfortable, I lingered. I've come to know a loving Creator/ God/Spirit for whom titles are not important. Call it whatever; it is that which is greater, more powerful than I am. I do not deny the power of evil, hatred, destruction, or obsession with control, but I believe that the Universe is slightly tilted toward that which fosters growth, that which is good. If it were not so, the human race would have annihilated itself long ago. It is easy to let violence, hatred, retribution, and spite be the focus of my life. Or I can choose a marrow of kindness, patience, acceptance, love, tenderness, and creation. I left the Bench because it was becoming increasingly difficult to see the good in the world and because I didn't like the person I had become. I was growing detached and calloused because I did not know how else to survive the waves of humanity and all of the negative forces that came to me for justice. Driving around the country alone, I hope to find another way to live this one life I've been given.

As I sit alone on the grass, a few people drive up and go into the building. I wait a bit; this is their world, not mine, and I don't want to talk. I slip into the back corner of the long, tall chapel just as the service begins. At peace, though without answers, I sit on the wooden bench as the monks chant. When the service is over, I leave quickly and go back home to Bruin.

I wake up the second morning knowing I've spent enough time lost in Dubuque. I call a campground in Iowa City near the university where I'll be in class and ask for reservations and directions. The owner asks, "Are you comfortable driving country roads?" Following his directions, I drive 50 miles through the backcountry without passing so much as a convenience store. I've spent my life being busy–working and being responsible–so I've seen very little of our country. Now that I'm traveling, the world is rewarding me. The countryside of Iowa is beautiful–huge farms, rolling green hills, zillions of cows and cement barns. They pour a cement slab at the cows' entrance because the ground gets very soupy in the winter.

On the road, I stay in close contact with a few folks by cell phone. I talk with Al a lot; it varies with his work schedule and my cell phone service but sometimes we talk a couple of times a day. These short conversations always include a laugh and encouragement for whatever problem I've gotten myself into next. We talk about mechanical issues, as well as loneliness, fatigue, and my short-term plans. He always says I can handle whatever I'm facing; he never says I'm too stupid or too female. I also talk with two close friends I met in our meditation group–Gwen, my wise Chinese friend and Cherry whom we both rely on for spiritual wisdom and a dose of non-judgmental reality. I stay in touch with my son, Clay, and then, of course, I talk with Bruin about everything. I'm also sending out an email travel log to a group that keeps growing; mostly, they're judge friends from around Florida. I get short responses in the form of jokes and encouragement, though many also assure me I'm out of my mind.

As I begin to back the trailer into my slot at the campground in Iowa City, an older man dressed in jeans and a green plaid cotton shirt comes from the RV next door. "Can I help, ma'am? Just come straight on back." With his help, I look like I know what I'm doing. When I turn the truck off, the edge of the cement patio and the steps to the RV are in a perfect line.

I enjoy being back on a university campus. I feel at home in the writing classes where I do not have to explain the draw to and fear of pushing a pen across the blank page. I sit with others who struggle to find words, who strain to learn the craft while honoring the art. From my favored instructor I learn a new mantra: "Show, don't tell."

When I'm not in class, the campground owner sends me off on side trips that often include serial dirt roads. On one outing, miles from pavement, I stop at a cemetery with graves dating back to the 1830's. I like to walk around old cemeteries, wondering about the stories the headstones could tell and wishing for inscriptions in the fashion of those in Edgar Lee Masters' Spoon River Anthology. I wander, looking for grave hints to the personalities buried there, watching for groups of deaths in a brief time span that may suggest a plague, while overlaying the cemetery and my imaged people with a limited knowledge of history (before or after the Civil War, during the Depression, World War I or II, etc.). But as I walk by the grave of a four-year-old little girl, my throat began to ache, my eyes burn, and my steps slow. I wonder where Autumn's small grave rests and what her tombstone says.

IOWA

❦ ❦ ❦

For Autumn

Autumn was a four-year-old murder victim, kicked to death in a fit of rage by George Broxson, her new stepfather. Autumn didn't want to die, so she kept crawling under furniture, to be dragged out and kicked again and again. Finally when she had no other choice, she died. Shortly after the noise subsided, Autumn's mother came home from work. Her husband had promised many things including a better life for her daughter. Now, he swore, "Autumn fell off the tree swing."

I had been on the Bench for less than two years in this tiny town in the backwaters of the panhandle of Florida when I found myself looking down the barrel of an impossible criminal docket that included three capital murder cases (a case in which the State is seeking the death penalty). When Autumn's stepfather came up for trial late that summer, I had completed two of the three cases and had imposed the death penalty twice.

The law in death penalty cases was complex and did not allow the State to kill everyone who kills another. Murders are committed for a variety of reasons, using a gamut of methods, and the Florida legislature developed a weighing process, a score sheet if you will, to be used by judges and juries when evaluating a specific murder for the death penalty. The judge and jury were to weigh aggravating factors (reasons to kill the defendant) against mitigating factors (reasons to not kill him).[2] If the jury found the defendant guilty of 1st degree murder, there was a second trial, known as the penalty phases, and the same jury of 12 returned a recommendation to the Judge on whether the death penalty should be imposed. If the jury recommended death, the Judge remained the ultimate decision-maker and could sentence the defendant to life in prison without parole. On the other side of the equation, if the jury recommended

---

[2]Aggravators were defined by statute and included a murder carefully planned or premeditated, one committed for money, and a murder that caused the victim great pain and suffering (as distinguished from a murder caused by a single bullet to the head of an unsuspecting victim.) Mitigating factors, a term more loosely defined by the Legislature, could include pretty much anything, such as a deprived childhood or a history of doing volunteer work.

life, there was a narrow set of facts and legal requirements under which a judge might override the jury's recommendation and impose the death penalty.

I was 44 years old, ambitious, and determined to prove to myself, this community and the rest of the world that I could do this job well. I was careful to stay current on the law, and I had attended the very technical course designed for judges, aptly named "Death is Different." The group of intelligent and well-trained judges discussed many nuances of the law in death penalty cases but we didn't examine what it would actually feel like to order that another human being be killed. Over after-dinner drinks, we still didn't get into the moral or spiritual issues involved in exacting "an eye for an eye" or the politics of revenge. But finally I asked one of my buddies, "Rob, what happens when you're stubborn as a mule, but have the heart of a poet?" He waited a moment, and said, "It's gonna be rough on you, Melvin."

At dinner, the casual conversations among my colleagues often included facts regarding the death penalty, realities unrelated to our job of applying the Law.

• The death penalty is not cost effective. It cost three times as much to execute a defendant as it does to imprison for life.

• DNA results increasingly show the fallibility of eye witnesses and other evidence.

• There is no study that shows that the death penalty is a deterrent to crime.

• There is racial bias in the administration of the death penalty

• Imposition of the death penalty is technical capricious; if you get arrested for the same crime with the same facts in South Florida, that jury is less likely to recommend the death penalty than a jury in a rural area in North Florida. I have a friend who sat on the criminal bench in Ft. Lauderdale for 15 years and never had the jury recommend the death penalty.

• In Florida all death sentences must be reviewed by the Florida Supreme Court. Death penalty cases make up 12% of the Supreme Court's docket yet, because of the complexity and finality involved, such cases usurp 50% of the Court's time, leaving the remaining 88% of its cases only 50% of its time and attention.[3]

The first man I sentenced to death is named Ernest Suggs. He was 37 years old; I was 44. Suggs was a twice-convicted murderer; I was a Circuit Judge. I sentenced Suggs to die in the electric chair, although the death penalty is three times as expensive as imprisoning for life, is not a deterrent, and is unfairly applied. I sentenced Suggs to death, although I believe that killing in retribution is wrong. I imposed the death penalty because I believed that was my job. And 20 years later Suggs still waits to be killed in the metal and concrete world of death row with 405 other in Florida and 3,300 others in the United States. Suggs is a unique defendant on Death Row in that he's upper-middle-class white in a group that is disproportionately black.

At the time of his arrest and early court appearances, Suggs was a middle-aged white male, 5 feet 8 inches tall, heavy-set but not fat, brown hair, and blue eyes. But when I saw him nine years later for post-conviction relief motions, he had aged, gained weight, and wore the signs of a human body long caged without sunlight, with skin so pallid it seemed translucent.

If the State is ever going to justify killing in retribution for killing–Suggs is it. Suggs was on parole for murder in Georgia. In the trial I handled, the jury found him guilty of a robbery at a liquor store, kidnapping of the female clerk to a remote area, and then murder by multiple sophisticated knife wounds, wounds described in the book on his shelf at home. The book, titled Deal the First Deadly Blow, was illustrated with black and white photos of a man and his female "victim" to show position and angle of the knife and described in chilling detail the depth required and specific results. Deal the First Deadly Blow is a how-to-book for killers.

At the close of the second trial, or penalty phase, the jury's recommendation was five for life, and seven for death.

On the day of sentencing, the air in the courtroom was charged– no one knew what my decision would be. In this small courthouse (three floors counting the basement) I avoided everyone. Later my

[3]"Take a hard look at the real cost of the death penalty" Florida Bar News, March 2010

secretary and security officer confided in me the courthouse mutterings. Some folks assumed I'd "do it," but others questioned my ability to impose the death penalty, me being a woman and all.

When it came down to it, I could not rationalize overruling the jury. Suggs met all the criteria under the law; as the Judge, I didn't feel that I had the option of voting my personal morals. As I struggled with my decision I recited from memory the jury instruction I'd read many times: "In closing, let me remind you that it is important that you follow the law spelled out in these instructions in deciding your verdict. There are no other laws that apply to this case. Even if you do not like the laws that must be applied, you must use them. For two centuries we have lived by the Constitution and the Law. No juror has the right to violate rules we all share."

So I did my job.

I had done my homework. I reread the course materials and reviewed the cases. I didn't know of any error in the trial.

I typed out the lengthy order for Suggs and basically read from it. I read, feeling distant from the words, from the reality. Sitting up there on the bench in this quaint Southern courthouse, a courtroom with tall ceilings and long windows on two sides—it was hard to perceive any actual connection between my mere words and this same man having a hood put over his head, being strapped to an antique wooden chair, and then the State, us, flipping the switch, frying his brains—killing him.[4] I read aloud the standard words "death by electrocution and may God have mercy on your soul" and then added "and on ours." I felt far away. I took much comfort in the nitpicking appeal process that would follow—knowing it would be years before everybody finished reviewing this job I'd done. I took comfort in feeling I was only a small part of the process, hoping that somehow I could feel less than ultimately responsible, trying to ignore the fact that I had the choice to impose a life sentence and reject the jury's recommendation. I ignored the legal

---

[4] In Florida, execution was by the electric chair until January 2000, when the Florida Legislature passed legislation that allows lethal injection as an alternative method of execution.

reality that the Supreme Court would not likely reverse a lower court's decision to impose a life sentence.

It was dark when I left the courthouse. I went for a long drive through the woods, riding slowly down dirt trails, without my headlights on, grateful for the moonlight and the quiet. Just riding.

And then I got up the next morning and went back to work.

The trial of George Broxson, Autumn's stepfather, was the third capital murder case I'd try that summer. Over the next few months Broxson came into my Chambers several times for various pretrial motions; each time he was dressed in a jail-house-issued green jumpsuit with brown plastic sandals. He was always quiet and respectful. He was in his early 30's, a tall white male of slender build, fairly nondescript. Someone you'd pass at the grocery store or gas station every day. He certainly didn't look like a baby killer.

I don't know how many other murder cases with a child victim I've tried as a judge. Actually, I don't want to know. I don't want to think back, because in that counting process I will recall graphic details of what it looks like when a baby is murdered. But protective amnesia has never worked for me when it comes to Autumn's case. It's been over twenty years, yet her memory will still blind-side me. Somehow, Autumn continues to prod me, to make my heart contract, and my eyes tear.

It was my job to conduct this trial without legal error, and because the victim was a child, that was going to be rough. The prosecutor announced he would ask for the death penalty, upping the ante, so to speak, in terms of the significance of the smallest mistake. And the facts involved in the blunt trauma death of a small child created an emotional mine field that was seeded with technical legal issues.

The State was obligated to prove that the stepfather had repeatedly kicked Autumn and that she died of blunt trauma. In doing so, the State would be allowed to present evidence, some of which would be gruesome. At the same time, the Defendant was entitled to a verdict that was not based solely on the emotions of the jurors, so I was not to admit evidence that inflamed emotions but proved no necessary facts. My job was to protect the rights of both the State and the Defendant.

When I had to hold and then look at the 5x7 autopsy photos of Autumn, it felt as though the world shifted, for each was a glossy reminder of the violent death of a young child. Each was graphic evidence that the case was not limited to legal arguments and historical facts recited by professionals. From an analytical standpoint, the photos were important pieces of evidence to which a finite set of legal rules applied. At night I spent hours researching the Evidence Code, other statutes and case law. I read on and on, comparing the appellant cases with the facts and photos in Autumn's case. I didn't want to make a mistake dealing with the violent death of a four-year-old girl.

As we went through Autumn's autopsy photos in my Chambers before the trial, the defense attorney argued why the jury shouldn't see any of the photos, and the prosecution argued why the jury should see them all. As we worked through the large stack of color photos, one by one, I was dealing with the technical aspects of the law and autopsy photos, but I was also trying to desensitize myself as a human being, a woman, a mother—desensitizing myself so the jury couldn't see on my face the horror of my soul as I looked at the dead baby, surgically dissected to show internal trauma and cause of death. I admitted into evidence photos that depicted the blunt trauma, primarily to the abdomen, but was careful not to admit multiple views of the same injury. If a photo that was less horrific accurately portrayed the trauma and force used, that one would be admitted. I required the prosecutor to show the specific legal purpose of admitting a photo that included more blood or one in which it was easier to recognize Autumn as a four-year-old. After going through all the photos, I ruled some would be allowed into evidence; some, the jury would never see.

DeFuniak Springs is a rural town in the conservative Deep South. The story of a four-year-old dying of blunt trauma and her new stepdad in jail for murder triggered strong emotional reactions.

Then the defense attorney filed a Motion to Remove the Ten Commandments from the wall at the entrance to the courtroom. I researched the law; he was right. If I allowed the trial to proceed, I'd be reversed and have to try it again, the second time without the Ten Commandments standing guard.

While doing the legal research on this conundrum, it was clear that these jurors could not walk past the Ten Commandments, but nothing said I had to remove the religious plaque. So I sent Ron, my bailiff, to the grocery store with an unusual request. At the end of the day when the courthouse was empty, Ron and I used brown meat wrapping paper and scotch tape to cover the Ten Commandments. The plaque then looked something like a Christmas present hanging there in the hall. The next morning I filed my order that the Ten Commandments would remain covered "until further order of the court."

The Bible Belt erupted. Details, such as the fact that the defense was legally correct, had no impact or relevance for the masses. The defense attorney received death threats; my name and address were published by various fundamental church groups, triggering boxes of mail. Strangers from around the country, and a few foreign countries as well, wrote me scathing analyses of the state of my soul and offered explicit details of what I would suffer in Hell–a place, they assured me, I was clearly destined to see. The County Commissioners held a special meeting at which the Walton County Christian Coalition presented a petition with 2,341 signatures in protest to my covering the Ten Commandments. The Board voted unanimously "to take whatever action" was necessary to protect the Ten Commandments. People who had been warm and friendly to me before would now avoid all contact if possible; if some exchange was required, they spoke in short, brittle phrases. Looking for the bright side, at least I had run for reelection the year before.

At one level it was interesting to watch all of this, for the defendant and I were both being fileted by the press and local community. Because I had followed the law and covered the Ten Commandments, I was now staring into the face of an emotional uproar spouting religious terms. I was protected from that mind set by the power of the Law and my robe. My job was to ensure safe space for the exercise of Justice. And that meant I was to defend the Constitutional rights of the man accused of kicking Autumn to death while also protecting the rights of the State and its citizens. It's a lonely job that requires copious amounts of intellectual impartiality.

Soon the defense attorney filed a motion asking that the trial be moved from DeFuniak because of all of the negative public sentiment and publicity about the Ten Commandments. There were many who grumbled and growled at the requested change; I wondered if they were angered by the possibility that the defendant might "get away" from them. I granted the motion and ordered the trial be held in Milton, my home-town and a rural community covered by different news media. We were able to select a jury in Milton who knew nothing of the hue and cry generated by my covering the Ten Commandments in DeFuniak Springs.

At the trial the defendant looked thinner in "civilian clothes" than he did in the baggy jailhouse jump suit he wore to the many Pretrial Motions. Each day George came to court clean-shaven, in a business suit and white shirt—wearing cowboy boots. Pointed-toe cowboy boots. Boots that could seriously injure or kill a small four-year-old girl. Every time I looked at him, he was still wearing those damn boots. Nothing was ever said on the record about his cowboy boots, and the Medical Examiner testified that the Defendant's rounded-toe, heavy work-boots found in his room were consistent with the injuries inflicted. My duty was to spend hours, days, and weeks working on the technical aspects of the Constitutional rights of the Defendant and the State of Florida. But as I worked, the cowboy boots hissed, "This is not academic. In a real bedroom, there was a real baby, a baby who is now dead."

Throughout the trial, I was braced and crossed braced, all my emotion and humanity covered by my robe and stored far below my resolve. My only focus was my duty to insure a fair trial, fair to the State and to the Defendant.

On the second day of the trial, Jan the Crime Scene Investigator from the Florida Department of Law Enforcement, was called to the stand. Jan had been a crime scene expert for more than 20 years. She was trained in chemistry and physics. She worked with blood splatters, fingerprints, tire tracks. You name it, and she'd analyzed it. It was her job to go to crime scenes and to autopsies, and she'd done that hundreds, maybe thousands of times. It was her job to testify professionally, accurately, with detachment. And she was very good at her job. When Jan took the stand, she knew this was a preliminary drill to show that she was at the autopsy and that she took the photos. All she had to do was to identify that group of photos, marked as State's Exhibit 22. She would testify on a later day about the specifics of those photos.

After Jan was sworn in, the prosecutor asked her name and occupation. There was a crisp, professional response. Then, while holding a small stack of color photos in the palm of his hand, he asked, "Did you attend the autopsy of Autumn Jean Doyle?"

The room was quiet. Jan didn't answer because she couldn't. Her face twisted and turned red as she tried in vain to stop the tears. Her years of training and experience had just been knocked out by an extreme wave of emotion, a rogue wave named Autumn.

As the silence deepened, the prosecutor looked at me in confusion, and I simply said, "We're going to take a ten minute break. Court is in recess." I murmured a prayer for Jan and the rest of us as I walked away.

Ten minutes later, the Bailiff barked, "Court is reconvened. All rise!"

Jan resumed her testimony with polished and authoritative responses.

The trial moved on through the week, with the testimony of the Medical Examiner, the mother, and law enforcement. For days, I sat in the courtroom on the edge of my chair with my back straight, both feet on the floor, straining to insure I heard, saw, and understood everything. Underneath my black robe, I wore the predictable and professional pinstriped suits. This was serious, *deadly serious; here, there was no time or place for Laura; I was the Judge, and nothing else.*

In a private hearing with the attorneys, the prosecutor agreed to schedule the introduction of the autopsy photos at the end of the day. Around 4 p.m., the State Attorney stood up with the stack of selected autopsy photos in his hand and said, "Your Honor, the State moves State's Exhibit 22 into evidence."

The defense counsel stood to say, "Your Honor, I renew my earlier objections but acknowledge that the exhibit contains only the photos detailed in the pretrial motion."

I responded, "Counsel, would you please hand the exhibit to Security."

The prosecutor handed the photos to Tim, my security officer who then handed them to me. With the jury watching, I slowly flipped through each of the photos in the stack. I didn't have to do that; the defense and I knew exactly which photos were there. But I wanted the jury to see me look at them; I wanted them to see that a woman and mother could study those photos. What the jury didn't know was that I didn't look at them, not really. I had already seen too much, and I didn't trust my face in public. With the jury watching, I held the stack in my hand and flipped through them, studying only the white border on each while carefully avoiding the images.

At the close of the case, the jury returned a unanimous verdict that the Defendant was guilty of First Degree Murder. With the same jury we began the second trial or penalty phase in which the State and Defense presented evidence and argued why the death penalty should or should not be imposed. At the close of the penalty phase, the jurors recommended by a vote of nine to three that the Defendant receive life in prison; I knew that under Florida law had I imposed the death penalty contrary to the jury's recommendation of life, the Supreme Court would find that I had not followed the law and the case would be reversed, after much expense and delay. I also understood that killing Autumn's stepfather, in her name, would do no good. So at the end of the week, I sentenced the George Broxson to life in prison without parole.[5]

❧ ❧ ❧

---

[5]On appeal, the higher court found no error, and the defendant is serving his life sentence

But that wasn't the end, of course. Things aren't that simple or straightforward. Years later, I think of Autumn, and my stomach tightens. My eyes fill with tears as I stand in a cemetery in Iowa, as I watch the fall leaves change colors, or as I sit quietly, doing nothing at all. And I have slowly come to understand that no matter how he tried, Autumn's stepfather could not force her to remain in his rage, fear, and pain, for he was not that powerful. Autumn quietly left him behind. She left him alone in his self-made hell.

Across the dirt road from the cemetery is a small field of prairie grass, and down the way a young boy, maybe seven, stands on the cement apron outside the family's barn, feeding a bottle to a calf. A child dressed in blue jeans and tall black rubber boots, going through the routine of his life, a short life that is already longer than the one Autumn lived.

After finishing the eight days of writing classes, I drive west into Nebraska, taking with me a slight boost in confidence, a renewed commitment to keep my pen moving, and a few technical skills. I'm heading to Denver to pick up my friend Sara at the airport; it feels good to be on the road again.

I'm fairly easily entertained, and as we approach the Nebraska state line, I have a grand idea. I explain to Bruin with a laugh, "Trust me, you'll have fun being my model." I pull into the Visitors Center and have him pose in front of the first of many state signs. He sits quietly as I back away to frame the photo just so. After a walk down paths he finds more interesting than I do, we drive on. This is another part of the country I haven't seen. Nebraska has more trees than Iowa.

I stop for the night at the Wal-Mart in Kearney, Nebraska. Soon a horrific thunderstorm roars in from the east, blackening the sky over the colossal cornfields that share the open spaces with Wal-Mart. The clouds are dense and the color of tar, moving in that eerie dance favored by tornadoes. I briefly consider waiting out the storm deep in Wal-Mart, but I know they won't let Bruin in, so I fix a cup of hot tea and settle into my recliner. As the world turns a pale shade of slime green, I take a macabre comfort in the fact that there are five other RVs in the parking lot. I explain to Bruin, "Someone may notice if we go missing. It'll be more newsworthy that six RVs were tornado'd back to Kansas." Thunder and lightning in Nebraska makes what we have in Florida look like sparklers! In the bowels of the storm, the wind rocks the 5th wheel so hard that the Venetian blinds thwack against the walls. I get mad at the banging sound of the blinds –an unreasoned response to my raw fear. I pick up Bruin's dish because it's sloshing water on the floor. From time to time I look through the dancing Venetians–just checking to see if any of the other RVs has flipped.

Of course, I can't sleep. When the winds finally die down, I go shopping for wine, Cheerios, chips, and dog treats. It's quiet in Wal-Mart at 4:00 a.m. I smile at a stockman, and he responds, "Man, could you believe that storm! The winds got up to 60 mph!" A nice round number that justified some of my terror.

I'm on the road as the sun comes up, driving through Nebraska and gazillions of cows standing around on bare ground, dying for someone to order rib eye. The smell of cloistered cows is strong. The odor of manure, urine, and fear packed into small spaces is not pleasant.

Riding west across Nebraska, the low light of sunrise brushes the underside of trees and shrubs. The face of the world has been washed by the thunderstorm, leaving all things fresh. I have a cup of coffee, my dog, my home, and a big smile.

"Train up a child in the way he should go, and when he is old, he will not depart from it."
Proverbs 22:6

CHAPTER 4.
THE STRUCTURE OF MY SMALL WORLD

I have no childhood memory of Dad other than as a revered figure who occasionally passed through the house. He was busy with his law practice and high-level state politics (he was a member of the Florida House of Representatives and then the State Senate from 1947 to 1956). I was ten years old when in 1957 he became a Circuit Judge, but that change in job title had no impact on my life or my relationship with Dad. Home is where Dad brought professionals for lunch and where he could sit quietly at the end of the day, without being disturbed. There were five kids in his house, but he didn't engage with us. Mom's rule was simple: "Do not bother your dad." And we didn't.

As he aged, Dad interacted more and more with the family, and as a young adult, I had a greater understanding of this gentle man who sat quietly at the end of a long day. Dad was patient and kind-hearted; he quoted Shakespeare, peppered his speech with Latin phrases, and whistled subconsciously when he was relaxed. He had a dry sense of humor, and his eyes would dance as he set up a joke. His laugh was contagious. When I was 12, my parents built a home down on Blackwater Bay and, except for one year in Tallahassee, lived there the rest of their lives. Dad was not a handy-man, mechanical, or remotely curious about anything that involved physical activity, though in his earlier years he enjoyed throwing the mullet net.

Though you don't find mullet on the menu at the higher-priced restaurants, it's a popular fish amongst the "natives" in this small geographic area (east of Mobile Bay to the Big Bend Area south of Tallahassee) where the bottoms of the bays are clean sand. But most people laugh at you if you say you eat mullet: "Mullet's a trash fish! You use mullet for bait. You don't eat it!" Mullet are not expensive; they're known as the poor man's fish. Mullet are a humble fish; the South's version of rhubarb. The term "mullet wrapper" refers to a newspaper with nothing in it worth reading so it's used for wrapping (cheap) fish. In this neck of the woods, mullet is a mild-flavored fish. Gary, my ex-husband and local mullet expert, explained that mullet don't keep well; they're good for four to five days max, which makes it more difficult to commercially fish for them. Festivals have grown up in this area on the image of mullet; there's the Boggy Bayou Mullet Festival in Niceville, Florida and the Interstate Mullet Toss, sponsored by the FloraBama Bar, held on the beach at the Florida-Alabama line where contestants toss dead mullet from one state to the other.

Most people fish for mullet by throwing a net, but some chum them up using cooked rice (they throw the rice into the water and the mullet come to feed) and then use cane poles with dough balls or mealworms on small hooks for bait. Dad always used a net; he would catch the mullet and clean them at the edge of the Bay. Mom fried them in deep grease and fixed a big meal that included cheese grits, hush puppies, and baked beans heavy with brown sugar and bacon. If Dad caught mullet early in the morning, we had them for breakfast, with grits and fried eggs. As he aged, Dad stopped throwing the net, but friends often gave him "a mess of mullet" for Mom to cook.

Though Dad liked to talk about mullet, Law was his life; it was his profession, his passion, his mistress, his hobby. He had no real interest other than the Law, and he wasn't interested in developing any. He spent his life studying the Law and was very well versed in its technical aspects. He had a knack for cutting through complexities of humanity and law to arrive at the central issue. He was accustomed to wielding great power and was known to wait quietly and announce his decision, with a soft- spoken Southern accent that brooked no argument. I never heard my dad raise his voice, at home or in the courtroom.

Dad was one of six sons, each born in the same bedroom in the house built by their father in Milton; Dr. Thames delivered each of the boys to my Grandmother Laura. In 1945 Dr. Thames was there again when my older brother Jim was born in that room. While in labor in 1947 in the same bedroom, Mother said to Dr. Thames, "Maybe this one will be a girl." He laughed, "Now, you know, Nita, girls can't be born in this house." Mom was inordinately proud when I proved him wrong. When she managed to birth two more girls, she quietly resolved to help us stem the tide of male dominance.

Mom attended Florida State College for Women from 1932 to 1934, and then returned to Milton at the age of 18 to marry Dad, her high school sweetheart. As was expected of her, she lived her life as a wife and mother. She raised her five kids on a deep appreciation for nature and a wide range of literature. Like the main character in Rudyard Kipling's The Elephant's Child– a book she had read so often that she often quoted huge sections by heart–Mom was full of insatiable curiosity. She studied a broad range of subjects, including physics, biology, astronomy, Biblical archeology, and genealogy. She grew Bonsai plants and fed several squadrons of hummingbirds on her front deck.

A soft-spoken woman, uncomfortable around crowds, and very sensitive to noise, Mom stayed away from the TV and radio; she had no interest in shopping malls. Her spiritual path crossed in and out of church but it always focused on a loving God manifesting in nature. Mother was slightly overweight and had beautiful skin; she saw herself as mousey. Those who met her saw a woman of gentle kindness, a kindness that came into full bloom with her grandchildren.

Mom was a gifted seamstress and made clothes for her three daughters. Later she sewed for the granddaughters, often adding rows and rows of colored rickrack to the hems of their dresses.

Always curious about the world, at the age of 79, she returned to college. We gave her a computer for her 80th birthday, and she immediately signed up for computer classes. The walls of her sewing room were stuffed with books, and she delighted in giving her favorites to young readers, a practice she followed for years.

Mom loved to travel; Dad loved to stay home. And so it was that she didn't see much of the world that fascinated her. When a child or grandchild would leave on a trip, she'd say, "Take my good-looking eyes with you, baby. And when you come home, tell me what you saw."

I inherited my mom's stubbornness, curiosity, and love of the road. I was raised in the same culture that taught her a lady was to be responsible but subservient. Much of my life I've bucked against those gender constraints that chained her to a predictable life in Milton. I also inherited my dad's ambition and love of the Law; I've worked hard to reflect some his wisdom and kindness.

"When you come to a fork in the road, take it."
Yogi Berra

CHAPTER 5.
COLORADO:
Guns, God, heights, and horses

I ride west on Interstate 80 through Nebraska and then take Interstate 76 southwest toward Denver. Mid-day, I top one of the many rolling hills, and there stand the Rocky Mountains. There are no words for their grandeur or the joyful impossibility of my actually being here. I can't think of anything else to do, so I begin to laugh happy tears while singing "America the Beautiful" at the top of my lungs.

My friend Sara is flying into the Denver airport to spend time with me, a joint gift from her dad and me for her 17th birthday. I first met Sara and her dad when she was eight.

Shortly after I became a judge, I was hiking through a state park on a trail that weaved through oak and pines as it snaked around the edges of Bluewater Bay. Rounding a corner, my jealously-guarded solitude was interrupted by the sight of a young girl and a man squatted down beside her as they looked at something in the leaves. They were easy with one another, and I assumed he was a week-end dad, enjoying that short time-line in which it is easier to focus on and be present for your child. He was tall and good looking; she was animated by a huge head of long, curly hair and a complexion that seemed to glow in the leaf-diffused light. They hadn't seen me, and I quickly turned down a side path to avoid them. I needed nature; I didn't need to chit-chat with strangers. My new path turned and abruptly ended at the water's edge, and there I was drawn to animal tracks in the sand, tracks I couldn't identify. Soon I heard the little girl and man coming down the dead-end path to my hideout; I frowned and followed an animal trail behind some tall palmettoes. The young girl scampered straight to the beach and squealed, "Look, Dad! Raccoon tracks." He walked to her with a laugh

73

and said, "You're right." He was cute, I liked what I saw of the energy between the two of them, and I really didn't know how to read the track, so I came out of my hiding place, stooped down beside her and asked, "OK, how can you tell it's a raccoon." Thus began a life-long friendship with Sara and a shorter but important romantic relationship with Ron.

For our first date, Ron, Sara, and I took his ski boat, on a cold Florida winter day, on to a large body of water. To Ron's chagrin, the engine died miles from the shore. As he and I took turns with the one paddle, I taught Sara how to speak pig Latin. And I learned that I could not have been more wrong about my weekend-dad assessment of Ron. Sara and her mom were in an automobile accident when Sara was eight weeks old; her mom was killed. Ron was a single dad, raising a motherless daughter in the Deep South, with generous support from his mother and sisters.

Sara and I developed a close relationship concurrent with and yet independent of my relationship with Ron. The three of us were united by an awe of nature and a love of experiencing the great outdoors. As Sara grew over the years, we discussed many things. I wanted her to see me as a safe person with whom to share feelings and questions. Of course, I talked to her about going to college. Her dad was on a very tight budget; Sara's good grades made a scholarship a realistic goal. But Sara only described herself as living at home and going to a local community college. She often explained, "I can't imagine living anywhere else."

There are quirky little ways you can see Ron's influence on Sara. She loves to go camping, and even at the age of eight, she insisted on sleeping alone in her separate tent. Like her dad, she has no interest in guns; unlike her dad, she's a good shot with the bow and arrow. Her dad taught her to defend herself and to do the dishes. Each year she gives her dad a card for Mother's Day.

As I begin the southwest jog of Interstate 76 to Denver,

thoughts of Sara and her dad get tangled with thoughts of Autumn and her step-dad, pricking memories that lead to other murder trials that then lead to trials of a personal nature. Such mental gymnastics are my blessing and curse for traveling long distances alone.

Shortly after going on the Bench, I received in the mail a permanent permit to carry a concealed weapon. It just came– without me even asking for it–like grits with an order of eggs in the Deep South. The permit assumed that a gun, like a robe, was part of my new uniform. Within a few days, a Highway Patrol Officer introduced himself and asked, "Judge, what gun do you carry?" I responded, "Well, I don't." He said, "You have to. I'll get with your assistant and set up an appointment. I'll show you some good options." A few days later, with my new .38 in hand, he took me to the law enforcement officer shooting range. He trained me well and often.

My new job included other unique twists. One was my own personal, armed deputy. Tim and I were certainly the Odd Couple in this small rural area–Tim, the only African American with the Sheriff's Department, and me, the only female judge in a county that had no female attorneys. I also had my own court reporter who wrote down basically every word I said. Another reality of my new life was the panic button located on the underside of my desk in chambers and the Bench in the courtroom. The little buttons looked like doorbells, and they set off an alarm in the Sheriff's Office that sent armed deputies running. As I sat in other courtrooms in the four-county Circuit, I found such silent alarms in each. Many of the courtrooms also had a small tray in the knee-well of the Benches to hold the Judge's personal gun. In our Circuit, it was common for male judges to wear a small pistol strapped to their ankle; this choice was not available to me as I wore skirts rather than slacks. If violence erupted in the courtroom, judges were taught to immediately duck into the knee-well of the Bench, some of which were lined with recycled bullet-proof vests from law enforcement agencies. This new job was about enforcing justice as currently defined by the Legislature; the work place was not geared toward peace, nature, smiles, or hope.

My robe was weighing heavy. I had completed two of three capital murder cases on my docket and was working on pre-trial motions in George Broxson's case, Autumn's step-dad, and was under siege in the community for having covered the Ten Commandments. I called Ron Saturday morning to say I wasn't coming over. "I need to take a long hike in the State Park, off the path. I've got to get out into the woods; it's almost like I need to go swimming in them." He replied, "I understand. But be sure to take your gun with you." Somehow the idea that I couldn't walk alone, safely, in nature without my .38 to protect me from the harsh world of man, that idea was just too much. I had been well trained to use the gun. I had accepted the need to keep it in my car and in my house. I carried it in and out of the courthouse; it lay close by in a drawer while I worked. But in the woods! When I needed to get away from violence?

I decided I had two options: run through the state park at a break-neck speed until I was too tired to think, or talk this through with someone who might understand. I called a new acquaintance, Dr. Thomas L. Butts, pastor of the Trinity Methodist Church in Fort Walton Beach, someone I'd met through our mutual friend, Scott Peck, author of The Road Less Traveled. I knew Scotty trusted Tom and so I said, "Tom. Could you meet me for breakfast? Today!" He was waiting for me at the IHOP, and during our first one-on-one conversation, I poured out my frustrations with my new life in general and my responsibility for three murder trials in particular. "So here I am. In a job that assumes I'll arm myself, off duty, in the woods. And I don't hunt!" Somehow, in the midst of it all, my humanity got the upper-hand. My voice cracked, my nose ran, and I stabbed at mascara-streaked tears

COLORADO

with a soggy Kleenex. I didn't look or feel very judicious as I sat with this kind stranger in the middle of a crowded restaurant.

As my emotional tide subsided, I accepted that I could trust Tom at all levels. We talked of the community building workshops that Peck sponsored and Tom's work there. Then I launched, "OK, Tom, it's like this! I was raised in a Southern Baptist Church with a judgmental, revengeful god, one I could never please no matter how hard I tried. And trust me, I tried!" Tom didn't reprimand me for such blasphemy. He just nodded with a smile and said nothing. So I continued, "I left the Baptist Church and was churchless for years. Then I found myself in a Unitarian church. I thought it was cool when they played a tape of Mack the Knife for the offertory. But I slowly came to know that I needed more than their focus on the intellectual; it was as though in their world everything can be defined and debated. I needed room for mystery and awe, things I see in nature every day." Tom nodded. "I left the Unitarians at about the same time I began going to Al-Anon meetings, a 12-step group that showed me a Higher Power of love, spirit, and mystery. Then I backed into a Unity Church, then a Catholic and Episcopal Church. I say 'backed' because that's how it feels–like I don't get a clear view of what I'm doing or where I'm heading. For the last 10 years or so I've meditated daily. That's really the most important part of my spiritual journey. For me, being still and breathing is the best way to quiet these critical voices, the committee that resides in my head. I loved my time in the Episcopal Church, but one day as we knelt singing, I knew I had to leave. Immediately. And I haven't been back. I have a prayer I don't recommend to anyone, Tom, yet I keep using it. It's 'Creator, please don't be subtle.' And, duh!–my prayer keeps getting answered."

Tom laughed softly, "Many spiritual people move across different paths at different times. My day-time job as a Man of the Cloth keeps me locked into the Methodist Church. At times I'd love the flexibility you have."

"But, Tom," I blurted, "What about this gun?! Now what! Does all this mean I have to learn to meditate with a fucking .38 in my lap?" He looked me straight in the eye and responded simply, "Yes." And though we were in a crowded restaurant, we sat together, alone, in silence.

He caught me totally off guard by his lack of recoil at my crude language and his candid acceptance of me and this new job of mine. A job that was clearly much bigger than I was. Another prayer answered, I guess, and the beginning of a life-long, deep friendship with Tom.

So I began to develop a relationship with this gun I'd rather not have in my life. Yet I wanted other options for self-defense, since everyone else seemed to think I was at risk. With a quick phone call by Renee, a new attorney who taught at the local police academy, I was signed up for Weaponless Defense, a course offered to teach the cadet everything he needed to know about defending himself without using a firearm. It was a 40-hour class that met for five hours on eight consecutive Saturdays. To put it mildly, the course was physically demanding; they taught us, among other things, a variety of take-down moves, a multitude of ways to throw someone regardless of your respective sizes, how to disarm someone who has a knife, and the art of using handcuffs. Renee took the course with me but we worked in random pairs, so I was handcuffed, flipped, and taken down for each time I practiced the same maneuver on rotating partners. I received no special treatment; I jogged every mile and did every push-up required of the cadets. Usually by Tuesday or Wednesday I could stop taking ibuprofen for the various muscles I'd pulled.

Near the end of the course, the lead instructor invited Renee and me to join some Air Force Rangers and firefighters who were doing recertification training that included rappelling down a fire tower. Somehow the Universe decided I needed a concrete exercise in fear, so a voice that sounded like mine responded, "Sure. When and where?" while my mind screamed "Are you crazy?!!" I've always been terrified of heights; I cannot go to the balcony on a second floor without my stomach lurching, my knees softening, and the world threatening to spin. Yet this invitation seemed to come with a unique unspoken summons that could not be declined. My friend Gwen often reminds me: "Rule number one is Show Up." I was afraid to rappel, but more afraid to miss an important life lesson. I was scared of heights; I felt daunted by violence, verbal conflict, guns, murders, autopsies, dead babies, and being required to decide whether someone would live or die. So I agreed to back off of a tall fire tower.

Ron went with me, and we met Renee and the small group of men at the base of a fire tower in the piney woods of Eglin Air Force Reservation. As we walked up the interminable wooden steps to the platform that loomed above the highest tree, Ron said softly, "You're OK. Keep moving. Look up at the next step. You don't need to look down. You're doing fine." At the top, I stood in the middle of the wooden platform, next to the enormous pole onto which the belay rope was tied, and watched the others back off the ledge one at a time. I stood perfectly still, for when I took even one step closer to the edge, my stomach lurched and I felt light-headed. Finally there was no one left on top except Ron, me, and the instructor. I was running out of options. I decided I needed Ron's support on the platform more than on the ground, so I offered to go first. The instructor double-checked my gear and then spoke calmly and slowly as he gave me step-by-step instructions to back toward the ledge. I looked straight ahead and did only and exactly what he said. As I moved slowly from the center of the platform, I felt the taunt rope and a deep trust for this burly guy who had taught me how to take a man down and how to fall when thrown. He spoke softly, "OK, keep backing up. Left foot, right foot. You're almost there. OK, now move your heels over the edge–a little further out. Stand with just the balls of your feet on the platform. Good. Now begin to lean back. You're fine–I've got you. Lean back against the rope. Good job. Keep your knees locked and your back straight." As I continued to lean backwards, I lost eye contact with the instructor but was greeted by an incredibly blue sky and an amazing sense of peace. At the instant I had gone too far to come back onto the platform, when I was totally committed, I was no longer afraid. Then the instructor said, "OK, now bend your knees and push off with your feet." And down I went, with a big smile, pogoing off the wall like a kid.

An hour or so later I stood at the bottom of the tower watching the men rappel down. Behind me was the guy holding the belay rope, a wiry-built, short man with tattoos and a few teeth missing. When he showed up that morning, he laughed about being hungover; when the group ran through the obstacle course, he stopped to vomit in the bushes. His buddies finished the course as he began the dry heaves; his friends yelled and teased him. But then when he got himself together, so to speak, he started the obstacle course over and finished it. I decided I didn't like him. Yet the person I easily dismissed soon turned into my sage.

As he worked the rope to steady the next man coming down the tower, the belay said to my back, "What do you think?"

Without turning my head, I responded crudely, "I think I'm pissed. I've been down that tower four or five times today, and it still scares the shit out of me. I came here to get over this fear thing, and it isn't working!"

The wiry little wise man answered, "If you ever get to the top of the tower, and you're not scared, turn around and walk back down the steps. Fear is good. It's your body's way of saying, 'I can't believe you're going to do this, but since you are, here's an extra helping of adrenaline to keep you sharp.' The trick is to put a saddle on your fear and ride it. Don't let it ride you. Let fear be your friend. Let it keep you safe."

I took a deep breath and watched several more rappel down the tower. As a female in the Deep South, I'd been taught that fear was my signal to either bolt or assume the fetal position. Yet I had ended up in charge of doing justice in a small world of intense violence, a world from which I could not bolt, and there was just no way to look judicious curled up in the fetal position. Yet this tough oracle with missing teeth offered me a very different view of fear.

And now at 53 years old, I've backed off a professional ledge that feels higher than the fire tower. I'm unemployed and heading to Denver to meet my 17-year-old friend, Sara. I pick up Sara from the Denver airport, and then to ensure she's properly introduced to the gypsy life, we spend the first night in a Wal-Mart parking lot at Pueblo, Colorado. From there we head south on Interstate 25, then west on Highway 160. As we start down Wolf Creek Pass at 10,850 feet with the 11,000-pound RV pushing the pickup, I realize I'm way above my pay grade. I'm from Florida where we don't have hills, much less mountains. The courthouse square in Milton sits at an elevation of 15 feet! I downshift to second gear and then first, but the steep grade is stronger than the transmission, and I have to brake again and again to keep us out of the rear end of the slow-moving log truck directly in front of us. I feel incompetent and very alone though Sara is sitting beside me. My stomach is in knots, I have a death grip on the steering wheel, and it feels hot inside the truck. I don't want to scare Sara, so I don't say much. She's a trooper, and if she's scared, she doesn't let me know. I white-knuckle my way down the mountain, and after pulling off to let the brakes cool, we continue west to Pagosa Springs, a small town east of Durango where we stay in an out-of-the-way campground. Sara has grown up with an adventuresome dad, so she's open to unexpected events. She loves the trip and makes an easy companion.

The next morning a wrangler, Sara and I take a four-hour

horseback ride along the Piedra River. Riding through a deep red cut in the earth, we approach a house on the opposite side of the water. A couple is sitting outside on their porch having coffee as we pass on a narrow and crumbly path. It's something like a display at the aquarium, but I can't decide who's being displayed. They speak, and we talk softly back and forth across the river, sharing our awe of the perfect weather and the way the light seems to ignite the red cliffs until a bend in the river puts us out of earshot. In the course of the ride, the terrain varies–tree-covered hills, rocky slopes with low, scattered vegetation, and narrow, rocky streams to cross. We hear a wild turkey calling. The river, much wider than the feeder-creeks, is crystal clear; the aspen and conifers are green; and the rest of the world is red.

The horses move like first cousins to the mules that work the impossible ledges in the Grand Canyon, a place I had yet to see. After an hour of riding I considered difficult, the wrangler says, "Now, don't let your horse stop, no matter what!" Then we ride out onto a rocky, sandy ledge maybe six inches wide, with a drop of a couple of hundred feet down to the river. About 20 minutes later as we approach a bend in the trail, the wrangler turns and yells across the rear of his saddle, "This is where one of our horses died!"

As my horse maneuvers the tight curve and uneven ledge, I glance down the sheer face of a cliff that seemed to have no bottom. It's at least 100 feet down to the closest toehold.

Sara asks him if the rider was a wrangler or a customer–actually she yells, "Was the rider one of ya'll, or one of us?" He shouts back, "One of you. And she bailed."

Rocks skitter, my stomach drops, and the three horses plod along.

Three hours later we ride the horses back toward the trailhead and splash through a shallow creek. I smile as a wild turkey calls–what a joy to share her pocket of raw nature.

"One does not discover new lands without consenting to lose sight of the shore for a very long time."
Andre Gide

CHAPTER 6.
UTAH:
Green dirt and gender roles

From southern Colorado, Sara and I drive over to Moab, Utah, and encounter green dirt, which we learn is a residue of volcanic action. We spend a couple of days hiking in Arches National Park–God's playground in the high, red desert, filled with zany rock formations. After years of listening to technical legal arguments with an eye on the clock and the cases yet to be called, it's a gift to spend days finding faces and shapes in the rock. It's a bit like the game of who-can-find-what-shape-in-the-clouds, except the rocks don't move. On the second day, it actually rains–Florida rain but a desert rain with drops smaller and much farther apart. After walking in the rain for two hours, my T-shirt is still dry in places. There are no puddles of standing water; every drop is sucked up for immediate use. Our footprints leave dry outlines in the almost damp sand.

Green dirt, zany rock formations, and feathery rain drops that fall inches apart–what a delightfully different world than the one I grew up in. Yet, like these rocks, I am shaped by my own microcosm.

Though both of my brothers had gone away to college, my parents assumed I would stay home. We didn't discuss it, but that was nothing new. Mostly I listened and tried to figure out what was expected of me and how to do it. Yet part of me longed to leave, to move to the unknown, a place where no one knew me.

But, like my mom, I did what was expected. I stayed at home and went to the local junior college. By then I was very straight laced, uptight, and full of Southern Baptist religiosity–the dutiful daughter still trying hard to be good enough yet never measuring up.

I had been going steady with Gary, my high school sweetheart, for three years. In a naive way I felt grateful and obligated to him simply because he paid attention to me. Everyone assumed we'd get married, and once we began to have sex, my unmitigated guilt could only be assuaged by getting married quickly–the only way to avoid Hell for my flagrant sins. After all, having sex was irrefutable proof that we were in love, and I had been programmed to become a married woman with a family. Plus, if I married, I could move out of my parents' house and enjoy guilt-free sex.

Like my brother Mac, Gary had a gentle, caring side; they were also both vain, controlling, and chauvinistic. Gary was intelligent with a smiling glint in his eye, and I adored him.

At 19, I was graduating from junior college with plans to get married and go to work to put Gary through the local college.

I focused on getting a job with federal civil service. Pay and benefits were good and because there were several military bases in our area, I didn't have to suggest moving to a husband I knew would never leave. I took the tests for clerk, typist, and stenographer. This was the Vietnam era of 1966, so business was booming in the military arena. I went to the Naval Air Station in Pensacola for an interview for one of several clerk-typist openings at base security. I told myself it wouldn't really matter that the building was painted a dreary gray or that the long wooden benches sat on dull linoleum tile in a not-well-lighted hall, but it was harder to explain to myself how mediocre the supervisor appeared or to imagine how boring it would be to type gate pass forms day after day after year in that gray, gray building.

I was stunned to learn they passed over me and continued to interview applicants. I was finishing up my Associate degree and working part-time at Pensacola Junior College; before I left work the next day, I asked to talk with my boss, a professor in the English Department. After everyone else had left we sat in his office, and I told him what had happened. I added, "I'm really confused. The job is not even a good one. A monkey could do it and would get bored. Why didn't they want me?"

He was quiet as he packed and lit his pipe, "Do you really want to know?"

I knew I could trust him; I softly answered, "Yes."

"Look at you, Laura. Would you hire you? You might take you on a picnic, but how about on a job? You're looking down, always. You speak very softly, and you don't move your lips. And that Southern accent doesn't help. Your speech communicates weakness and lack of confidence. You're a damn good secretary, but you hide behind this Southern Belle image of helplessness."

I listened; we talked. Though he pulled no punches, his suggestions were specific and focused on helping me. "Hold your head up–look people in the eye. Don't act like a door mat if you don't want to be treated like one."

Then he handed me a pencil and told me to hold it between my teeth and talk out around it. He didn't condemn, belittle, or judge me. He seemed to say exactly what he meant. Because I knew at a visceral level that I could trust him, he didn't frighten me. I began to practice speaking up and not being a doormat. Two weeks later I got a civil service job at Whiting Field, a Navy base north of Milton.

The summer that I was 19, I began another life as the Dependable Wife. Instead of going away to college, I went to work as a secretary 30 minutes from the 10 foot-wide trailer in which we lived on Blackwater Bay, next to my parents' house. I was married and had left home, sort of.

I married a fantasy that looked a lot like the Ozzie and Harriet TV series, a story depicted in black and white with no complications. My marriage was a fantasy but not my dream; my dream was to go away to college and travel. My fantasy marriage wasn't Gary's dream either. I didn't know his dream; he didn't know mine. We didn't talk about important things. Instead, we each played our roles, bolstered by the culture of the Deep South in the late '60's. I was passive-aggressive and subservient; he was aggressive and controlling. I was self-righteous and self-deprecating; he was fun loving and social. Sometimes, late at night we shared common ground.

Three years later, Gary graduated from college and went to work as a math teacher. I quit my good-paying civil service job and went to the University of West Florida, about 45 minutes from our trailer. My plan was to get a degree in Elementary Education and teach, but I quickly found I couldn't sit through those classes. I had been bored far too long in my drab civil service job to be bored by college. I was taking elective courses in Spanish, a longtime favorite, and soon I changed my major.

At the University I took a philosophy class with Dr. Mike McGraft. This was 1970, so the rest of the country had seen many changes, but my small world had not evolved. I was still living in a trailer next door to my parents, still trying hard to be responsible and to please others. Mike was an excellent instructor who facilitated independent thought, and I thrived on his challenges to my beliefs and thought patterns. But Mike didn't do well in the good ol' boy department of academia, and the University announced he was being fired. I wanted to write a letter of support for Mike, and my dad, the consummate Southern politician, helped me draft a letter to the university president. The letter was artfully ambiguous, crafted to offer no offense to The Establishment, with phrases such as "I appreciate the work you do for this University and our community" and "as you look at personnel issues, I'm sure you will make the best decision for the University." Mike read it and simply asked, "Is that what you mean?" I'd never considered saying what I truly meant, without filters or apologies, without factoring in angles and political permutations. I rewrote the letter, without my dad as editor, saying what I meant–that Mike was the best teacher I'd ever had, that he challenged his students to think independently and supported them as they struggled to understand their world, that he made a lasting impression on me, and that firing him was against everything we, the students, were attending the University to attain. Mike was still fired, but he left me with an important lesson. A lesson I still struggle with today–to say what I mean, without apology or filter.

I've always loved kids and animals and feel more patience with them than with grownups. When Gary got a teaching job, we could finally afford a baby. It took two years of testing, timing, and trying but when I graduated from UWF with a bachelor's degree in Spanish, I was also pregnant, much to my delight. Dad's secretary had left, so after graduation, I went to work for him.

Because the baby was due in August, I couldn't teach that fall as planned, but that was OK because what I really wanted to do was stay at home and be a mother. Gary was adamant that I go back to work immediately, but I hoped he'd give in since we'd never really lived on two paychecks anyway.

While in college, I had done some sporadic court reporting using shorthand as most reporters did at that time. Our son Clay was four weeks old when the State Attorney called me. He explained that the only court reporter in the county had gotten mad and quit Friday morning, and he had a grand jury coming in on Monday to review what appeared to be an accidental shooting. "Laura, would you please report just this one?" And that's how I gave up my dream of staying home with the baby to reluctantly begin a new career as a court reporter. I was miserable because all I wanted to do was rock, feed, pat, and love on Clay. Instead I reported grand jury proceedings, trials, and depositions, and transcribed the work from home. I had never hired or fired anyone in my life, yet I had to fire two babysitters. I cried—a lot—and then found

Renie, a widow who loved and doted on Clay for several years.

Although I was able to work out of my home, I didn't really like court reporting. It was interesting hearing the testimony the first time, but boring by the time I typed and proofed it. Finally when Clay was about three, I went to work as my dad's secretary at the Courthouse in Milton. Dad was the only Circuit Judge in the county; he was also Chief Judge of the four-county Circuit, Chairman of the statewide Judicial Qualifications Commission (the policing agency that can recommend removal of a judge from office or other sanctions for improper conduct), and for two years Chairman of the statewide Florida Conference of Circuit Judges. The legal and political significance of my dad's office belied the unobtrusive courthouse sitting on the square of this small town. When Dad's court schedule was too tight for him to drive home for lunch, I'd go to the Quick Burger and get two orders of fried mullet, to go. Then Dad and I would go down to the picnic tables at Pond Creek to eat.

Dad was many things. He was wise and gentle; he was bright and uniquely able to cut through complexities to arrive at solutions that were fair, well-reasoned, and recognized by others as just. He was polite and respectful. Dad was powerful, both politically and personally.

Mom and Dad were private people who did not entertain often; they preferred the quiet of Blackwater Bay and the company of family. The few friends who came to visit at our home were often, like Dad, powerful, influential men. Growing up, I saw Dad and his friends through the eyes of a child; I was impressed by kindness, not by power or money. Living with my dad–his greatness and his faults–I learned that as in the dream of Nebuchadnezzar in the Old Testament, exalted men have clay feet; they are both strong and fragile. I grew up, watching powerful men continue to do great things, clay feet and all.

And now, at the age of 53, as I stand in the high deserts of Utah, I wonder if these far-flung dreams will wash away my clay feet and leave me in a mud puddle beside a deserted back road. Can I rise like the phoenix from the ashes of the expectations of others, or like Icarus will I fly too close to the sun, melt my new-found wings, and crash back to earth? I'm not naive, and I've certainly had other dreams crash.

As Clay grew, so did my desire, my longing–perhaps my animal instinct–for another child. I talked to Gary about how much another baby mattered to me; I told him I was going off birth control. He didn't say anything, but he wasn't listening. I was delighted when the doctor confirmed a second pregnancy, but then I was frightened. Things weren't the same with my body; I knew that something was wrong. Soon I had a miscarriage. A year went by; Clay was four years old. I very much wanted to get pregnant again but now Gary was vehemently opposed. Reluctantly, I abandoned all hope of a second child, but the death of that dream wrenched a deep hole in my soul. Over the years I've learned to fill that complicated void by loving and helping other children. But when I relinquished that dream to Gary, my previously unshakeable belief in our marriage began to erode.

My parents did not share my life-long passion for horses, and so I was 26 years old before I got my first one. Kracker was a chestnut quarter horse, incredibly fast, spirited but gentle. At times Kracker was quiet; other times he was quite the handful, bucking or trying to run away. But slowly I learned that I could handle him; I gradually learned to trust him and to trust myself. I learned that I could to do things, even hard things. Gary would caution me, telling me not to run Kracker when I took him out for a long ride. I'd listen quietly, ride off, and then we'd run like the wind down a red clay road, far from the barn, far from the rules and the "should's." We'd return much later, both of us very tired and happy. We trained each other to run the barrels, and we competed in horse shows and rodeos. Kracker opened the barn door, and the tomboy was on the loose again.

At about that time, Clyde Wells began to influence my life. Judge Wells lived and sat on the Bench in DeFuniak Springs, about 60 miles to the east of Milton. He was a close personal friend of our family, and he often came to Milton to hear cases. Judge Wells was bright, candid, humorous, and well liked; he was a big man with an easy smile who never lost his country charm.

Somehow, Judge Wells took an interest in me and began to prod, though not always subtly, as we worked together at the courthouse, "What else are you going to do with your life? Laura, how long are you going to sit here? You know, if you stay here too long, you'll have to have that phone surgically removed from your ear. Is this all you want?" He was striking a deep chord; I had again become terminally bored with my work. I felt a festering restlessness and had no idea how to scratch this incessant itch.

Though I was very close to my dad, I don't think it ever crossed his mind that I could or would do anything professional. And I think his prejudice was gender-based. His world had no ambitious women in it. Women were helpers, supporters of men, employed only if they insisted and then on the side as a teacher, nurse, or secretary. So, it was Judge Wells, not my father, who planted a seed, who nudged and teased me. It was Judge Wells who believed in me. And my day-to-day world as a judicial secretary continued to close in, suffocating me as court reporting and civil service had done.

The discomfort with my life grew. Our office at the courthouse was on the second floor, and as I ran up and down the marble steps, I noticed the wear pattern from 100 years of feet, heavy-laden with problems. I began to tell myself, "All's not lost. I can stay here 'til I die, and then maybe they'll let me use one of these worn steps as my tombstone, as a testament to all my hard work and how many trips I've made on these stairs."

Shortly after Clay's 6th Christmas, Judge Wells was assigned to hear a trial transferred from Miami that involved a high publicity murder-by-bombing. The trial was in Shalimar, about 50 miles to the east of Milton, and I took off from work to drive over to listen. I'd sat through countless trials, but this was a day of epiphany. From the audience I watched the out-of-town attorneys question a witness. A large beam of light passed through the skylight in the ceiling and played across a section of the floor. And I thought, "I can do that. I can ask those questions. I can be a lawyer." Up until that moment, the idea had never crossed my mind; my family certainly never suggested such an ambitious leap. I was the dutiful daughter, responsible mother and wife in the Deep South in the late 1970's. But now, I asked, "Why not be an attorney?"

When I told Dad I was going to take the Law School Admissions Test (LSAT), he was surprised but totally supportive. During this time, a young female attorney, Nancy Gilliam, argued the penalty phase of a capital murder case that Dad tried. He spoke of her intelligence, hard work, and strong presentation. He saw Nancy as a competent attorney and a good role model for me. The LSAT was not scheduled again until February. I knew it was getting late to apply for the fall term of law school, but having decided I wanted to be an attorney, I wasn't going to slow down. I would finally go away to school, and then I'd speak as an attorney rather than write down what others said or schedule them for trials.

As I drove over to Mobile, Alabama, to take the LSAT, I started my period. I grumbled, "Great! Is this the wrathful god showing me what happens to good little girls when they try to act like men, instead of staying where they belong?" As I sat with a miserable case of cramps and obscenely difficult test questions, I wanted to mark the unoffered multiple choice of "d: Who gives a damn!" I did well, but not well enough to get into law school for the fall term. My dad's good friend, Florida Supreme Court Justice B.K. Roberts, was the founder of the FSU School of Law. Dad made a phone call; Justice Roberts made a phone call. When Dad told me, I hesitated with, "But I can do this by myself!" Dad responded, "Yes, you can. Next year. And you can go this year if you want to. Either way, remember that neither Justice Roberts nor I can take one exam or make a single argument for you. You're on your own."

I started law school that fall in Tallahassee. I was 30; Clay was in the first grade.

And that fall, at the age of 65, my dad accepted a gubernatorial appointment as District Court of Appeals Judge in Tallahassee, an appointment he had declined several times before. He and Mom made arrangements to rent an apartment in Tallahassee. Dad was leaving his beloved Milton, his only home. Dad said little about his career change or its timing, but I understood that my parents made their choices in order to support my decision to go to law school and to be in a position to help with Clay.

Gary moved to Tallahassee with us, leaving his job with the school to work in tax and accounting, his field of study. Dad had made another phone call, and Gary had a good job. Gary was very unhappy in Tallahassee and stayed in close contact with his friends in Milton. His position had not been filled, and he left the night before my first semester exam to return to the only place he could comfortably call home. Clay stayed with me in Tallahassee; he completed first through third grade, and I completed three years of law school.

Clay and I lived in an apartment complex in Tallahassee, and although my parents were only 10 miles away, I felt tremendous pressure, on my own for the first time, a single mom of a six-year-old, new in a city, trying to figure out this law school scene.

I loved Tallahassee and flourished with new female friends,

none of whom were interested in the traditional Southern female role. But my joy of learning was quickly besieged by law school professors whose philosophical and analytical views of the Law left little room for the realities of the work-a-day world of the legal profession, a real world of messy ambiguity and ordinary people with real problems. Slowly I gave up trying to square their ivory-tower view with my personal experiences and began to focus on regurgitating their answers.

I learned in the first semester not to volunteer a response in class. My Criminal Law professor had been discussing the various purposes of punishment and asked if anyone could suggest any others. I remembered a case Dad handled in which a young mom shook to death one of her twin babies. Her husband had left her; she was alone in an apartment in a strange town a long way from home. She had no money, no friends, and no prior criminal record. The mom had a crushing migraine, and the baby had colic. Mom was in jail awaiting sentence when Dad ordered a psychological evaluation. The psychologist opined that if Dad put the mother on probation without prison, she could not survive her own guilt; he suggested that the mother needed Society to punish her and without that she was likely to commit suicide. I raised my hand and briefly suggested there could be defendants who needed Society to punish them to help diminish the guilt they felt. Before I could give a few brief facts from the case of the shaken baby, the professor broke out laughing in ridicule, made several snide comments about my suggestion, and adjourned the class that was by now an echo of his derision. I didn't raise my hand again.

The turning point, or give up point, came the second semester of law school. The same professor was discussing aspects of criminal procedure when one of the 200 students in the lecture hall asked if there were any cost considerations in pretrial depositions. The learned professor said, "No," and

199 heads bowed and reverently recorded his truth. I just sat there dumbfounded because I had earned a good living taking those depositions. The professor had never tried a case; he had never had to schedule or pay for a deposition. He was brilliant and well read, with no clue about the real world of practicing law. When class was over, I picked up Clay; we went to his T-ball game and then to the apartment to fix supper and finish his homework. After Clay went to bed, I studied the law according to my professor, for that's what the test would cover. I knew I had much to learn about the Law; unfortunately some of my professors thought they knew it all. They had never had their heart broken by the Law and had never met a problem that could not be resolved through proper legal analysis.

Dad was not happy in Tallahassee; he, like Gary, had left his heart at home in Milton. At the end of my first year of law school, Dad retired from the District Court; he and Mom moved back to their home on Blackwater Bay. Clay and I found a one-story, wooden duplex that backed up to a cow pasture, a welcome relief from the parking lot mentality of the large apartment complex.

When I began to be honest with myself and others–when I stopped trying to be the smiling Harriet and began being me– Gary and I became more honest and respectful of each other. Though the relationship improved, our connection was too tenuous and too much time had passed. We divorced. Gary put a lot of time and effort into maintaining his relationship with Clay; their bond remains strong today. And more than thirty years later, I can still call Gary if I need a strong arm to lift something, a reference for a good mechanic, or information about mullet. Now, we bump into each other at the grandchildren's ball games and take turns playing taxi in the kids' hectic schedule.

Clay and I lived in Tallahassee on a very limited income but I had taken my horse, Kracker, with us. I didn't have time to ride consistently, but I always knew he was at the nearby stables. After I graduated from law school, I accepted a job as an assistant prosecutor in Shalimar 50 miles to the southeast of Milton and made arrangements to have Kracker trailered there. Clay and I were to leave Tallahassee two days before Kracker would be trucked over. The night before we left, the owner of the stable called to reluctantly explain that a bolt of lightning had killed Kracker during a summer thunderstorm. Clay came to me as I hung up the phone, and I stood in the kitchen confused and sobbing. Kracker who taught me so much about myself, taught me to trust myself, to reach long, that falls are not fatal, that I'm stronger than I thought. Kracker who taught me to laugh. But how could I argue with death by lightning? I had never experienced death before. My two maternal grandparents had died, but I had no affection for them or grief for their leaving. Kracker, I loved in a deep important way. Clay wouldn't go to bed; he explained, "It's OK, Mom. I'll just sit here with you." At age eight, Clay was a gentle comfort. I tucked him in and lay across his bed; in spite of himself, he fell asleep. I cried, muffling the sounds in a pillow so I wouldn't worry my young bed fellow. A few times, I dozed off but the sleep wasn't deep enough to alter my nightmare, hold back the tears or fill up the hole in my heart.

The next morning I cried off and on during the three-hour drive to my parents' home in Milton. I was feeling stronger as Clay and I walked into their home and hugs; Clay quickly asked, "Are you going to tell them what happened yesterday?" Mom and Dad were startled as my knees buckled and the tears flowed. I think in his eight-year-old way, Clay wanted my parents to help him take care of me. And he knew that was something they would do well.

Many years have gone by, and I still miss Kracker. I have a special spot in my soul for that small chestnut quarter horse with one white stocking on his left rear foot. Sometimes, I close my eyes and run with him down a clay road, wind whistling, and our hearts rising.

"I travel not to go anywhere, but to go. I travel for travel's sake. The great affair is to move." Robert Louis Stevenson

CHAPTER 7.
THE LONG WAY BACK TO DENVER:
Fast landings, 2% milk, and closet gypsies

From Moab, Sara and I turn south to take the long way to the Denver airport. We loop back through Pagosa Springs to visit Pat Parelli's horse training center. In the late afternoon, we climb up on a wooden fence with mountains to our back and watch the horses and owners work together. It's easy to breathe out here.

We continue east on Highway 160, find that crossing Wolf Creek Pass is much easier from west to east, and then turn north on Interstate 25. Next stop is Front Range Skydivers, a drop zone[6] outside the tiny town of Calhan, Colorado, population 896. I plan to skydive at the Lost Prairie Boogie[7] in Montana the end of July, and I'm nervous about landing my parachute there at an altitude of 3,560 feet.

Landing at a new drop zone presents challenges, like playing golf on an unfamiliar course, but the consequences of a mistake are more significant under a parachute. In the South, I was familiar with landing on level grass and plowed fields, while dodging swamps, cows, trees, and highways. I don't see any swamps around here, but I see a lot of unleveled ground. I get on the jump plane with a few local skydivers, and as we climb to altitude, I watch the rocky ridges below us lose their menacing angles; the terrain flattens into a grey/brown blanket that rolls out to the east as far as I can see. To the west, the ground lifts into rocky backbones that climb up to grey cliffs.

Because air is thinner at higher altitudes, the parachute behaves differently, and the landings are very fast. I had only jumped above sea level a couple of times (my home drop zone is at 110 feet), so I picked the Front Range Skydivers, thinking

---

[6]Drop zone – a parachute landing area, also referred to as the DZ
[7]Boogie – a skydiving event widely publicized to draw a large number of jumpers, often from great distances

it would be a good warm up to Montana. Wrong! Front Range sits at 6,500 feet, which is 3,000 feet higher than Lost Prairie!

I jump out with a few new friends, and we play around in free fall. I open my parachute and am settled in under canopy by 1,800 feet; I make a few playful turns and enjoy life. The closer I get to the ground, the faster I seem to be falling but that's an illusion, "ground rush" we call it. At 500 feet I realize that maybe the ground isn't as level as I thought, but now I'm absolutely committed to land directly below. There's no way to fly, for example, to the softer-looking spot on the other side of the hangar. Oh shit! That's cactus, not clumps of grass! A little to the right and I'll miss them. There's nothing soft around here–lots of small rocks and too many big ones, but at least the rocks don't have thorns. Brake! OK, forget the pride because you're not going to have a tip-toe landing. PLF–bam!–feet, knees, hip, and shoulders roll across clumps of dry grass and small rocks. My god that was fast! Nothing is painfully broken, so get up quick, before someone thinks I'm hurt. Quick is easy with this much adrenaline flowing. Yahoo! Survived that one! Guess I'll go try it again.

I'm laughing at myself because instead of warming up for Montana with some gentle jumps, I'm landing at lightning speeds at the highest civilian DZ on the continent. The local jumpers gather to watch my rather dramatic landings; typical of the black humor among skydivers, they call out bets on which bones this flat-lander from Florida will break; they also give me pointers. "Next time, flare[8] 10 feet higher." At this altitude the art of flaring takes on new dimensions. After four jumps, I almost have the hang of the fast landings, I've practiced my PLF's[9], I have broken no bones, and I'm still having fun.

The next morning, Sara, Bruin, and I head north and west

---

[8]Flare - pull down on the brakes of the parachute, reducing your forward speed and creating a brief lift of the canopy. When the flare is timed properly, a jumper can make a tiptoe landing. If a jumper flares too late, she will not reduce the forward speed on her canopy and can land so fast as to break bones. If a jumper flares too high above the ground, her canopy is likely to collapse and drop her like a rock.
[9]PLF or Parachute Landing Fall - the drop and roll maneuver designed to equalize impact on landing.

with the first skydiving bumper sticker on the rear tire cover of my RV.

As Sara and I wander around Colorado, I continue to notice, with delight, that people do not notice me. I love the anonymity of this new life and don't miss the fish bowl I left behind.

❦ ❦ ❦

2% milk

The first time I walked into a courthouse as Judge Laura Melvin was in May of 1990. In a harsh turn of events, Judge Clyde Wells, who had pushed and prodded me out of my complacent role and into law school, was killed in a single-engine plane crash, and I was appointed by Governor Bob Martinez to fill his unexpired term.

A local attorney announced he would run in the September election against whomever the Governor appointed. Though I grew up in the legal world, I had never been involved in a political campaign. Suddenly I was both a fledgling judge and a green politician. I enjoyed the challenge of the Bench but the campaign trail was not fun.

I've made my living working with people. I enjoy people, and I'm not shy. I'm a good listener and am comfortable speaking to large groups. But I'm also an introvert, hard-wired at birth to prefer quiet, nature, time to think things through, and time to be alone. An extrovert is energized by people; for me and other introverts, being with crowds is draining. It took extra effort for me to wade off into a crowd of strangers at a political rally, smiling, shaking hands, introducing myself, handing out pamphlets, and I always left weary. Like most introverts, I do not like to draw attention to myself; I cringed the first time I saw my face on a billboard along the highway.

It was less than a week before Election Day, and I was exhausted. I'd maintained my court docket as best I could while giving serial speeches, meeting with groups and individuals, doing TV and radio shows, and canvassing neighborhoods. I'd done everything I could, and it had reached the point that I didn't care if I won or lost. I just wanted it to be over. My brother Mac, the attorney from Miami, came up with his wife, Elaine, to help me through those last days, bringing energy and enthusiasm that I'd lost. They were like hyper cheerleaders, egging me on, looking for things to do. I explained there were two campaign options remaining that I had decided to skip; I had just enough energy left to laugh at their zest and then agree to their plans to go for it. The first morning, we met the 6:00 a.m. shift change at International Paper Company, north of Pensacola. Elaine had fun talking to the streams of workers as they left the factory; I just smiled and shook hands. The three of us had a big breakfast at a local diner, and then I drove 85 miles to handle my docket in DeFuniak. Before dawn the second morning I was reluctantly standing beside the crowded highway waving at people as they drove to work at the Pensacola Naval Air Station. Mac and Elaine were ahead of me, waving signs. The traffic was heavy and moving slow. I could hear Elaine call out to the cars with a vigor I didn't feel. It was still dark; the passersby could see me in the street-light but I knew he couldn't get a good look at my face. People would beep their horns and wave at me in what was meant as an affirmation. But the sound of their horns, riding on the glaring beams of headlights, stabbed me. Exhausted and protected by the poor lighting, I began to cry. Too much noise, too many people, too tired. I knew not to wipe at my tears; that motion would betray the image I was to project. I stood, waved, and cried. But soon the sun began to come up, so I sucked up my tears and my dismay, and continued to wave, dry-eyed, until the traffic subsided. Then I walked back to Mac and Elaine. Elaine was bubbling over with enthusiasm and having a grand time. Elaine is an extrovert.

I carried all four counties in the election, winning a six-year term and communicating to future would-be judges that I had strong voter support. I threw a crowded celebration party that night and spoke on TV and radio. I was ever so glad when it was finally time to go home.

The title Circuit Judge once described a jurist who rode horseback to hold court in various locations. It is no longer efficient for judges to crisscross the Circuit, passing each other in route to the various courthouses, so the Chief Judge[10] assigns each to a particular location and division, though judges continue to move through the Circuit on a limited basis to help with special cases and cover dockets when a colleague gets sick. There were 19 Circuit Judges in the First Judicial Circuit, each authorized to hold court throughout the four-county area. An election or gubernatorial appointment is to the Circuit Court, not to a particular courthouse or division.

I was initially assigned to the courthouse in DeFuniak Springs, the county seat of Walton County. Because of its smaller population and caseload, I was the only Circuit Judge in the County. Rather than being assigned to a specific division with a focus on one type of case, I heard it all—family law, criminal, civil, probate, and juvenile.

Walton County, a delightfully diverse region, straddles Interstate 10 between Pensacola and Tallahassee in the Panhandle of Florida. The sugar-white beaches of San Destin, Seaside, and Rosemary Beach on the Gulf coast are popular with tourists. Driving north on Highway 331, you pass through hardwoods and rolling hills, uncommon sights in Florida. DeFuniak Springs, just north of I-10, had a population of less than 5,000, a handful of traffic lights and only two elevators, one in the old hospital, the other in the courthouse.

Though I grew up in a rural county, I was surprised by some of what I encountered in DeFuniak Springs as I began to live the life of a big fish in a little pond. For instance, after a few weeks on my new job, I went into Sun Bank to cash a check. As I approached the window, the cashier did not say, "May I help you?" Instead she looked at me quizzically and said, "Who are you?" "I'm Laura Melvin. I've just moved to town." She responded, "I knew you were here, Judge, but I hadn't met you yet. Welcome! How may I help you?"

I was renting a house three blocks from what is advertised as one of two naturally round spring-fed lakes in the world (the other is near Zurich, Switzerland). DeFuniak Lake is surrounded by homes built

---

[10]The Chief Judge, elected by the judges in the Circuit, acts as the administrator responsible for assignment of judges and other administrative decisions.

in the late 1800's and early 1900's with white clapboard siding, tall windows, high ceilings, and long porches. The houses sit on their deep yards along the quiet road. Moss hangs from massive oaks and in the spring azaleas bloom on bushes ten feet tall. The Chautauqua Building stands by the lake as a reminder of busier times. DeFuniak Springs, selected in 1884 as the winter home of the New York Chautauqua, was one of the cultural centers of the Southeast through the late 1920's. The library, established in 1886, and two churches rest around the lake.

Our family home faced Blackwater Bay with its back to the edge of the woods, a quarter-mile from Ward Basin Road that ran five miles to the north to the small town of Milton and dead-ended a mile to the south at Yellow River. My parents raised five kids in the peacefulness of this home, which they never locked and for which they owned no keys. It was several years after Dad retired from the Bench that I watched his discomfort when law enforcement explained they had received a tip that someone had a contract out on his life—the tip had not said who, why, when, or how. Later I answered the door at my parents' to find a stranger who politely explained, "I've been hired to kill the Judge. But I've changed my mind. Would you see if he'd talk to me?" I asked him to wait on the steps; I shut the door, realizing the futility of locking it when there were three other unlocked ones. I went to Dad as he sat in his big chair in the TV room. He got up, called the Sheriff, and then invited the stranger into his home. They were sitting on the couch talking when the deputies arrived. The stranger explained he had been hired to kill Dad and that after watching his routine, they had decided to put a bomb in his car. Dad didn't remember the guy who hired the killer, for there was nothing memorable about him; he was one of thousands Dad had sentenced over the years—a second-rate criminal who received a not-particularly-long prison sentence. The stranger from the door steps turned State's evidence and fairly soon the guy with the grudge was arrested. We all slept better after he went to prison. That experience and others with Dad taught me the practical vulnerability of being a judge away from the courthouse, the robe, and security.

I often did a three-mile run through the neighborhood and around DeFuniak Lake. Shortly before the election, I was jogging around the lake when a car came up behind me on the quiet street. It began to pass me, but then slowed to a crawl. I pretended to ignore the darkly tinted windows; I didn't know what else to do. I was uncomfortable with my new role as judge and was having trouble knowing what was and wasn't a potential threat to me.

I jogged on, concerned by the car and reassured by the daylight and people out in their yards. The car drove away, but circled the lake to come by me again. As it slowed beside me the second time, a back window rolled down. I didn't know whether to run or ask for their vote. Then a male voice boomed from the dark interior, "Now, that's what I call running for office!" The car sped away, leaving me confused and alone in the deserted street.

Several weeks after the election, I went into Food World near Interstate 10—a chain grocery store with multiple registers and scanners, unlike the Mom and Pop store in town where items were individually priced and the floors were wooden. I was deep in thought as I put my groceries up on the belt.

The cashier interrupted my foggy solitude. "Judge, when did you switch from 2% to skim milk?"

I went home and made plans to move to a place where unknown cashiers didn't call me by my new first name or keep track of the minutiae of my life. Within a month, I had left DeFuniak to live in a large subdivision 35 miles to the west, where I didn't drive the only sports car and where I could get lost in the crowds. And from my new home, I drove my Mazda RX7 into the fish bowl of my new life.

❈ ❈ ❈

But now I'm just one more diesel pick up, riding through the Rockies.

As we pass road signs for Littleton, Sara and I become quiet. Remembering the fear and death at Columbine High School, my mind tumbles to other lives shredded by raw violence, and I'm reminded of my personal violence quota–that individual saturation point, the level of awareness of violence beyond which my psychic says, "No, we're not going any further." I drive on, feeling helpless, knowing there are many who will never be able to drive away from the horror and loss of that day at Columbine. In the early evening I continue to feel at odds with the beauty of the mountains and the comfort of Sara's friendship. I pull out an old journal and stumble backwards, riding on earlier words, in an effort to describe my inability to resolve a world filled with violence.

❖ ❖ ❖

No answers

As we finished our weekly writing practice at the home of a friend, several people wanted to stay and lament the horror of 15 children dying violently the day before at Columbine High School in Littleton, Colorado. But I bolted, leaving without explanation. Not because I was unaffected by those deaths, but I had to be careful. There seemed to be a limit to my capacity to deeply feel violence, and I felt pushed to that limit and beyond. The last two days had been rough–too many cases, too few solutions. Four of the cases I heard weighed heavier than the others. After leaving the group, I went to a city park at the edge of Pensacola Bay and sat at a picnic table to write, seeking some relief, some comfort, maybe even an answer by pushing my pen across the blank page.

I can handle a routine plea and sentencing in a Violation of Probation in ten minutes or less, but yesterday I spent more than an hour with one defendant, the most unruly I've dealt with in nine years. Howard was on probation for aggravated stalking–an unblinking, bone-chilling stalking that began at church 10 years ago and continued as his game of cat and mouse until he was arrested for violation of probation. Howard is not crazy by our technical, legal definition, but he's damned sure scary–very bright, violent, stubborn, proud of his quick anger, and still focused on the Garcia family after all these years. Security had discussed with me their concerns about Howard's volatility and threats. Though he would be handcuffed to a waist chain, we agreed it would be too easy for him to charge toward the Garcias if he were standing at the podium. So I had him sit in the jury box with a deputy on each side; the Garcias spoke from the podium in the middle of the courtroom and then returned to a seat on the pews. There is a strict catalog of issues that must be covered in a plea and sentencing, and failure by the judge to cross the proverbial T or dot an I can generate a reversal on appeal. Howard's plan was obvious—push me with the hope that as I became tired and irritated, I'd make a legal error he could reverse on appeal; push me until I lost my temper—do whatever it took to get a rise out of me, a rise that he would count as a "win" whether it won him a reversal or not. Both the prosecutor and defense attorney stepped aside, and for an hour it was just Howard, sitting in the jury box with a deputy on both sides, and me, sitting on the Bench in my robe in an uncrowded courtroom—me checking off all the legal requirements prior to sentencing him; Howard rambling, maneuvering. I used that old trick that I learned from my dad – speak softly, politely—and eventually Howard calmed down some, interrupted less. Under the sentencing guidelines, I could only give him four and a half years in State prison, but he needed at least 40. As I verbalized the required legal litany for four and a half years in prison, I watched the muscles in his arms twitch and his eyes narrow without blinking as he glared at me. With his hair-trigger violence bubbling, I anticipated mayhem in the courtroom, with Howard yelling and turning over furniture, while swinging his head and torso. To my surprise he didn't erupt, but he was only biding his time. When security walked him to the heavy doorway leading to the holding cell, he spread-eagled his legs so they couldn't get him through the opening, and he began a screaming tirade of expletives. Security was ready. They folded his legs, pushed him through, followed him in, and slammed the heavy metal door behind them. I expected to hear the unique sound of bodies hitting metal and cement, as well as Howard's screaming, but by the time the clanging of the metal door waned, there was only silence. I found out later there were two *more deputies waiting on the other side of the door, and that the four of them quickly put Howard down on the cement floor. No one—including Howard—was hurt.*

I called the next case. Robert was to be sentenced for two serious sexual batteries. Robert was a blond 17 year-old whose mom was crazy—not in a humorous, engaging way but in a way that failed to protect Robert, and Robert was raped at age eight by his mom's boyfriend. Robert's mom was crazy in a way that had screwed up a little boy who grew into a teenager and then at the age of 16 raped two eight-year-old little girls. Family values: "Will the circle be unbroken?" Even the hardened, cynical prosecutor saw hope for Robert, and the plea agreement was for 23 years in state prison, with the prison sentence suspended, conditioned upon satisfactory completion of 30 years of probation, sex offender treatment, etc. etc. I added a provision to his probation that he have no contact with his mother until further order of the court. Mom stood beside him at the front of the courtroom, holding his hand and draping her other arm around him. When I said "No contact with your mother," she began to wail, turned, walked a few steps, and dropped to her knees with her head and torso erect.

Andy, the deputy, walked to her and said, "Stand up."

She looked up over her shoulder and said in a clear voice, "I can't. I'm praying."

Andy responded, "You can pray sitting down over there. Get up."

She stood up, went to a seat in the front row, and hunkered there for a few moments. Then she walked back to Robert as I continued with the sentencing. She took his hand and began to rub it, then interrupted me to beg, "Don't take my baby from me. I'm not a bad mother."

She wasn't impressed by the fact that I was not sending him to prison; all that mattered to her was the no-contact provision of his probation.

As I ended the hearing, I said, "Robert, you can't leave the courtroom yet, so have a seat in the jury box." I wanted to give him a fair chance of avoiding his mom in the hallway. None of us knew what chance he had of making it on probation. But we would let him try.

She snuffled as she moved to the back of the courtroom, stopped at the wooden double doors, looked back at me, and announced, "I'm going to kill myself!"

I took a deep breath but said nothing. She retrieved something from her purse, slowly opened the doors, and walked out. I called the next case.

After finishing in the courtroom yesterday, I went back to my office to sign papers. There was a warrant for Violation of Probation on a 19 year-old kid named Christopher. The warrant read, "New law violation, to wit, Murder."

Two years ago Chris and two other kids were arrested for armed robbery of a victim they selected at random from a crowded restaurant parking lot as part of their initiation into a gang. At gunpoint they demanded the victim's wallet and then snatched a blue bandana from his neck. The victim resisted, and a co-defendant shot him two times, severing an artery in his leg. Through no fault of the robbers, the victim didn't die, though he has a permanent limp.

At sentencing on the robbery, I'd heard the familiar argument, "Judge, Chris is only 17, it's his first arrest, and he's the perfect candidate for Youthful Offender Boot Camp. Judge, Chris can be rehabilitated."

Boot Camp is intense but short. I followed the recommendation, and six months later he was released from Boot Camp on parole. And now, two years later, there's a second warrant for Chris' arrest.

The violation of probation warrant described another armed robbery of a random victim in a restaurant parking lot. Again the victim resisted. This time the aim was better or the luck was worse, for this time the man is dead. Yesterday I sat in my office with the new warrant in my hand knowing that had I sent Chris to prison, not Boot Camp, on his first robbery, this particular unnamed man would be alive.

Two of the kids at Columbine—Eric and Dylan—like Chris,

107

thought they had it all figured out.

I signed Chris' warrant and ordered that he be held without bond.

Earlier today I sentenced William S. in criminal court after the jury found him guilty of firing a pump-action shotgun into a crowd. No one died in the shooting. One man was slightly injured. Why were there not several deaths? Just because. When you work in a high volume of violence as I do, you see no injury, slight injury, and unfathomable injury. This one just happened to fall into "slight injury," but William gets no credit for that. That was Grace, or blind luck. The evidence showed that after firing into the crowd, William remained furious at whatever, and two and a half hours later fired the same shotgun into a car occupied by two men. Incredible as it seems, in his second shooting, there was no injury at all. Again, Grace or blind luck, at no credit to William.

William's girlfriend was in the courtroom today and asked to be heard before I imposed sentence. I listened as she explained that she was 19 years old and the mother of his two children. She held the little girl, two months old, while the older brother, not yet two years, held onto her leg. William has been in jail on these charges since she was three months pregnant with the baby. The mother is a hard worker—she's a manager at Burger King—and a survivor. She asked that William be put on probation so his financial support could improve the lives of the children. "I'm making it, Judge, but barely." As she talked, the baby wiggled, and she adjusted the pink blanket on her shoulder. When the toddler scooted between her legs, she maintained her balance and gently guided the little guy back to open territory. She didn't frown, jerk, or snap at her kids. Her eyes were soft and brimming with tears.

Then it was William's turn, and he droned on about having learned his lesson—yadda, yadda, yadda. Though he certainly didn't mention it, I knew from the reports that William as a juvenile went to reform school for Attempted 1st Degree Murder with a Firearm (perhaps his aim or luck was the same at age 15, because again no one died.). As an adult, he was put on probation for Possession of a Firearm by a Convicted Felon.

108

Now 22 years old, William was again before a judge for sentencing, this time for firing a shotgun into a group of people twice, because he was angry. I listened to him without interrupting; when he was finished, I took a deep breath and sentenced him to 30 years in prison as a Habitual Offender, knowing that as a Habitual Offender he won't earn gain time for an early release. As I spoke, I watched the girlfriend begin to weep softly and then sink down toward the floor; the almost two-year-old whimpered, his tiny face contorted in confusion as he pulled on his mama's skirt. William's eyes hardened and his body stiffened as he glared at me. His jaw twitched. I know my ruling means William will not live with, will not truly know, his two children until they're old enough to have children of their own. But I also know William won't shoot anyone out here where we live, at least not for the next 30 years.

Does it make me feel good to sentence a 22-year-old father of two to 30 years in prison? No, and that makes no difference. And I'd rather feel this concern for a 19-year-old mother of two, than live with the knowledge that there's one less father in the world today because I did not send Chris to prison two years ago. Prison does not rehabilitate but it will keep Chris and William away from guns and regular people, at least for a while.

After lunch today I had a two-hour hearing on a Defendant's Motion for extended furlough from the Florida State Mental Hospital at Chattahoochee where he was sent after being found Not Guilty By Reason of Insanity. Several years ago he shot his sleeping wife to death, and the experts at the hospital feel he's improved to the point that I should let him come home. One witness was not present, so that particular story is "to be continued." I didn't have to make that decision today.

I don't have the answers. Today I'm not in the mood for solutions or explanations reduced to sound bites. I don't want to sit around and hypothesize about violence, guns, and trauma. I only wish I could back all that into a hypothesis. Today, the best I can do is write, sitting at a picnic table, watching the sun set, and the Bay turn a bright reddish orange, watching the world tone down through pink and purple to settle into the blue-black of the night.

The park was not well lighted, and I didn't see the drunken weirdo until he crashed his bicycle through a clump of bushes and teetered to a stop at my picnic table. He mumbled to me and then stumbled; I left, fast. There were too many guns and too much bad luck for me to feel comfortable enough to finish a thought on paper while sitting in an isolated spot with a drunk.

I got back in my car and drove to a car wash where I sat with water drumming on my Nissan 300ZX. As I waited, I read the day's paper. I was careful to only scan the story of Colorado. But on the second page of the local section, another land mine went off beside me. Yesterday I signed an order that a man be picked up for an involuntary psychiatric exam; his mother said he was mentally ill and would not agree to go for treatment. The paper said he stabbed her to death, after I signed the order and before the officers arrived. Apparently she tried to explain it to him, and he didn't like what he heard.

I understand. I don't like what I hear either. I want to simply, quietly leave this war zone, this craziness where somehow I've ended up In Charge. In Charge of pick up orders delivered too late, prison sentence without solutions, real wives with broken hearts and needy kids, men and boys who use real guns to kill real people. Tonight I sit alone at the car wash, with a heart too heavy and too full for 15 more dead kids.

❧ ❧ ❧

Sara doesn't comment on my long quiet spell at the kitchen table; she's been reading and doesn't look up from her book until I tell her that dinner is ready.

Sara loves animals, especially horses; she talked of becoming a vet tech and working near her home. I knew that Sara was brighter than that; I also knew there was a veterinary college in Fort Collins, about 70 miles north of Denver. This is the summer before her senior year in high school, and we have time before her return flight to Florida, so we ride up to

Colorado State University. We spend a long morning talking to a counselor about admission requirements for undergrad and vet school; we discuss class schedules and financial aid; we tour the campus, with special attention given to the horse barns. We stop for a late lunch near the college at a café with tables outside on a cobbled sidewalk. As we eat our pizza, Sara looks down the street at the college and up at the mountains; then she announces, "I can do this." I watch her closely, and after several quiet moments, she adds, "I can live here. I can go to school here." I feel like turning cartwheels on the brick sidewalk, but trying to act like a grownup, I just smile and say, "Yes, you can." For me, that one "I can" from Sara makes the entire trip.

Showing kids a bigger picture challenges cultural and familial concepts and may not always be appreciated on the home front. Back in Florida, Ron was not impressed with her new vision because it was dauntingly expensive. I stepped back from their discussion. Sara set her own course, and a year later, with an academic scholarship, she began her freshman year at the University of Florida, 300 miles from her home and light years away from the world she had known.

A closet gypsy

I say with pride that I was born with the soul of a gypsy. For me, the term "gypsy" is one of endearment. It speaks of fierce independence, curiosity, restlessness, and a willingness to try most anything. A gypsy is unwilling to be shackled by expectations and doesn't like to color within the lines of life. But given when and where I was born, for years I felt forced to live parallel lives–the dutiful daughter and gypsy. And the dutiful daughter generally succeeded in keeping the gypsy stifled and stuffed in the closet. The good thing about gypsies, though, is that we are stubborn and refuse to be reprogrammed.

This jaunt in an RV around the country wasn't my first solo trip. The summer after the first grade, I somehow convinced my mom to let me take the train alone from Milton to Tallahassee to visit my dad in the Florida State Senate. I rode with the conductor to Marianna, 115 miles to the east. In Marianna I changed trains and kindly conductors, arriving in Tallahassee 65 miles farther down the tracks with an unwavering love of trains and travels. As a young child, I was a tomboy, independent, and more curious than fearful. I played tackle football with the boys and refused to wear a dress to school. I broke both arms and had multiple gashes stitched, but I was undaunted. I often took a small skiff alone into Blackwater Bay to be gone for hours. I wore my hair in a long ponytail that I could make swing left to right as I walked.

As I "matured" I was taught to ignore the rowdy characters of Tomboy and Gypsy; I was growing up, and it was time to assume the respected role of Dutiful Daughter. Later the fourth role would fall into place–Ambitious.

I skipped the fourth grade; 5th grade was housed on the high school campus. Though I was only nine years old, I was at the Big School, with big people, and I did not take the sudden transition lightly. I was serious about being serious, about being responsible and grown-up. My mother was not one to get the family up in the mornings. Soon I took on that obvious need, with a flare. We had a wooden tray with handles on each end and a faded floral pattern across the center. I'd set my alarm, get up, and make everyone a cup of coffee or tea, just the way they liked it (Daddy–coffee with milk but no sugar; Mama–hot tea with less than a teaspoon of sugar, etc.) I carried the tray from bedroom to bedroom waking each family member, leaving a steaming cup beside the bed. On the backside of my life, I still enjoy the quiet ritual of fixing coffee and delight in taking a hot cup to a loved one in bed.

I'd been in the 5th grade a few weeks when Mom took me for my first trip to the beauty parlor, and with her encouragement (she explained that my long hair was too much trouble), I came home with my ponytail in my hand. My hair was cut in a short bob called a DT (duck tail) and plastered down with setting gel. When I went to school the next day, Mrs. Hollingsworth said, "Oh, it's you. I thought we had a new boy in the class." Instead of being a cool chick, I looked like a skinny boy. I felt sick to my stomach; I wanted to run away but there was no place to go. I said nothing and stared at the floor. I had no idea how to be a proper young lady, yet that was the role I was supposed to assume. Somehow, I bought in–hook, line, and sinker–to a world of rules. Basically, the rule was–if it were fun I should quit doing it because it wasn't lady-like or proper. So at the ripe old age of nine, I consciously and intentionally resigned from childhood and began trying to be responsible and grown-up. My laughter, confidence, ponytail and grit were packed away, and I began in earnest to please–trying hard, and then harder, but never quite getting it right. There was always someone there to tell me that I was wrong, that I wasn't thoughtful enough, that I was letting the Devil control me; there was always someone who said I wasn't smart enough. My maternal grandmother led the list of critics, a list that also included my teacher and brothers. The more time I spent being wrong–no matter how hard I tried–the more time I spent looking down, looking away.

Mother always referred to my sisters as "The Little Girls"; one sister was in the first grade at the elementary school and the other was home in diapers. Even if I wanted to, I couldn't be one of the Little Girls because I was at the school with my two older brothers. Jim was two years older but suddenly only one grade ahead of me. Mac was a junior and a big man on campus–President of the Student Council and editor of the Panther's Paw. He was also very good looking, popular, vain, and chauvinistic. I knew his gentle side and worshipped him. Growing up, it was Mac who listened and believed me. When at age five, a cousin told me the scary, disgusting things our maternal grandfather had done to her–things I learned later were called digital penetration and sexual abuse–it was Mac to whom I ran. For my 10th birthday, he gave me a five-pound box of Whitman's Sampler chocolates and convinced Mom I didn't have to share with my four siblings, my first experience of indulging Laura. I ate the whole box of chocolates, all by myself. If I bit into a piece I didn't particularly like, I put it back and chose again. When I got down to the already-tasted pieces, it was easy to tell what was in which one. I didn't share, and no one told me I was eating it wrong. Two years later, Mac was working in a jewelry store, and I'd walk over to visit him. He let me try on a sterling silver ring with a white and black pearl. Mac talked to my parents about them buying it for my 12th birthday, but they were too practical and distracted by other things. Mom baked me a cake, and Mac bought me the ring. I still have it.

One day Mac explained, "Boys don't like girls who giggle," and so I stopped giggling. I didn't know the difference between giggling and laughing, so I stopped laughing, too. Some 20 years later, my son Clay said, "Mom, you smile a lot, but you don't laugh." Oh…

When I was in the 8th grade, a dance teacher moved to town, and Mom let me take ballet and acrobatics. I loved the feel of the hardwood floors; I moved to the music with my head high and remembered I could do difficult things well. But the teacher left at the end of the school year, and the closest class was then in Pensacola. I didn't even ask, for I knew my parents saw no reason for ballet and certainly no reason to drive me 30 miles to class; they complained when the classes were in Milton.

Milton was a backwater town, rural, chauvinistic, and heavily colored by fundamentalist beliefs. Milton was a place for proper young ladies, not for aspiring ballerinas, rowdy tomboys, or gypsies. My confidence and free spirit went back into hiding for years while I went to the local junior college, married my high school sweetheart Gary, and went to work as a secretary with Civil Service. When I finally returned to college and encountered people and situations that challenged my rigidly defined life, the tomboy and gypsy began planning to make a break for it.

In my senior year of college I went alone to the University of Lima in Peru as an exchange student. My experience with Spanish had been strictly academic; I wrote and read it very well but had virtually no exposure to the spontaneous spoken language. I flew to Lima, a city where I knew no one, and negotiated the large international airport. I lived with a family who spoke no English. I walked in a plaza one day and watched a maid pushing a baby carriage. The maid spoke sharply in Spanish to the family dog—words I couldn't understand—and the dog obeyed. Even the dog spoke more Spanish than I did! The first few weeks I was overwhelmed, exhausted, challenged, and enchanted with the foreign and beautiful culture. I stuttered and stumbled along until I was fluent in the language I love. A new friend and I flew to Arequipa and took a cross-country train ride to Cuzco and Macchu Picchu. I saw stucco walls painted with colors that radiate a life unknown in the predictable palette touted in the United States. I tried spices, foods, and drinks that asked questions, often with an exclamation mark. I had only lived in Milton, the town in which I was born, yet there I was in a country in which I was a white-faced minority. I experienced a world that challenged my stodgy reality. The world I'd been taught was the best—wasn't.

The hard kernel of my tiny world in Milton, Florida, continued to crack. Gary was supportive of my decision to go to Peru and glad when I came home. But I'd had a taste of the open road, and it was a flavor I wouldn't forget.

After our visit to Fort Collins, Sara and I return to Denver. From there we head west and ride up Boulder Canyon on 8% and 10% grades, numbers that acquire significance when pulling a heavy RV. There was no place to park in the pint-size mining town of Nederland so we head over to Kelly Dahl National Forest where I manage to back the trailer into an impossible spot–a narrow obstacle course made of trees, boulders, and poles so short you can't see them before you hit them. I'm pretty smug about that back-in and figure I don't have to do it right again, for years. We dry camp for four days; the park has no electricity, no water, no sewer, and no showers. And then it's time for Sara to go. I leave Bruin in the RV at Kelly Dahl and drive her to Denver to catch the plane home. We laugh, hug, and cry; I wave as Sara walks to her gate.

I get back to the 5th wheel after dark to find Bruin has had diarrhea. I'll skip the details of how bad it can be when a 100-pound dog in a 30-foot RV is violently sick at his stomach. I do the best I can to clean up, and the next morning I hook up and pull out in desperate search of a town large enough to have a professional carpet cleaner. Driving down through mountains that are not cell-phone-friendly, I stop several times to use a pay phone and phone book, hoping to make an appointment with a carpet cleaner. The big companies offered appointments days or even weeks later. As the sun heats up Bruin's fertile frosting in the tin can I call home, I consider leaving the whole smelly mess at a recycle center. I finally find a one-man operation, and he agrees to meet me at the Clear Creek Campground in Golden, Colorado. At the campground, I set up the 5th wheel and disconnect the truck, but I don't dare go back inside the RV without a gas mask. The carpet cleaner arrives with his magic wand, and soon a small throw rug hides the one stain he couldn't remove. The odor gone, I remember what I like about this house on wheels.

A few days later I go back to the Denver airport; Al is flying in to spend his vacation with me. We hook up the RV and pull north. For the first time since leaving Florida, I sit in the passenger seat and relax. I've learned to pull my home around the country alone, but I've missed sharing sunsets and laughter with him. We stay at Estes Park with a view of 14,000-foot mountains under permanent snowcaps. As we ride up to the Rocky Mountain National Park Visitors' Center at 11,800 feet, we pass a large herd of elk grazing next to a pullout above tree line. By mistake, I bolt out of the truck and run up the path with my camera. I thought the running would keep me warm (I'm wearing shorts and T-shirt, and there's snow on the ground). I don't know what I was thinking I'd do for oxygen. When I stop, my heart is beating so fast I can barely stand up. But the view is worth it. And I get some good photos of the elk.

Too soon it's time to bring the RV back to the Clear Creek Campground in Golden, Colorado, and take Al to the airport. The void he leaves is palpable; the view of the mountains eases the ache. Though lonely, I remained convinced at a visceral level that I need to keep moving. After six weeks, I have no regrets about leaving that prestigious job or paycheck. The freedom and changing views are still worth the cost of occasionally being lost and lonely.

The next day I sit by the fast-moving creek that borders the campground, watching kayakers maneuver the white-water course. Then I notice bright-colored floating objects–paragliders atop a high bluff across the creek. The wind inflates their oversized parachutes so they can soar with the vultures and play in the air currents. They don't have to pay for lifts on a noisy airplane, and they can stay airborne for hours on good thermals.

Monday morning I drive over to Camping World with my bicycle in the bed of the truck. They are going to install an exhaust brake and a Banks power pack; $3,000 for more stop and go. I leave the truck and ride my bike the eight miles back to my RV. For a biking enthusiast, the ride would be nothing, but I haven't been on a bike in ten years. But the ride is fun, and I'm rather proud of myself as I ride back roads past a railroad museum and the Coors Brewery. Without my truck for two days, I plan to explore the small town of Golden, on foot.

That night I'm invited to join two couples at the campground for a dinner of salmon tacos with cabbage followed by a wine tasting. Beau and Barbara, full-timers from Texas, are wine connoisseurs, and they share from their stash of German wines, stored in the under-belly of their 5th wheel. Then Barbara opens some tequila (the real stuff with a worm in the bottle), and we do shots. We talk into the night; we swap addresses and phone numbers. They explain their loose schedule (as they say, one cast in jello) and invite me to winter-over with them in Texas. I walk home with a buzz and a contented heart. And who knows, maybe I'll spend some of the winter with them.

The next day, Bruin's hind end begins to fold up on him as he walks. Though he doesn't seem to be in pain, he falls down while walking or just standing. He's nine years old, orthopedic problems are common in German Shepherds, and he had spinal surgery two years ago. Now, alone at the campground with no way to take him to a vet, I take the easy way out–I freak. He's been such a friend and supporter; the idea that something is very wrong, so far from home, is just too much. Finally, he looks at me as though to say "Get on with it, Laura. This is life." Sara and I had just been to the Colorado State University Veterinary Hospital in Fort Collins, so I knew who to call for an appointment.

After some delay the truck is ready, so Bruin and I finally leave Golden with the RV in tow, drive up to the veterinary hospital at Fort Collins, and park in a pull-through space, beside horse trailers. Then we spend the rest of the long day having tests run; they even shave Bruin's belly and do a sonogram.

While waiting for Bruin, I go out to the RV and make a peanut butter and jelly sandwich for breakfast/lunch. Adjacent to the parking lot is a paddock with perhaps a dozen llamas and a couple of huge dairy cows grazing on hay. The cows have been modified for teaching purposes; they each have a large hole or fistulate, cut in their side, sealed off with a plastic sleeve; the vet students are taught to reach inside the cows' bellies, to learn about cow-belly things.

As I gaze across the parking lot, I remember an eight-year-old who used a yellow legal pad to teach me a few things.

❦ ❦ ❦

"Pretty much all the honest truth telling in the world is done by children."
Oliver Wendell Holmes, Jr.

A child's mask

Before going on the Bench, I did contract work for the State, representing the Department of Health and Rehabilitative Services (HRS), the agency in Florida that prosecuted cases in Juvenile Court involving allegations of child abuse and neglect. As their attorney, I would represent the State in its attempt to prove that a child was in need of court intervention. Depending on the case, HRS might ask the Court to remove the child from the parents and place custody with another relative or in foster care, or ask that supervision and services be ordered for the child in the parents' home.

I knew from talking to the caseworker that in this incident the stepfather was accused of anally raping two young brothers over the last two years. Their mother said they were lying, and she didn't believe the graphic physical evidence that supported her sons' story. She was regularly visiting her husband in the county jail.

The brothers were now six and eight years old. The caseworker had all the details—when, where, and how the sexual abuse occurred. But the trial was coming up, and I needed to know in advance exactly how well the kids would handle testifying in court. I also knew how hard it was going to be on the boys to tell that story yet again.

The caseworker agreed to bring the kids to meet me at the courthouse coffee shop. I was sitting at a small table on the sidewalk when the caseworker walked up with two young boys—not hollow-

119

eyed victims but two kids wearing T-shirts, jeans, dirty tennis shoes, and yellowed baggy socks. The six year-old was a small child with gentle eyes and a soft face that said it wasn't so long ago that he was a baby. The eight year-old had grown out of that baby-face stage and had begun to get lanky with long arms and skinny legs that hinted of the man he would be.

I took them into an empty courtroom. First I showed them where they would sit, and then I told them who would be in each of the other chairs. They sat in the witness chair and called out to imaginary people in the courtroom. We went up behind the Bench, and I let them sit in the judge's chair. They took turns spinning each other around and around. I showed them where the court reporter would sit and told them that she would write down every word that everyone said. I explained a little about the stenograph machine—how the court reporter wrote phonetically with lots of shortcuts so that by pushing her hands down one time she could write a whole phrase. I told them to be sure to answer out loud with a "Yes, sir," or "No, sir," because the court reporter may not be looking at them to see in which direction their heads moved. I explained that everything would be typed up later and it was hard to read the difference between "Uh-huh" and "Unh-unh" so to use "Yes" and "No." They nodded and smiled. They held their hands out in front of them and pretended to be typing; they asked more questions about the court reporter's job than any of the others. They commented on almost everyone who would be in the courtroom, and they clowned around. This could have been a simple field trip, a civics lesson for two young kids in how our court system worked. But it wasn't.

When I thought they were comfortable with the room, the process, and me, we sat on the front pew of the empty courtroom.

The caseworker said, "OK, guys, you know we've talked about this. And you need to tell Laura what your dad did. She needs to hear it from you."

They looked down, and they shook their heads, "No." It was as though the little guys who had been clowning around moments earlier were gone, and two stiff, shell-shocked shadows sat in their places.

Although they would no longer respond to me, I continued to talk and then added, "You don't have to look at the judge when you talk, you can just look at me. I know this is hard, and you can do it." I had a yellow legal pad for notes—the kind that comes pre-punched with two holes centered at the top. Larry, the eight year-old, reached over without speaking, took the legal pad from me and hid his face behind it. I said, "Larry, it's OK, you don't even have to look at me. But tell me what happened."

Larry began to talk, haltingly, from behind the pad. As he fidgeted with the pad, I watched one small eye and then the other dart to a hole. He bent the pad slightly; now both dark eyes peered at me. He sat up straight and looked me in the eye. From behind his mask of cardboard and yellow paper, he calmly told with chilling simplicity how the man he called dad had repeatedly raped him and his little brother.

❧ ❧ ❧

That was 25 years ago, but I can still see Larry, sitting in the empty courtroom, his bright eyes peeking at me through the holes at the top of a legal pad. I have forgotten the details of his horror story; that was just too much for me. But I'll never forget those eyes.

At the veterinary teaching hospital, each of the animals brings a human with them, people who love their animals. There are big dogs and little dogs, cats, a snake, and even an iguana. All of the animals are in medical need, some seriously. The mood of the people varies, but everyone here cares—the owners, the students, and the vets. My time here feels authentic.

There is a couple in the waiting room who sit near me for hours while their dog is being treated. Though others in the room share conversation and magazines as they wait, this couple sit with their chairs pulled away from everyone else but close to each other. They sit quietly, without reading, talking, or moving about the room. Their faces are strained with red resolve. The woman suddenly gets up and leaves with choking tears; several minutes later she returns to her chair without speaking. Soon the man bolts from the room to take his turn with inconsolable sadness. I am reminded of the time I spent in the ICU waiting room just before Dad died, watching another family deal variously with grief over the imminent death of a loved one. I didn't know the family; I knew something of their pain and confusion.

As I glance at this couple waiting for word of their four-legged loved one, my throat begins to close and my eyes fill with tears. Tears for them, tears for Bruin, for me, for that unnamed family five years ago, for Dad, for our family. As I sit alone in the vet hospital in Colorado, the floodgates open to uninvited memories of the day my daddy died.

Except to make jokes of himself, Dad seldom gave his health much attention. I'd been on the Bench in DeFuniak Springs for three years when Dad was diagnosed with cancer of the gall bladder–a condition as unique as he was. He was optimistic and very focused on whipping that invader. Chief Judge John Kuder granted my request for a transfer to a vacant judicial slot in Pensacola.

Dad handled the treatment well and laughed about the new tattoo that marked the focal point for his radiation. We had photos taken together, each in our black robe. And it was clear that his steps were slowing. Mom had always had various health problems, but she was now stronger than Dad. Though he had stopped drinking, Dad's heart problems got worse. He kept nitroglycerine in his pocket, and I kept hoping we could go on forever.

My role was always that of the Dutiful Daughter, the one you called, the one who took care of things. One night two years after Dad's cancer treatment, Mom called, "Your dad is having chest pains. We don't know what to do." When she told me how many nitro tablets he had already taken, I said, "Mom. Hang up and call 9-1-1. I'm on my way, but don't wait for me. Call now." I hung up with an empty feeling that grew colder and larger as I drove the five miles home. The ambulance was there, and Dad was lying on the gurney outside in the driveway. The EMT's backed away as Dad and I talked. He looked old and frail. This was the first time in my 48 years that I'd seen my daddy scared. He tried to make jokes but his sentences would trail off without a punch line. Neither of us knew what to say. I just stood there and held his hand. One of the EMT's spoke to me, "We need to load him up now, Judge." Funny, this stranger calling me Judge when THE Judge was there on the gurney. I stood back as they lifted him into the dark belly of the ambulance, then I climbed in. He took my hand, "Thanks for coming, baby. I guess your mother will ride with me. Be sure she gets home OK." I kissed him on the forehead, checked on Mom, went to my car, and followed the howling and flashing ambulance as it moved slowly to the local hospital. Dad was quickly transferred to a large hospital in Pensacola; it was hard to take that as a good sign.

The next day Dad explained they were scheduling open-heart surgery. He was optimistic, almost enthusiastic, "Let's get this show on the road." He insisted on signing a Living Will.

At the appointed time, I sat with my siblings in the waiting room. The doctor finally came out and said everything went well, and that Dad would be in recovery for a while. Everyone else left, but I needed to see and touch him before I went home. About an hour later, a tired, worried-looking doctor came out and explained that Dad had developed a bleeder on the back side of his heart, and they had no choice but to operate again and immediately. I sat back down, alone in a room full of strangers. I didn't call anyone; I didn't trust my voice, and I saw no need to worry them until we had more news. After what felt like several life-times, the doctor came out to say they'd stopped the bleeding, and Dad would move to recovery soon. Finally I got to see him; he wasn't awake and he was all wired up, but I kissed him on the forehead and then left to call everyone.

After the surgery Dad developed lung problems and remained in ICU while they tried to clear that. In the meantime the metal sutures used to close his chest cavity somehow pulled through the cartilage in his 82-year-old chest. More surgery would be required to close him up again, but first they had to clear his lungs.

Time dragged on, and for the next six weeks Dad was in ICU. I was very grateful to be sitting in Pensacola rather than DeFuniak Springs, 80 miles away. I went by the hospital on the way to work and on the way home. I called on each shift change, setting my alarm at night. I came to know the staff well–who worked which shift and their days off. The nurses were kind and candid. I remember once when I called on the 11:00 p.m. to 7:00 a.m. shift. The nurse said that Dad was agitated and disoriented. I knew that they had put Dad on morphine and he had begun to hallucinate. She explained that another patient in ICU had flat-lined and that the area was quickly crowded with medical staff and machines as they tried in vain to revive the man next to my father. I asked the nurse if I should come over, and she responded, "If it were my dad, I'd come." It was only a 30-minute drive. It was close to Halloween, and Dad, unaware of his hallucinations, told me about the trick-or-treaters, in costumes and masks, who had been in the hallway. Though obviously disquieted, he tried to make jokes. I didn't try to explain the doctors with masks or the equipment rolling by. Over the weeks, I spent more and more time at the hospital, often very early or late in a day. It is one of my life's greatest blessings to have shared that special time and space with Dad–often at weird hours– laughing, telling stories, or just sitting together quietly. Mom went to the hospital every day, sitting with him and doing her needlepoint.

Finally a doctor suggested that time on a tracheotomy may help clear his lungs. Pulmonary problems were not new to Dad, and he was sure he could defeat this known enemy. The last thing I heard my dad say was, "OK, let's get this show on the road."

Initially he seemed to handle the trach and drug-induced coma, but after a few days his facial features changed. He seemed to not be there in his body. Something was wrong–bad wrong. I asked the various specialists but each assured me their particular body part was not an issue. I cancelled hearings and spent most of my time at the hospital. Mom also knew something was wrong, in spite of what the host of doctors was saying. She said, "Your dad doesn't want to be like this. Find out, Laura." After leaving several messages that went unanswered, I managed to catch the neurologist as he made rounds around 5:00 a.m. He had few words to say and even fewer bed-side manners. The bottom line was that Dad was in an irreversible vegetative coma. I drove to my house and just stared out the window, numb. Mid-morning I rode to my parents'. Mom was sitting by the sliding glass doors watching the Bay. I stooped down by her chair and began, "Mom." She looked away and raised her hand to stop my words. "Don't tell me. I already know. Just take care of it, Laura. I don't want to see him like this. You take care of it. I'll wait here."

Even with Dad's Living Will, it was important that I talk to each of my siblings. The phone calls were placed and answered. Each child made arrangements to come home. Dad waited at the hospital in an unresponsive body, and Mom waited quietly at the Bay.

Finally with his five children with him, it was time to unplug the machines. All the paperwork was done, and the nurse was ready.

Mac, the oldest, said, "Dad, the nurse needs to work with you for a bit. While you're busy, we'll all go downstairs for breakfast. We'll be back." I was in the far corner and watched the room empty. No matter what my big brother said, I wasn't leaving. Not now.

I stood at the end of the bed with my hand on Dad's foot as the nurse turned off the ventilator and put oxygen tubes under his nose. Then I watched a big old tear run down my daddy's face, and my throat closed on a lump on confusion. The doctor said he was a vegetable, but vegetables don't cry. I leaned close but Dad seemed to be looking over my shoulder. I fumbled as I wiped away his tears, and I uttered trite, empty words that I regret to this day, "Is that oxygen cold, Daddy? Cold air makes my eyes water, too."

Always a lover of life, unplugged, Dad didn't die. Slowly my siblings returned with their spouses. Then a few grandkids joined the crowd. I stood silently in my corner. About noon, it was as though a Big Hand took me by the nape of the neck and walked me to the bedside. I kissed him on the forehead and calmly said, "Dad, I'm leaving now. I love you." And I walked away, without looking back.

Dad died before I got out of the parking lot.

I look around the animal hospital; somehow this is a more hopeful, honest place than the waiting room in a people hospital. It makes me wish that 30 years ago I had chosen to work with animals, instead of people.

Hours later I'm called to the Consult Room. The vet and three vet students carefully explain what they've done and the results of the tests. Bottom line: Bruin is nine years old with lumbar-sacral disease and hip dysplasia. Nothing imminently fatal. He's had a few bad days and will again. We leave with a new prescription that he must take with hamburger and the recommendation that I take him swimming. Aside from being embarrassed by his shaved belly, he's fared pretty well on this adventure. An adventure that painfully reminds me of his mortality, how much I enjoy him, and how I rely on him for companionship and a sense of security.

Bruin and I walk out of the hospital at 6:30 p.m. With nothing better to do with all of this pent-up energy, I decide to drive hard–just go–head on down the highway. As I pull away from the parking lot, I'm still entangled with thoughts of my dad. I've never second-guessed or regretted my sudden leave-taking from his people hospital. I simply had to go. It was time for him to get that show on the road, and he couldn't do his dying with me in the room. Leaving can be an act of love. Over the years and down many a highway, I've learned to trust that my faltering words don't crowd out kindness or love in those sacred places where words don't really matter.

Fort Collins is near the northern edge of Colorado, and the geography begins to change as I head north. The Colorado Rockies drop away, to be replaced by mesas that are surprisingly green and studded with rock. Wyoming mountains appear in the twilight, with a different persona than those in Colorado. In the mountains of Colorado it was easy to imagine a stooped miner with a long beard walking down a steep trail beside his mule, but in Wyoming I watch for a lone cowboy on top of the mesa. I drive until after dark, breaking the silent promise I'd made to my dad as I stood in the Milton Cemetery.

Driving through the now blackened mountains with bottled-up energy and memories, I remember an affirmation I received from the Supreme Court that didn't feel so affirming.

❦ ❦ ❦

When the job is well done

I was sitting as a Juvenile Judge in Pensacola when the Florida Supreme Court issued its ruling on Suggs, the man I had sentenced to death almost four years earlier. The conviction and sentence was affirmed; there was no error. Not even what they call harmless error. Nothing was wrong, legally wrong, yet the ruling really took the wind out of me. Suggs is now very likely to die because I'd been well trained and did a good job. Had I been sloppy or short tempered, Suggs would live.

I called in Jody, the deputy assigned to me for Security. Jody was my friend; we trusted one another. He sat with me in the heavy silence of my office, and then I asked, "Jody, have you ever killed someone?" He said, "No, I shot somebody but I didn't have to kill him." I said, "Did it make you feel like shit? Like you were somehow wrong for doing your job right?" Jody nodded yes.

Shortly after the opinion came out affirming my death sentence on Suggs, Toni made the headlines in an aborted pizza robbery. Toni, one of my juvenile delinquents, was a skinny, immature fifteen-year-old, living in a rough area, trying to act big. As he came in and out of court on various charges, his grandmother and I believed in Toni and prayed he'd make a life for himself. During that same time, the two officers described now on page one of the newspaper had sat at my kitchen table in the middle of the night as I signed various search warrants. The officers are good men, the kind I'm proud to know are "out there." Because of a series of armed robberies of pizza deliverymen, the officers were assigned to respond in an unmarked vehicle and plain clothes to Toni's late night call for pizza; it was their job. They watched a shadowed figure level a shotgun at them; they fired first. Killing a fifteen-year-old was big news, and the two officers caught hell in the paper. Lots of folks were sure the officers could have done something else. "OK." the public screamed "so Toni pointed a shotgun at them, but he was only fifteen!" Yet everyone thought I was a hero for sentencing Suggs to the electric chair. The officers answered Toni's call; they showed up. The officers are alive and Toni is dead— because they were well trained and did their jobs carefully and with attention to detail. Like me.

But instead of the officers' split-second decision to shoot, my killing will be incredibly slow coming. Very focused, fully intentionally, with time for life times of wonders and questions. I have no question of Suggs's guilt, or that if anyone legally qualifies for the death penalty, it's him. But will killing Suggs make the world a better place? I don't think so.

You can't pay someone enough money to live with the decision the officers made in responding to Toni's call or the one I made in Suggs' case. It's a very lonely place—one where my soul echoes and aches—one where I found no true answers but a place from which my job description required that I act decisively. The State— my boss—told me that killing in retribution is not wrong, as long as I did it right.

❋ ❋ ❋

"It is when we all play safe that we create a world of utmost insecurity."
Dag Hammarskjold

CHAPTER 8.
LOST PRAIRIE, MONTANA:
Skydiving and clarity

I park at the Wal-Mart in Missoula, Montana. I spend an hour talking to my new RV neighbors, Leonard and Marilyn, full-timers from Texas who travel from golf course to golf course. Like me, they are here only for the night.

Marilyn asks, "Are you tired of traveling alone? I'm not sure I could handle it."

I laugh, "Remember Dorothy in the Wizard of Oz and those ruby red slippers she got from the Wicked Witch of the West? All she had to do was click her heels together and say, 'There's no place like home.' And, zap, she was back on the farm! Well, I walk around pigeon-toed, like this," I point my toes in and heels out and walk a few feet, "because I don't want to accidentally click my heels together and wake up back in Northwest Florida. I'm exactly where I want to be–in a Wal-Mart parking lot in Montana talking with two people who get it–people who don't need to go back to the farm but need to check out lots of unknowns on crooked roads." As we talk and laugh, they invite me to winter over with them in the desert and to meet them even sooner, somewhere down the road. I know their offers are genuine, and I hope to meet them again. RV'ers are like that, important friendships, made on the fly. I don't make any commitments, of course; I'm still recoiling from years of tight schedule and structure. But Leonard and Marilyn are heading over to Glacier and will park their rig at Hungry Horse; the name of the town is a good enough reason to go there.

From Missoula, I pull the 5th wheel to Lost Prairie, 35 miles southwest of Kalispell. From Highway 2, I turn right at McGregor Lake and drive north four miles down a rough, dusty, rocky road to a prairie that is as beautiful as it is lost. At the drop zone, there's a long dirt runway that butts up to a cow pasture. During the day, the cows are elsewhere; jumpers are free to land in the pasture and careful to avoid sliding in on a cow patty.

I made my first skydive at a drop zone in Deland, Florida. It was a tandem jump; I wore a harness that was attached at the shoulders and hips to Pine, my very good-looking instructor from South Africa who wore a special parachute large enough to handle two people. The first jump was a carnival ride on an E ticket; after a brief class, all I had to do was pay my money, walk to the plane, and then nod yes when Pine asked, "Are you ready to skydive?"

"Creator, please don't be subtle." That's a prayer I can't recommend to anyone, yet I continue to use it. And my prayer continues to be answered. How I managed to fall out of a perfectly good airplane is just one example of how unsubtle the Creator can be.

I was attending a faculty planning session for the Advanced Judicial Studies in South Florida when Rob, a fellow Circuit Judge and instructor, explained to a group of cohorts over dinner how much fun he had skydiving. I'm terrified of heights and can't stand at the rail of a second floor balcony without my stomach dropping, my knees loosening, and the world threatening to rotate around my dimming eyes. I said nothing to Rob but was aghast at him for even talking of jumping out of a plane. I had no concept of terror being fun. I had recently rappelled down a fire tower, to silence my fear of heights, but the plan didn't work. Though I'd learned a lot in that cram course of fear, I wasn't interested in any more lessons, especially those that required I fall down from two miles up.

Sitting in the restaurant with seven other judges, as Rob talked on about skydiving, I thought of the videos my young friend Sara and I often watched together and the one that consistently freaked me out. Rescuers Down Under is a Lilliputian-style video by Disney that includes a piece in which a mammoth-size eagle is captured by the equally large bad guys and roped to the top of a dizzy precipice. A young boy, tiny in proportion to the others, begins to saw through the maze of ropes lacing the eagle to the rock, using a knife that fits his hand but is smaller than the eagle's eye. With only a few ropes remaining, the eagle struggles to free himself and accidentally knocks the boy from the pinnacle. As the boy falls, the camera zooms in on his face filled with sheer terror. The eagle swoops down to catch the boy mid-air; within seconds the air games begin as the eagle flips his tiny passenger onto his huge back and from there tosses the child into the air. The boy is no longer frozen in fear but is giggling; he intentionally slides off the eagle's back to fall until his feathered friend catches him. OK, I could feel the raw terror, but my reaction to the boy's playfulness and unabridged joy was one of anger. How do you do that!! I'd watched the video with Sara many times; my reaction was always the same— terror and then anger.

From across the dinner table, Rob interrupted my quiet angst, "Melvin, you can jump tandem with an instructor. You won't believe how much fun it is." He had no idea.

For weeks, night after night, I'd wake up startled, with my heart racing and my mouth dry, as I tried to shake the dream of falling, falling, falling. I didn't talk about it. No one said I had to fall out of a plane. And the dreams racked on.

Within a month Rob and I were back in Orlando as Judicial Education instructors. He explained he'd brought his parachute and that I needed to go make a jump with him in Deland. I didn't answer.

Our courses ended early afternoon, and as we loaded our cars, Rob asked, "Well, Melvin, are you going to jump?" I responded, "I don't know yet." He retorted, "What do you mean? You have to know! We're leaving." I said, "When we get to the stop sign, if I turn left and follow you, I'll go jump. If I turn right, I'm heading home." We drove across the parking lot to that stop sign where Rob stopped, hopped out of his car, and sprinted back to me to say, "Follow me across the street. We have to talk." So I turned neither left nor right. Instead we drove straight into the parking lot of a restaurant, less than a hundred yards from where we started. We went inside the mostly deserted bar decorated in a Disney theme and ordered cokes. Rob barked, "OK, Melvin, this is ridiculous. Are you going with me!?" I responded, "Turn around and watch this video for a minute, and then I'll answer you." Rob swirled his bar stool to look at a large screen; the video showed a young boy with a knife smaller than the eagle's eye, sawing through a maze of ropes. We watched quietly as the child fell in fear but then soared playfully with the eagle. Then I said, "Rob, I don't get it. But, yes, damn it, I'm going to jump." As I followed Rob to the drop zone, I knew I could delay this lesson in terror. I also knew that the Universe would only become more direct, less subtle. And this scenario was scary enough.

My first ride to jump altitude was one of mind-crippling, nauseous fear. There was no room for fantasy about all the fun I'd have; this was deadly serious business! There were four of us sitting on the floor of the small plane (seats are space and weight hogs so they are often taken out of jump planes). As the plane began to climb, I had to concentrate to breathe; even then my breaths were jerky and forced. When I finally screwed up the courage to throw a darting glance out the window, I saw a rainbow off to my right. I thought, "Nice touch, Universe. OK, OK, I'm going." Typical first-jump style, fear sucked all my juices dry; I had cottonmouth and my teeth stuck to my lips when I forced a smile. I leaned over and said to Pine, "I'm scared"

He patted my leg and smiled, "That's good."

I was puzzled; it didn't feel good. Later, I screwed up my courage to confess, "Pine, I mean I'm really scared."

Again, he smiled, "That's very good, Laura."

Now I was petrified and dumbfounded. How could being filled with terror be "very good?" Seconds or hours later someone yelled, "Jump run!" and the jumpers began moving around to adjust their gear. When the altimeter on Pine's wrist read 10,500 feet, I watched in disbelief as a jumper opened the door of the plane, leaned his head out, looked back at us with a smile, waved, and fell out of the plane. The wind noise was so loud I could barely hear Pine yell into my ear, "Are you ready to skydive?" I nodded yes; the only thing I was sure of was that I was going to get this over with. I knew I could have said no and ridden back down with the plane; I also knew that all of hell could not make me say no, not now.

Pine shouted, "OK, move to the door," and we waddled like a four-legged duck, joined at the shoulders and hips by high tech equipment.

My knees were limp, my stomach churned, my heart raced, my breath was shallow and irregular, my hands were clammy, my eyes dilated, my mouth was dry, and my mind screamed, but I moved toward the door. Standing in the open door, breathing in and out was not an option; it took everything I had to simply be there. They told me I'd have no sensation of height, but I looked out that howling hole at the curvature of the earth and thought, "You lied!"

With my hands crossed on my chest, we fell forward into what could be hell. Within three seconds of clearing the door, my sheer terror disappeared, and the little tomboy was free again. I had absolutely no sensation of falling, not even that slight lift I get in my stomach in a fast-moving elevator. I felt totally secure, falling through more than a mile of open sky. She who was and still is terrified of heights, of losing her grip, of losing control, was lost in playful freedom. I was disappointed when I felt the chute open, like a kid on the carousel who feels the engine shift and the horse slow down. But then under canopy, a different joy burst into bloom. We could see for miles; Pine made gentle turns with the parachute, orienting me to locations on the ground–Daytona Beach, Flagler Beach to the north, the Space Center to the South, and the St. Johns River wearing aprons of saw grass. Then he was quiet so I could take in the experience without the clamor of words. The air felt crisp and cool like mountain air. At our feet lay Central Florida, gilded by the late afternoon sun–a green blanket with patches of blue lakes, citrus trees lined up like toy soldiers, and wisps of white water birds in swamps of cypress and pine trees. From the moment I left the plane until I was back on the ground, there was no room for thought, as that word is normally defined. There was no time to worry about what might happen or to brood over the past; there was no time to consider work, personal relations, or the future. There was only The Now and my body's immediate, joyful response to it.

I was a little antsy as we came down the last 75 feet because it looked too much like the stomach-dropping view from high balconies. But Pine's landing was perfect, and within seconds I was standing on the grass with the brightly colored parachute dropping around us.

Shortly after we landed, all my old fears returned–my fear of heights, my fear of falling, my fear of dying, my fear of failure, my fear of not being good enough, my fear of not being able to handle it, my fear of fear. That didn't seem fair; I thought one jump would dispel all that raw terror, but no. The fears were back with a vengeance, and to their screaming tirade they had added recently acquired facts about the risks of jumping out of an airplane. But it was too late; the tomboy was out of the box, and she wasn't going back. I'd learned I could do the impossible, that I could walk through my fears and jump out of a plane two miles above terra firma, and I learned it was a lot of fun. A couple of weeks later, I made another tandem jump and then went through the certification classes to jump alone. My fears stalked my every move, but they never followed me out the door.

I bought my own gear, and I jump regularly. I skydive the way I live–intense, analytical, contemplative, deep, and full of questions. The last two minutes of the plane ride and the walk to the door continue to be my personal Armageddon. But once I'm out the door, I'm an eight-year-old tomboy; my mind is alert, focused and unclouded. The world in free-fall and under canopy is clear, beautiful, rapidly changing, and brutally honest. Even after hundreds of skydives, when I'm safely back on the ground, the Critic picks up as though she had not been temporarily ousted, and she calls in the dragons for reinforcement.

As I moved toward leaving the Bench with the complex financial, professional, and personal consequences entailed, I was as terrified as on that first plane ride up to jump altitude. I looked out at the risks. My Critic screamed, "Why would anyone jump from such security into the howling unknown? Are you crazy? You're not going to make it, you know." Fear glued my lips and teeth in a cottonmouth smile, and I couldn't swallow. Occasionally I could remember to take a deep breath; at times I held my breath so long I choked. I wished Pine were there to tell me it's OK, that it was very good to be this afraid.

Skydivers are a delightfully eclectic group; they pay little attention to social status, education, race, or income, but they focus on trustworthiness, cool gear, fall rate, and attitude. Gravity is the ultimate equalizer; a plumber and physician, a dentist and ditch digger, an international fashion model and a guy who's lived in his van for two years all jump together because social distinctions don't mean squat once you go out the door of the plane. I'd been jumping most weekends for three years at Emerald Coast in Elberta, Alabama, when Michelle, a close skydiving friend, called Carolyne on the phone, "I just watched the news. There was some woman in a robe who looked like Laura. What's going on? Is she a judge?!?" The laws of gravity show no respect to last names and job titles so they're seldom used at the drop zone.

Michelle and Carolyne, like other skydivers, are hard to pigeonhole. Michelle is young enough to be my daughter but not even slightly deferential to me. She has long dark hair, an easy smile, and a gentle, positive manner. Michelle works in Human Resources, packs her parachute with a confidence I lack, and laughs a lot. Carolyne is a petite, attractive software developer who spends much time and energy on her appearance. Her makeup must always be perfect, so she reapplies it between skydives. Both Michelle and Carolyne keep plastic wine glasses in their sports cars for emergencies, often change clothes in the car in a flash, and believe in eating from everyone's plate at the restaurant. Carolyne and Michelle are members of an inner circle of female skydivers who lovingly refer to each other as Gypsy Trash, a small group who understands the call of adventure and the need to wander, a group whose members shun much of conventional life, appreciate a certain degree of trashy, and are sufficiently unpredictable and nonjudgmental. Gypsy Trash are known to be fiercely independent, preferring to work alone and bust knuckles rather than ask for help.

Several years earlier, Carolyne and I were two of 18 jumpers on the twin-engine Otter[11]; we were to jump over the Gulf of Mexico from 13,500 feet and land on the beach at the FloraBama Bar, a redneck institution with wooden floors, multiple bands, and packed crowds. Each jumper was required to wear a flotation device because we would fly over water. Gaining altitude, the plane flew a pattern that took us over the Gulf and a number of miles south of land. As we flew south, at an altitude of 7,000 feet there was a sudden, ear-splitting metallic sound as the plane convulsed and then skidded into a 70-degree turn. The lively banter between 18 skydivers

---

[11]Otter - a twin engine plane, customized with a large sliding Plexiglas door on the side for exits. On exit as many as eight or nine jumpers can hang outside the plane, holding onto various objects to wait while other jumpers line up inside. It can get crowded out there, but it's fun and helpful when building larger formations. The Otter is powerful enough to get the load of up to 21 jumpers to exit altitude (13,500 feet) in about 20 minutes.

stopped, and we waited in silence.

Finally the pilot shouted the magic words, "Exit! Exit! Exit!" and we all stood up. As part of our emergency training, we accepted that, based on many factors unknown to the rest of us, the pilot alone would decide if and when to put us out. And "exit, exit, exit" meant, Get out, now! A jumper opened the door, leaned out to look toward the white stretch of sand in the distance, and yelled, "I think we can make it from here!" We lined up and moved toward the door. In an emergency exit, you go out one at a time with about three seconds between each jumper, get stable, and open your parachute immediately. Though we had sufficient altitude, this was not the time to fly formations or play around. This was an emergency, and no one was laughing. Carolyne and I held hands as we moved toward the door, waiting our turn. We were cautious and curious but not afraid. At the door we smiled at each other, and then without thinking, we went out together. Just out the door we accidentally bumped into each other, which caused us to flip and spin. Instead of being stable and appropriate, we were upside down and laughing because we'd blown our first emergency exit. It's not necessarily dangerous to bump, flip and spin in free-fall; in fact, it can be a lot of fun. Carolyne and I were experienced jumpers, and we understood that with more than 7,000 feet in altitude there was still plenty of time and space to straighten up, fly apart, and open our parachutes. But this was not a routine jump; it was an emergency and not a time to goof off. We were supposed to be serious, since seriously we'd just jumped out of a disabled airplane over the Gulf of Mexico, and even skydivers have some rules. Still laughing but at least now trying to act like grown-ups, we flipped over belly to earth and tracked[12] away from one another. We opened our chutes and flew toward land. All of the jumpers landed uneventfully on the beach at the

---

[12]Track - to fly horizontally, like Superman, to create a safe separation between each other to open the parachutes

FloraBama Bar. We were right where we were supposed to be, it's just that we were there a little early. The spectators didn't realize anything unusual had happened, and the pilot landed safely at the DZ. And the ember of my confidence in my true self–long buried under layers of responsibility and the expectations of others–flickered a little brighter.

Over the years I bolstered my professional confidence with training, long hours of hard work, and increasingly difficult jobs, but I did little to encourage my personal confidence. My horse Kracker taught me to trust myself at a physical level as we rode together in the world beyond Law; years later, falling for two miles at 120 MPH before opening my parachute, I learn more and more about relying on me.

It feels like high adventure, traveling in an RV with my dog, heading to a skydiving boogie in Montana, a place I've only read about in Wild West novels and travel brochures. But I also feel uncomfortable, even shy about checking in at the drop zone by myself. In Florida and Alabama I jump with friends into familiar wind patterns, weather conditions, and terrain. Nothing feels familiar in these mountains of Montana except the law of gravity. I had not shown up at a drop zone alone, before I started this trip. I remind myself that I very much want to be able to skydive here and there while traveling. I'd jumped in Colorado, and I'd jump in Montana.

At the end of the long road to Lost Prairie I park and unhook the RV, plant my pink flamingo outside (a delightfully tacky metal bird that was a going-away gift), and go to check in at Manifest.

Manifest does a safety check of my skydiving gear and gives me a stack of waivers to sign. The waiver forms are long and legal; basically they require that you agree to die while having fun. I was there to jump, and the forms were there to keep me from suing them after I voluntarily jumped out of their airplanes. I don't read much of their legal jargon, except with a passing curiosity. I do read the bold print "Do not sign these waivers without reading!" One question is, "Who to call in case of an emergency," and I put down the info for my son.

A couple is sitting nearby at the picnic table, filling out their paperwork. She asks, "Who should I put down to call in case of emergency?"

He answers, "I always put down 9-1-1. Don't know why they even ask that question! Hell, if they don't call 9-1-1 first, I won't care who gets called later!"

As the weekend approaches, the number of skydivers and plane loads increases. On Saturday they put up 46 Otters loads and 16 loads on the Sky Van,[13] (assuming 20 jumpers on each load that would be 1,240 jumps in one day). Rainbow-colored parachutes moved like bubbles across the sky. The air was punctuated by soft puffs as nylon parachutes popped open, followed by a swoosh as the parachutes landed. Planes took off and landed, leaving whiffs of AV gas. Lost Prairie is just south of the Canadian border and slightly east of the Pacific Time zone; the sun didn't set until about 9:30 p.m., and it wasn't dark until 10:30 p.m. If you wanted to, you could jump 12 to 15 hours a day.

People often ask, "Why would you want to jump out of a perfectly good airplane?" It's hard to explain the child-like raw joy of running out the open door of a plane with a wad of grinning friends. Perhaps part of the initial draw is that you're not supposed to do it; just ask your mother or your big brother and see what they say. After that first jump I was happily hooked on the sense of freedom and empowerment, the joy of being in the air, and the camaraderie of the jumpers.

They don't let children skydive, so all jumpers are required to show up for the planeload in a grown-up body. But once at the plane, eight-year-old spirits emerge and the ruckus begins. The load of jumpers sounds like unsupervised campers and

---

[13]Sky Van - another twin engine plane that is VERY noisy and not as quick to altitude, but favored because of the rear-belly tail gate that can easily handle eight jumpers at the door, with others charging the door when the first ones are out. Jumping from the tailgate of the Sky Van is like running off the end of the pier or railroad trestle, but at an altitude of 13,500 feet.

silliness reigns. There's a lot of laughter and corny jokes; it's acceptable to flap your elbows on take-off to increase lift; loud yelps and whoops are almost mandatory. Because the planes are not pressurized, flatulence is common and farting becomes an art form. When the inevitable smell begins to spread, someone will yell, "Door!" and the accusations begin. A jumper will open the door to let the smell out, as the discussion continues about who had what for dinner based on an analysis of those particular smells. Onions and beans are easy to identify. Sometimes the farts are claimed; more often they are vigorously denied.

The community of skydivers is tight-knit and fairly small; a mobile lot, they often go to boogies on commercial flights with their parachutes in an unobtrusive backpack. Skydivers from around the country converge on Lost Prairie, knowing they can jump long hours on fast planes. Carolyne joins the migration, flying up from Florida. We make several jumps together in this unfamiliar place. Life is good.

After sunset, I walk over to use the only pay phone. (There's no cell phone service at Lost Prairie.) I meet a guy who landed under his emergency parachute that afternoon and then took a trip to the hospital; his right arm and shoulder are in a sling. I ask, and he explains he had dislocated his right shoulder a couple of months before, and it went out again on exit from the Sky Van. They had chunked a piece, meaning several jumpers left the plane holding onto one another's wrists, shoulders, or legs. Things don't always go perfectly on an exit, and there can be a lot of pressure put on body parts as the group stands motionless inside the plane, jumps into an air speed of 90 to 100 MPH, and then transitions to terminal velocity[14] of 120 MPH, without turning loose (known as dropping a grip). Dislocated joints can be a hazard of the trade. With his right shoulder out of joint, he couldn't use his right hand to open his

---

[14]Terminal velocity, or the rate of constant vertical speed, is about 120 miles per hour (192 km per hour) for a human body falling belly to earth with arms and legs outstretched. Terminal velocity is not reached immediately upon exiting the plane; jumpers refer to the fall time before reaching terminal as "on the hill."

main chute; with his left hand he pulled the release on his left side for his reserve parachute.

He describes how he flew and landed the reserve with only his left arm. "You release both toggles high enough to deal with the initial spiral, hold both brakes with your left hand and push them in the direction you want to fly. It's not all that hard. I'd figured this out 'cause I had a student jumper a few years ago who had no right arm. So, I'd actually practiced it."

He's still a little groggy from the anesthesia to reset his shoulder. He laughs about the intense pain and settles comfortably into a large crowd of skydivers who understands why he'll jump again soon.

Walking back to my RV, I remember Wanda, a child caught in her family's emotional storm–a child who, like this skydiver, reached for strength and clarity.

❧ ❧ ❧

Wanda
Wanda was 16, and her parents were embroiled in a bitter custody dispute. With the attorneys and parents waiting outside, she and I talked alone in my office. At first she sat up very straight and spoke slowly, carefully, saying negative things about herself like, "I'm not the brightest." I knew from earlier testimony that she was on antidepressants, following three episodes of suicidal ideation. As we talked, she relaxed her shoulders, sat back in the chair, and the tone of her voice softened.

When I asked about her parents she said, "I can't tell Mom if I have fun at Dad's 'cause it upsets her. Mom always asks questions about everything we do at Dad's. She can't just let me be, no matter what I do. She's afraid. At Dad's, I can laugh and smile without a reason."

As was often the case in custody disputes, neither parent was bad. Whether I ruled with the mom or the dad, this was another decision where I would be right as a matter of law, so long as I made appropriate factual findings and conclusions. It was also another case with no clear answer.

I said "Wanda, you're 16, mature, and the reason we're all here. I've never let a child sit in while I announce my decision in a custody case. But maybe it's time. Do you want to hear it all, straight from me?"

She looked at me quizzically then softly answered, "Yes, ma'am."

"OK, Wanda, but you know it may get rough. There're a lot of things I need to say for the record. And your mom may cry."

"I want to hear it, Judge."

"All right, and remember they both love you very much."

She returned to the lobby and then came into the hearing room with her parents and the attorneys. As I made my way through the factual findings and conclusions, Wanda's eyes darted back and forth, taking in her mom's silent tears and her dad's subdued looks as I announced that I was placing Wanda in the primary custody of her father, subject to liberal visitation with her mother. The attorney for the mother got little snippy, asking questions that revealed in form and tone how hard it was for him to lose. I interrupted, making it clear that he would not change my mind simply because he was overbearing or rude. As the less-than-pristine process continued, I began to question the wisdom of letting Wanda sit through this, but it was too late now and she seemed OK. When I finished announcing my ruling, everyone stood up to leave. Wanda—and only Wanda—walked over to me, looked me straight in the eye, put out her hand, shook mine, and said in a firm, quiet voice, "Thank you."

✦ ✦ ✦

My last jump at Lost Prairie is a once-in-a-lifetime, if-you're-lucky jump. A sunset cross-country jump in the mountains. As the sun begins to slide toward the horizon, 60-plus jumpers load into the two Otters and the Sky Van to fly in formation about six miles from the DZ. From the left side of our plane I watch the other Otter, painted an orange-ish tint by the setting sun. The Otters play tag; first one, then the other is in the lead. Ahead and slightly higher is the Sky Van, dancing in and out of view through the forward windows of our plane. On cue from the Sky Van, the jumpers in the three planes get out at 13,800 feet for a hop and pop, meaning that the jumpers exit about three seconds apart and open parachutes within about three seconds of exit. When it's my turn, I add my canopy to what looks like bubbles popping from the end of three wands. Soon the sky is full of 60 bright-colored canopies, back-lit by the setting sun.

The view is as unconventional as the opportunity; I look down at my shoes floating two and a half miles over mountains dotted by glacier lakes that reflect the orange, pink, and purple trail of the fleeting sun. The valleys are filled with long shadows; the mountains are a darkening green. It brings to mind Peter Drucker's remark that "There is the risk you cannot afford to take, (and) there is the risk you cannot afford not to take." I had stuffed a disposable camera down the front of my jump suit, and when I could finally stop drooling on the tops of my shoes while shouting "Oh My God!" I take several shots. Then I get cold feet, thinking of those 60+ other jumpers up there with me, also goggling at the scenery, so I stick the camera back into my jumpsuit and resume flying. It's a magical time and worth the entire trip. We have no trouble making it back (I was over the DZ at 9,000 feet), and the jumpers understand why it was a short cross-country ride. Management preferred to be conservative so that if there were a sudden change in wind or a jumper opened too low, it would not be dark when they plucked skydivers from distant hills and mountaintops.

The next day I hook up the RV and pull out–a tired, happy camper with a Lost Prairie bumper sticker pasted to the spare tire cover on my 5th wheel.

"He who trembles is not bored." Stendhal

CHAPTER 9.
GLACIER NATIONAL PARK:
Angry men, bumper cars, and grizzlies

Leaving Lost Prairie, I decide to spend some time in Glacier National Park before heading to the West Coast, so I turn east on Highway 2 and drive to a commercial campground at Hungry Horse, Montana, northeast of Kalispell. The route takes me around Flathead Lake, an emerald green, glacier-fed lake with hills and mountains snuggled against her wet edges. I drive past miles of cherry orchards. The narrow country road is heavily punctuated with roadside stands, selling the cherries picked from the owners' yards. Pulling off the road with a 30-foot RV in tow takes some forethought and puts a damper on impulse stopping, but I manage to pull into a stand manned by two girls, maybe 14 years old. Barely off the road and out of traffic, I walk over to their makeshift market. "This is the first time I've seen cherries growing on trees," I explain. They look at me as though I had dropped in from Mars. In self-defense I add, "I'm from Florida. And I bet you've never seen peanuts growing!" They wait a second and then laugh. They explain to this uneducated adult that Bing cherries are sweeter than Rainiers, and when I can't make up my mind, they sell me a large bag, mixed.

About 10 miles from Hungry Horse, the truck suddenly jumps and bucks as though I were trying to start off in 4th gear on this standard transmission. The 11,000-pound RV lurches back and forth in response to the jerking action of the truck. The truck and RV are not in sync with their bucking and are soon careening off each other like huge bumper cars. I check; there's no traffic behind me so I'm not in danger of ramming someone with my lurching rear end. With clammy hands, I pull over into a large center section of the road, marked off with yellow lines. My only guess proves to be wrong–the brakes to the trailer are properly plugged in, and, as proof, all the trailer lights are working. Brake lights, flashers, and turn signals. I have no idea what's wrong, and I'm scared–scared it will happen again, scared I can't figure this one out, scared I've finally met the problem I can't overcome, out here all by myself. I don't really have a choice so drive the 10 miles to the campground. A new neighbor listens intently as I explain what happened and gives me the name of a local RV repair shop. I'm surprised there's a mechanic who can work on RV brakes within a day's drive. The services in the area are so minimal that when I asked the sole employee in the one-window post office at Hungry Horse about receiving my mail there in care of General Delivery, she shook her head. "It might work, but I have all my mail delivered to Kalispell."

After parking, I realize I'm directly behind a familiar-looking rig. It's Leonard and Marilyn, new friends from the Wal-Mart parking lot in Missoula, Montana. I unhook my home on wheels and go next door to visit.

The RV park fronts the Flathead River where several campers saw a bear feeding this morning. I'm nervous about not being at the top of the food chain in a land that is so strange to me, so I don't go down to the river to check their report.

The next morning I pull the 5th wheel gingerly into the mechanic without incident. Without incident, that is, until I go inside. I explain the lurching, and the owner is instantly angry because when the problem first occurred, I had not unhooked the trailer brakes and tried stopping the 5th wheel using only the truck brakes.

He explains in disgust, "That's the way you find out if it's the truck or the trailer!"

I respond in an even tone, "It never crossed my mind, and I wouldn't have done it even if I thought of it. That's dangerous. My trailer weighs 11,000 pounds; there's a reason they put a separate set of brakes on it."

He grumbles, "Great, and now what do you expect me to

do? Take the time to drive your truck and trailer around for four hours to find out what's wrong? So you can bitch about the bill!"

I want to tell him off, but I'm in serious need of mechanical help, and he's the only game in this remote crossroad. So I practice my diplomacy skills. While telling myself he's an idiot and an asshole, I tell him he seems to be having a bad morning, that I need mechanical help for which I am willing to pay a reasonable fee, and that if he doesn't want to work politely with me, that's fine, because I'll leave. (It isn't really fine, because my home is sitting in his parking lot, I'm afraid to pull it down the highway, and there is no other mechanic for miles.) He calms down, but he never improves the initial impression he gave of being a chauvinistic asshole. I drive as we take a test run in my Dodge, and I use the long-handled floor shifter to change into each of the five forward gears on the standard transmission.

He barks, "OK, now put it in overdrive! And I guess I better call my friend at the Ford dealer."

Using my best female voice, I respond, "Why don't you call the Dodge dealer instead. My truck would be embarrassed to be around a bunch of Fords."

He mumbles, "Oh, is this a Dodge?"

Then I pat the stick shift and ask, "Where is overdrive on a standard transmission?" He looks out the window and doesn't answer. But he certainly isn't the first angry man I've had to work around; I've met more than a few sitting as a female judge in Family Court.

Judges sometimes say that in Criminal Court we meet the worst at their best, and in Family Court we meet the best at their worst. Perhaps an overstatement, but it's clear that emotions and attitudes are raw in Family Court, and the underbelly of society often shows itself. Although the rational purpose of Family Law is to amicably resolve disputes associated with marital relationships, the culture that has grown up there is often one of emotional warfare rather than respectful communication and joint resolution. Humans, acting like animals they consider themselves to be above, often like a good fight, and in Family Law I watched too many otherwise good people take scathing shots at the person with whom they had shared their life, using as ammunition intimate and visceral information unavailable to strangers, with the calculated goal of emotionally plundering the other. In Family Court, anger and aggression are the unnecessary norm.

❖ ❖ ❖

Another day, another docket

There was nothing unique about that Monday—another docket crowded with people and problems. I had flown to Ohio for the weekend, a long trip for a short speech. I left Bruin at the kennel early Friday morning; I had to pick him up by 6:00 p.m. on Monday or leave him 'til after work on Tuesday.

In the afternoon there was a particularly petty and caustic hearing on reciprocal Motions for Contempt in a divorce case. When I granted the divorce a couple of months earlier, I gave the house to the husband and gave the wife 30 days to move out. When the ex-wife moved her stuff, for spite she also took the shelf brackets from the entertainment center that I had given to the husband as well as the light bulbs. But the ex-husband was not to be outdone in the sewers of revenge. Seven days before the court order gave him sole possession of the house, he changed the locks. When his wife returned for the last of her things and found the door locked, she tried to climb in through a window. The husband was waiting inside. He slammed the window on her arms, and pinned her there awhile to leave deep bruises as proof of his spite.

Each had lied during the hearing, and they clearly enjoyed the energy of their mutual hate. At the conclusion of the testimony, I spoke to the parties, "You win the weekly prize for mean spiritedness, spite, and vindictiveness. It seems only appropriate that you each pay for your follies. Neither party is awarded attorney fees; you will each pay your own. The ex-husband's Motion for Contempt is denied. The ex-wife's Motion for Contempt is also denied. And Court is adjourned."

The next hearing was a temporary request for support in a divorce case. The husband was not represented by a lawyer, though he was obviously affluent. He wore Italian shoes, a rich-casual golf shirt, and pants with a knife pleat down the front. He brought to court his red-hot anger and disgust. He couldn't or wouldn't get past his anger and I–a mere woman–seemed to be making it worse. He had an attitude that's hard to work with in a 30-minute hearing. I bent over backwards to give him a chance to be heard, but resolution and reason were the last things on his mind. He was furious and proud of it. Near the end of the hearing, the wife's attorney asked him a question about some papers in his hand, and in response he threw them across the table at the lawyer. I watched him, as if in slow motion, thinking "Shit! I know I can go ahead and put him in jail for contempt of court, but it's five o'clock. I've got to get Bruin from the kennel by six. If I do a legally correct contempt hearing, I'll be late leaving and the kennel may close. And I want Bruin back home. Plus a day or two in jail might cost Mr. Attitude that job that nets him $6,200 per month." So instead of jailing him, I jumped in, chewed him out, and threatened him, "You don't want to know what happens next, if you even think about doing something like that again."

After the hearing, as I gathered up files, the deputy assigned to me as security for the day said, "I can't believe you didn't put him in jail!"

I didn't even respond. I bolted out of the building and picked up Bruin as the kennel was closing.

So the sun set on yet another routine Monday, another not-fun day. This work doesn't fill or energize me anymore. I feel no sense of accomplishment in locking someone up, no joy in "winning." There is no challenge or satisfaction in dealing with light-bulb thieves or those who slam the window on the mother of their children, after changing the locks on the home they built and lived in together as a family. I'd rather spend time with my dog than try to teach manners to an angry man.

❖ ❖ ❖

As we ride around a small section of northwestern Montana, the mechanic-with-an-attitude talks a lot, and I'm quiet a lot. There's little I can say without alienating the only help available. The guy finally decides the problem is not with the truck or trailer brakes but with the exhaust brake Camping World recently installed on the truck. Some time and several phone calls later, he gets instructions from the manufacturer to disconnect that brake, so I could later take it back to Camping World. But, as I pull the rig out of his parking lot, the red light comes back on, indicating that the exhaust brake is still functioning. I drive the rig back to the campground, without incident and without confidence, and then I make an appointment with Camping World in Tacoma to let a real mechanic tell me what's going on. The bottom line is I don't understand machines and mechanical problems scare me, even back in Pensacola, where I know people and the lay of the land. After 4,000 miles of traveling alone around the country, I've learned some things, but my interest in mechanical issues remains limited to "Does it work when I turn the switch on?"

Carolyne drives from Lost Prairie to Hungry Horse and stays a night with me in the 5th wheel before catching a plane back to Florida. She's late getting in and has to leave early. It's great being around close friends and sharing common, known interests. But I'm not ready to go back to Florida or to the world of Law. The lonely times have grown some, in both intensity and longevity. The novelty of seeing new places is not as compelling. I'm acting less like the perpetual tourist. But the freedom and view are still worth the cost.

After Carolyne leaves, I drive back to the Visitors' Center at Glacier National Park and ask about hikes I could make alone.

150

The Ranger doesn't smile as he responds, "We don't recommend you hike alone–period. This is prime season for huckleberries, so the bears are active. Hiking alone is dangerous."

He would say he was just doing his job, but I wonder how many people he's influenced with his knowledge of bears, how many he's saved from encounters with angry grizzlies. He reminds me of the police officer who taught a little boy what child abuse is and saved three children with one short lesson. I also remember a fourth child whom no one helped.

❦ ❦ ❦

DARE

On Monday I signed warrants to arrest a father and his girlfriend on felony charges of Child Abuse by Caging and Withholding Food. The affidavit said that the adults required the nine-year-old son to stay outside on a small stoop until 8 p.m., regardless of the weather. (Though it seldom snows in Northwest Florida, we often get a hard freeze during the winter and the allegations were made in February, not July.) After 8 p.m. the boy was allowed in the house where he was to lie down in the hall on a bathrobe–no bed, blanket or pillow. Food was often withheld from him as punishment; he was caged for hours in a wire dog carrier "as needed." His two younger sisters could come into the house earlier, but they were locked in a room with no toys, no TV, and no books. Their food was often withheld, too. The nine-year-old attended a public school to which a police officer was assigned through a program known as DARE. With his classmates, the boy sat through the officer's presentation that explained and discussed child abuse. Bolstered by this new information, the child approached his teacher, explained he needed to protect his sisters, and then told how he and his sisters were treated at home. An investigation followed, and the three children were removed and placed in a foster home. During the investigation, the father and his girlfriend admitted to locking, caging, and withholding food to "discipline" the children. Then their arrest warrants ended up on my desk as Duty Judge. As I read the warrants, I thought of the four-year-old girl in Santa Rosa County 10 or 12 years before who was caged and deprived of food. The parents were just about to exorcize the Devil from her, but she died first. There was no DARE officer to help that little girl, no one who listened to her cries, no one who cared to notice things were bad wrong.

❖ ❖ ❖

I heard what the Ranger said about the bears, but that stubborn part of me brushes him off because I am alone, so to hike means I hike alone. Otherwise, I have to leave this beautiful place without experiencing the tranquil beauty that waits away from the crowds. I scope out the brochures at the Visitor's Center for some short hikes closer to the road, which I assume, would be less grizzly-friendly, yet as I leave the Center there's a faint echo of a growl taunting my enthusiasm to hike.

My first hike up to Sunrift Gorge is perfect. There are several other hikers around for safety, yet I can enjoy the quiet beauty alone. Watching the sheer power of the water gushing past the rocks, I feel peacefully insignificant.

Then I drive to another trailhead that leads along St. Mary's Lake to waterfalls of touted beauty. There's only one car in the large parking lot. As I cross the pavement, I pass the first sign warning of grizzlies in the area, but I think, "That doesn't mean anything. They have those signs everywhere." A hundred feet down the trail from the parking lot, a second sign says the same thing. The signs don't really bother me, but I'm acutely aware that I don't see anyone, anywhere around. I climb a tall pile of rocks jutting out into the lake; I scan the area, assuring myself I would be able to see a bear if it approached my promontory. With a sudden flashback to Davy Crockett, I note that the wind was blowing from the lake to the mainland, so the bear would smell me from the mainland and steer away. But my feigned complacency is jolted by two older women who suddenly appear out of the rocks, only a few feet from where I'm standing. So much for my seeing a bear before it walked up on me. When my heart stops racing and I figure I can speak without sounding freaked, I ask for directions to the waterfall. We speak briefly, they leave to return to their car (the only other vehicle in the parking lot), and I start down the trail that followed the shoreline of the lake. I walk and walk; I see no one and hear no one. As my hands began to sweat and my heart pounds, I start to sing and talk to myself, loudly. (Rule Number Two: "Make noise and don't startle the bear!" It follows Rule Number One: "Don't hike alone.")

But the waterfalls were supposed to be beautiful. I round a corner and enter a natural tunnel made by the trees bending low over a path, a path covered in straw. Very quiet straw. I sing louder and keep going. I'm going to make it to those waterfalls!

I walk out of the tree tunnel; back on the rocky trail, I see an orange sign, "DANGER! GRIZZLIES TRAVERSE THIS PATH AT ST. MARY'S LAKE!" Orange. The other signs were on a white background.

I walk on, kicking stones, singing, and talking to myself about that orange sign. Farther down the trail and closer to the edge of my barely controlled panic, I hear rocks skidding down the embankment above my head. Suddenly I can't think of any more songs to sing, and I decide the waterfalls aren't that big a deal. I turn around and head toward my truck. I leave without seeing the waterfalls. I turn back because I'm alone, lonely, and afraid of the grizzlies. I walk with a metallic taste in my mouth and a visceral fear in my heart. As I return to the parking lot, the two women I met earlier are pulling out.

The driver stops the car beside me and asks, "Did you see the falls?"

I confess, "No. The grizzly bears won. I turned back because I got scared."

The passenger replies, "That's a shame. They're beautiful falls."

I drive two hours back to the campground, feeling at odds with the world and myself, for how could I be surrounded by such grandeur AND feel afraid? Back in my RV, I'm still haunted by the imagined face of a snarling grizzly, a face that morphs into primordial fears, and I want to huddle in the corner in the fetal position. Of course, the hike in Glacier isn't the first time I've felt the hot breath of a violent threat. I confront violence with resolve, strength, and defiance when I'm protecting someone else, especially a child. But when the threat is directed only at me, and I am alone–with no one watching or caring–then I'm not nearly so brave. Then, my blood runs cold, my resolve folds, and the fetal position seems the most reasonable. As I sit safely in my rocker with a cup of hot tea, I placate my fears with a resolve to return to Glacier when the grizzlies are not so active; maybe I'll go on a guided hike, or with a friend. But for now, there's a sense of foreboding on my coat tail, and I'm ready to leave Hungry Horse.

I decide to drive hard, to get out of grizzly country, to get to Washington. I have no schedule; no one even knows I've decided to go to Washington. But I feel a strong pull from the ocean. Choices! I very much wanted to spend time in Idaho because I was fascinated by the stories of a friend from Coeur d' Alene, but I decide to put Idaho on the list with Wyoming: "Must do on the next lap."

Bruin and I pull out of Hungry Horse, Montana, on my son's 29th birthday. As soon as I get into cell phone range, I'll call. As I ride through remote mountains, I remember another phone call I scheduled; the call didn't go as I planned.

✦ ✦ ✦

Phone call to the Supreme Court–Hello! Is anyone listening?
If you wake up in the middle of the night with an unfathomable

154

urge to leave everything you've known and worked for, there's a prayer and a book I do not recommend, for neither will lull you back to the sleep of complacency. The prayer is the one I've used much of my adult life; "Creator, please don't be subtle." The book is Callings by Gregg Levoy. It was this prayer and book that catapulted me from security and prestige onto a very long road. Just as Levoy predicted, acting on my dream of quiet time, writing, nature and travel was playing havoc in my well-upholstered world.

The summer of 1999, I took my last vacation while on the Bench—a two week trip that was to include skydiving with friends in Virginia and then a meeting in Tallahassee with one of the Justices of the Florida Supreme Court. Things did not go as planned. A tree attacked the RV, punching a large hole at the roofline; I covered the hole with duct tape and drove on. The RV's brake and electrical cord slinked from the bed of the truck and bounced down the Interstate until it was a shadow of its former self and my running lights were toast; I drove on, daylight only, and had it repaired. I threw my back out so I couldn't skydive; I had a massage and spent two days on the floor of the drop zone while friends jumped. And my trip south to Tallahassee didn't go exactly as I had pictured it, either.

The Justice, whom I will call John Smith, was a kind, gray-haired fellow whose quiet wisdom reminded me of my father. Justice Smith had known my dad well and had unwittingly become my father figure. Since Dad was dead, I wanted to go to John. I wanted to rationally explain face-to-face what could not really be rationalized—this inexplicable need to leave all I'd worked for, all I'd known. I decided it couldn't hurt to look good for my swan song, so I bought the classic business outfit: a black silk Ann Taylor suit.

I wanted John to listen deeply, and I wanted him to care that I was leaving. I even fantasized his response, "Laura, you're a good judge, and we need judges like you. Go if you must, but is there anything we can do to keep others like you in the future?"

While in Virginia, I called the Justice's office for an appointment. His assistant was cooperative and friendly, but John was out of the office for the next two days. I had to be back for my docket in a week, so I left Virginia and began driving south toward Tallahassee, saving a couple of vacation days to accommodate this important meeting.

After several more calls from the road in which I offered to meet him wherever, whenever ("We can just meet for a quick cup of coffee, if he'd like."), his assistant relayed his response:

"His schedule is full, but he can talk to you on the phone tomorrow morning." I swallowed what felt like a brush off and scheduled the phone call. I pulled in for the night at an RV park on Interstate 75, a couple of hours north of Tallahassee and considerably east of Pensacola. There was a gaggle of RV's parked under the shade of a pecan orchard; the park was quiet and family-oriented. But I felt disoriented, for suddenly I had a week before my docket resumed and only a phone call to complete the beginning of the end of my life as a judge.

There was no cell phone service in the park, so the next morning I called the Justice from a pay phone that hung on the edge of the bathhouse. As I dialed the number, I felt exposed to the strangers walking by, going to and from the pool. But no one saw the panic in my eyes or the knots in my stomach. No one noticed as I steeled myself to announce the decision to leave the world that had defined me.

I had written out and practiced my speech; it was important that I not let my voice crack, for a crack might open the floodgates and leave me in a wet wad—embarrassed and most unprofessional. I knew I had to leave to live, but I was also deeply invested in the legal system, an institution that was my life and world, one worthy of deep commitment though fraught with its own foibles. And, oh, yes, I was very comfortable with the prestige, power, and money that came with the robe.

As the phone rang in the Supreme Court building, I stood barefoot on the grass, facing the swimming pool where half a dozen kids launched themselves as cannon balls and the tallest spray triggered the loudest approval. As I spoke though the black receiver and into the ear of the Justice words that would end a well-maintained life of professionalism, a boy maybe 10 years old climbed out of the pool and ran up to the bathhouse. Skinny and awkward, he danced a *silly movement, slinging water as he laughed and called back to his buddies in the pool. He paused mid-stride when he realized he'd sprayed me. "I'm sorry!" he said.*

I smiled and waved him on as I listened to the Justice respond, "Oh, OK. If that's what you want to do, Laura. You know you need to send your resignation to the Governor. You may want to wait until the first of the year before submitting it, though, in case you change your mind or something."

John didn't understand and didn't know what to say; I didn't think my dad would either. The kid darted by and threw up a rooster-tail of water as he vaulted back into the pool. I hung up the phone, shaking. It was done. And I didn't need that expensive outfit after all.

There was no reason to return to Pensacola a week early, so before noon, Bruin and I were heading north on I-75, returning to the Smoky Mountains.

❖ ❖ ❖

The mountains of Montana are taller and more rugged than the mist-covered Smokies. It's good to be here. Finally I'm in cell phone range and reach Clay. He's busy with his own life in Florida; his job and marriage are going well. Joan enjoys her job, and there are no complications with the pregnancy. Clay often doesn't know what state I'm in, and that's become a joke between us. He seems comfortable not knowing where his mom is for days at a time, yet so much freedom can feel lonely.

I head west on Highway 2 through Kalispell, Montana, and pass the dirt road that winds to the drop zone at Lost Prairie. I briefly consider stopping by for a jump, but there's that long bumpy ride in and out, all that dust, and today I'm not up to being alone in a crowd of people. I'm still feeling like I flunked Glacier National Park, and I just don't have the energy to meet and skydive with yet more new friends. Sometimes, I do alone better, alone.

On a whim I turn into the National Forestry Park at the edge of McGregor Lake. There's only one car in the parking lot, and I easily maneuver and park the truck and trailer. Bruin and I go into the 5th wheel, I change into my bathing suit, and we walk down to the small dock on the lake. There's a family at the edge of the lake, with a blanket, picnic, two dogs, and a small bonfire. We speak briefly. With Bruin on his leash and shoes on my feet, I wade knee-deep into the icy water; Bruin loves it. The bottom of the lake is covered with irregular shaped rocks, not smooth like those in a mountain stream, and the rocks shift on the sand as I walk. After Bruin swims, I somewhat dry him off and put him in the truck. Then I walk back to the dock, with a towel around my neck. The family chuckles, and although none of them are swimming, they each assure me it would be easier if I jump off the end of the pier rather than trying to ease into the glacial water. I smile remembering a pier that stands above warm waters in Florida, a pier from which I'd jumped, alone or first, many times.

❖ ❖ ❖

Just do it
Growing up we swam, crabbed, fished, and boated from the wooden pier in front of the house. (I slept on the pier a few times, just because.) A visitor used heavy fishing gear with bloody bait, caught a shark from our pier, and hooked all of our childhood fears. Shark! A fear never mentioned around the grownups but never forgotten. Of course, we kept on swimming, though after that no one wanted to jump off the pier first. But there were times I wanted to swim, and no one else was around. Or I had to go first because the others were younger or more afraid. Or because I had to, to prove to myself I could. Later I jumped out of a plane for the same reason—because it scared me so bad I had to, to prove to me that I could do it.

❖ ❖ ❖

I jump into McGregor Lake and pop up laughing, "I bet there're no sharks in here." I swim out a good distance before turning around. Back at the shore, I dry off, return to my RV, change into clothes, fix a peanut butter and jelly sandwich with a glass of milk for the road, get in the truck with Bruin and drive west toward Washington. An hour's delay and worth the smile.

Back on the road, I remember another time I had to do something, something uniquely difficult.

❋ ❋ ❋

My dad's charge

The ceremony of swearing a new judge into the Bench is one of pomp and circumstance. All of the Judges in the Circuit attend the Investiture in their robes, and the ceremony includes several rituals such as the oath, the charge, and the robing. The charge is a brief speech designed to welcome and challenge the new judge. Dad was held in high esteem and had been asked to give his charge to many new judges over the years. His speech included such wisdom as "if a judge is to only have one positive attribute, it should be that he possess a kind and understanding heart. The Bench is no place for a cruel, boisterous, callous person, regardless of what other qualities or abilities that he may possess," and "If you believe in a Supreme Being, as I do, you should pray for guidance. Judges need all the help they can get."

I've known Mike Allen for a long time, and like many attorneys, he had a deep respect for my dad. When Mike was elected County Judge of Santa Rosa County, he asked and Dad agreed to give him the Charge. But Dad died two weeks before Mike's Investiture, so he couldn't keep that commitment. To my bewilderment, Mike asked if I would read Dad's Charge. My grief was so raw, I thought it would be impossible to speak Dad's words, sitting in his chair, in his courtroom in Milton, but soon I understood that it would be impossible to refuse. The day of Mike's Investiture came, and a sea of black robes flowed into the courtroom in Milton to acknowledge a new comrade.

I wore Dad's robe; the sleeves were too long and the collar a bit frayed. I held his speech in my sweaty hands and prayed for the emotional distance to do him justice. At the end of the last page I had added to Dad's language a brief explanation of the source of my material. I figured if my voice was strong I'd read my closing; if I was shaky, I'd end it as Dad always had. As I began to read those rehearsed phrases, I carefully avoided making eye contact with Dad's many friends in the crowded courtroom who would immediately realize what I was doing and why. At the end of Dad's words, I took a deep breath and read my tribute to the man whom I adored and mourned. Then sitting heavy in my dad's chair, I tucked my shaking hands deep within his black robe and went on emotional autopilot. By the time the Investiture ended, I had a blinding migraine and a sense of accomplishment.

❖ ❖ ❖

The drive across the northern panhandle of Idaho is too short. The country doesn't feel as harsh or dry as Montana.

"I came to explore the wreck. I came to see the damage that was done and the treasures that prevail."
Adrienne Rich

CHAPTER 10.
ORCAS ISLAND, WASHINGTON:
Listening, believing, and surviving

I drive west until we get to Whidbey Island, a place without grizzlies. Leaving the RV at the campground, Bruin and I take the truck to catch a ferry to Orcas Island, one of the San Juan Islands off the coast of Washington. In route, I stop at a charity thrift shop and drop off items that violate my Rule of Fours. It's easy to accumulate stuff, and I now have six coffee cups and five plastic glasses. I leave the extras, together with a couple of T-shirts, and head to the ferry landing. I've read of Orcas Island for years, and now I'll see it for myself. The deck hands direct traffic and park us below, squeezing cars and trucks together like sardines in a can. Bruin has to stay in the truck, but I go up to look around. This should have been a glorious, happy trip–a ferry ride to an island that draws mystics and artists to its natural beauty and the simple life required by its isolation. Yet standing on the wet metal deck, I fight off tears as I wrestle with a deep sadness, an aching loneliness. I fuss at myself, "Buck up, Laura! Tears under the Christmas tree? This is what you asked for, remember?" After a cup of latte, I stand outside on an upper deck, watching the smooth waters slide by, wrapping like gray silk around small islands and an occasional boat. I'm standing near a family: Mom, Dad, older brother (maybe 12), and younger sister (maybe 7). The brother is wearing the family binoculars around his neck.

The brother looks through the binoculars and interrupts the sounds of the engine, "See the seal!"

The sister strains to see and answers, "No. Where?"

He points again, without lowering the binoculars, "Over there."

"I can't see it. Let me use the binoculars."

Without moving he responds curtly, "Well, it's over there, and it's a big one!"

The sister doesn't answer. Sometime later she begins squealing and hopping around, "I see a whale! I see a whale! Give me the binoculars! I see a whale!"

He holds the binoculars with a straight arm, just out of her reach, and in a haughty, disbelieving tone says, "Where!"

"Over there! Over there! Give me the binoculars. Over there!!"

The dad walks away, and the mother stands quietly staring at the opposite horizon. The sister asks repeatedly and then begs, but the brother keeps the binoculars just out of her reach.

As minutes pass and the boat pulls further and further away, the sister begins to sob, "I did see one, Mama, I really did." Mom doesn't answer. "Mama, I did see one. Don't you believe me, Mama?"

I wince and walk to her to say, "A whale! That's really cool. Show me where."

She points but says nothing. I'm not her mama—I'm not her family—I don't count.

Then the mother turns to the son, "Let her have a turn with the binoculars." Looking down at the daughter, she barks, "But don't you drop 'em!"

The small child stands on the metal deck with binoculars heavy around her neck. All whales, real and imagined, have left the area, and her joy has drowned in tears. I look down into the gray waters, into the eyes of other little girls ignored, disbelieved, and discounted.

✤ ✤ ✤

"Courage is what it takes to stand up and speak; courage is also what it takes to sit down and listen."
Winston Churchill

Survivors
We sat at the round oak table in my hearing room on the 6th floor of the courthouse, with an east wall of windows overlooking rooftops, live oaks, and Pensacola Bay. I was to review why these three children were still in foster care, two years after they were last removed from their mother. Stephen, age 17, and Mary, 16, sat on either side of their mother, the three of them holding hands. Michele, the youngest, age 9, was at school.
The facts were fairly straightforward. From the age of 11, Mary had been sexually abused by her mother's boyfriend. Mary told her mother what was happening, but her mom didn't believe her and did nothing. The boyfriend continued to rape Mary. The sexual abuse only came to light when Mary went to school with visible bruises from a "spanking" from the mother's boyfriend. From a legal standpoint, this was not a weak case for there was physical evidence of violence and sexual activity consistent with Mary's testimony and the onset of Mary's serious emotional problems. The Juvenile Court became involved, and I removed all three kids from the mother. "Failure to protect" is how the Law labels the mother's role. Within the week, Mom came back to court and agreed with the court order that custody be returned to her, that the boyfriend have absolutely no contact with any of the children, and that she was to contact law enforcement if he showed up. And so I sent the kids back home to the mother. With Mom's apparent change of heart and an active arrest warrant for the boyfriend on a charge of rape, I was hopeful that the kids could stay at home. But soon the youngest let it slip that they had recently spent time with the boyfriend. When the caseworker asked, Mom reluctantly admitted that the boyfriend had been by but spoke with assurance, "I'm not going to let anything happen to my kids. I love 'em!"

Somewhat assured, the Department left the kids with the mother but scheduled a hearing for the next day. Overnight, the mother disappeared, taking the three children with her. After a couple of years with the boyfriend, she came back to Pensacola. I took the kids away from her again and found placements for them. That was two years ago. Back in the System, Mary changed her story about the sexual abuse. Finally the State Attorney decided to not prosecute the rape charge. Mary's multiple stories and her psychiatric history didn't make for a good witness. "Plus," the prosecutor added, "she's sexually active now," as though that would somehow disprove the earlier rapes. After the State Attorney closed its criminal case, the boyfriend magically reappeared, and he and the mother were married.

I had been involved as the Judge of this sick soap opera for almost five years. From time to time I had to move the kids. The two girls went from foster care to their grandparents; Mary didn't get along there so she returned to a state foster home, but is now living with her aunt. The grandparents didn't have a separate room for Stephen (a requirement of the Florida agency overseeing abused children), so he stayed in a foster home, visiting often with his sisters and grandparents. Michele, the youngest, had consistently remained with the grandparents and was doing very well. I wondered, "The boyfriend was sexually attracted to Mary as an eleven-year-old, but Michele was only seven when we moved her out the last time. Was Michele still too young to catch his eye? Did we get something right?"

Basically nothing had changed in the six months since our last hearing. The mother continued to live with the Perpetrator, who was now her husband, and she continued to deny there had been any abuse. Mom refused to go to counseling with Mary or by herself. The mother would disappear for weeks or months and have no contact with her kids, then reappear to cling to her "babies" and blame the Court for all her problems. And now she was again sitting in my Chambers, glaring at me, her eyes filled with hatred and resolve.

Stephen, 17, had always tried to be The Man of the House and take care of his younger sisters, though he had taken time out to get arrested for burglary and be sent off to a juvenile facility. He was *"home" again, back with the same foster parents. He sat in my hearing room, holding his mom's hand, with tears running down his face as he explained why he had to go back to live with his mother and step-dad.*

When the explanations didn't change my mind, he began to beg with the voice of a young child, "Please! Please let me go back to mama!" Then he glared at me through tears and said, "The worst mom in the world is better than the system!"

Keeping my inscrutable mask intact, I thought, "Some days I'd agree with you, son." Stephen added, "Don't get me wrong. My foster mom's a good person but I can't hold her hand like this," and he raised his mother's hand up in the air with his. "I know my mom made mistakes, but I love her! I just want my family together again!"

I quietly wondered, "Who can argue with that dream?" I looked at the mother's distant eyes and swallowed hard, but my anger remained stuck in my throat. Mom's plan remained fixed—blame the system, the court, anybody except herself and her lover, the man who repeatedly raped her daughter. The mother would do nothing else.

I said, "Stephen, I wish I had that much power. Son, when I became a judge, they gave me a black robe, but they didn't give me a magic wand. I wish I had one, and if I did, I would put your family back together. Your mom can do that, but she won't. No, I don't understand why, but she won't."

For the last couple of months, Mary had been with an aunt she adored. I turned to the aunt and asked how Mary was doing. While shaking her head, "No," she said quietly "Mary is doing very well in school and causes no problems at home. But she so desperately wants to be with her mother that she is making herself physically ill." I'd read the reports; Mary had begun self-mutilation, with thin scars showing now on the insides of both arms between the wrist and elbow. She had also been hospitalized twice in the last year for attempted suicide. As the aunt talked, the mother released her grip on Stephen and moved her chair even closer to Mary's. With the exaggerated affections of a sentimental drunk, she smoothed hair from Mary's face, rubbed her arm, and

165

then held Mary's hand with both of hers.

I took a deep breath and said, "Mary, tell me why you can't live with your mom." (I work on the theory that it's important that the older kids know the Plain Truth, even when it's brutal. It's just a theory, though. Sometimes there's not much I can do in Juvenile Court, except call something by its true name. Maybe, sometimes that's enough.)

Mary shook her head and whispered in a brittle voice, "I don't know."

I had to take two deep breaths to steel myself, and then I said," OK, I'll tell you." (The kids knew all of this; I had been very candid with them over the years. It's just that they kept losing reality in their agony to belong, a hunger so pervasive in the face of cold facts that it must be an instinct, an animal urge tied to the survival of the species.)

"Mary, your stepfather sexually abused you." Her eyes filled with tears, and she looked away. "But your mom still acts like nothing happen. She still chooses to be with him instead of you. She has always refused to go to counseling with you—even before she married him. I've told her over and over that she has to give counseling a try if she wants you guys to come home, but she won't go. She won't listen." Mary looked back at me, her face leaking silent tears. "And you know you can't count on anything she says. She tells you she'll see you on Saturday, but then she disappears into thin air. And it doesn't matter if it's Christmas or your birthday, she's just gone. You don't know where she is for weeks or months. And then, pop, here she comes again, acting like nothing happened. Mary, it's sort of like this - your house is on fire. There are flames, smoke, and heat. The roof has begun to fall in. But your mom says, no, the house is just fine, there is no fire. And I can't let you go back into that burning house just because your mom says everything is fine. It's not fine; it's dangerous. You know what happened to you, and you know it could happen to your sister. I can't pretend there is no fire. Your mom talks a lot, but she doesn't do anything about that fire, about the danger of her husband hurting you again, or your little sister. I don't know why

she won't keep you safe. If I could make her, I would." As I spoke, the mother's eyes watered a little but I knew better than to hope I was getting through. I'd nailed her to the cross before, and nothing had changed. No, my sermonet was for Mary. I was throwing verbal hand grenades at the mother with the hope that Mary could more clearly see her mom and her mom's choices; I prayed that Mary could give up on her mom and decide to live for herself.

But all Mary could see was that she wasn't with her mother. Her mama didn't believe her, so Mary changed her story. Her mama still would not come to get her, so she changed the story again. All she wanted was her mama. Even if it meant living with her rapist. She could accept anything - anything - except living without her mama, except living without that hope of belonging.

Looking at Mary, I thought of a young gazelle, all alone, seriously injured, moving slowly at the edge of the herd as it crossed the plains. "I'm afraid this little one is not going to make it. And I don't think there's anything I can do about it," I worried.

As the mother petted and hugged Mary, I ended the hearing, "The children will remain in their present placements, subject to protective services supervision." Then I left, quickly and quietly. I had to be careful to contain the mother lion pacing around inside of me, this fiery instinct that wanted to tear that woman's face off, that wanted to roar that the mother of no species—much less this that pretends to be the "most developed"—no mother would allow her child to be repeatedly raped and then choose to sleep in the arms of the rapist rather than hold her own babies.

And yet I've seen other kids who are survivors. Other kids you might expect to perish as injured loners on the edge of the pack. But they don't. Somewhere along the way, someone listened, someone believed. Someone had the courage to protect the child.

Star was reluctant and shy, but then she was only five years old. She was also the State's key witness in the capital sexual battery case. She was four when the State said her dad raped her, ripping her vagina, cervix, and uterus. The State's case depended on her testimony. The physical evidence alone was not enough to convict; the Defendant would argue that Star had fallen onto the broken post of a seat-less bike. Her father was charged with capital sexual battery—if convicted, the sentence would be life in prison without parole.

After jury selection I sent the jurors to lunch and began the inquiry to determine if Star was legally competent to testify. She came into a courtroom that was empty except for me, my deputy, the attorneys, the Guardian ad Litem, her dad, and the court reporter.

She was small for a five-year-old. She was wearing a red jumper with a white T-shirt and black patent leather Sunday School shoes with white lace on her socks. Her hair was plaited in cornrows with a white barrette dangling from the end of each braid. The prosecutor picked her up and sat her in the witness chair. She swiveled the chair around, then reached over and touched the microphone. I began with the easy questions. "What's your name? What's your teacher's name? Do you have any brothers or sisters?"

She responded each time but in a faint whisper.

The prosecutor said, "Star, we talked about the difference between your inside voice and your outside voice."

She nodded.

"OK, we're inside now, but this is a big room. So use your outside voice, OK?" She mutely nodded.

I began again, and when I asked, "What's your favorite color?" she picked her head up and spoke clearly, "Red!" I laughed and opened my robe to show her my red dress. She smiled at me. After more questions, I was able to find her competent to testify—able to observe and recall past events, able to distinguish between a truth and a lie, and able to understand the need to tell the truth.

We took a short lunch break and then began again with the jury.

While Star waited in another room, the grown-ups testified - her mother, her grandmother, law enforcement, and the doctor.

Star's mother testified she had left Star with her dad early that morning and had come home to find Star "bleeding a lot" from between her legs and crying. The mother called the grandmother who lived next door; this is the Defendant's mother. The grandmother *came over and, rather than calling 9-1-1, she ran down the street to a police officer she had seen minutes earlier. The officer came to the house and called an ambulance.*

The arresting officer testified that the Defendant gave several stories of what happened that early morning while he babysat. One was "I musta blacked out cause as I come to, I was pulling myself off of Star. She was screaming and shaking her head, 'No!'"

As the officer testified, I sat deep within the stoic folds of my black robe. I'd been on the Bench for eight years and heard many things, but in that moment I didn't feel very judicious. Part of me just wanted to scream and shake my head, "No!" I made no sound, my face was its practiced blank, and I absent-mindedly twirled my silver thumb ring. But my mind was racing. "How, why would a father, or any man, impale a four-year-old on his penis? What anger, what ego engorged his penis? And so early in the morning! Why with such force? If this, what else? I can't believe that in one giant step the Defendant went from Father-of-the-Year to a pedophiliac rapist—other less traumatic abuse would surely come first. And if at the age of 25, he includes in his repertoire the ability to rip his own four-year-old daughter on his rigid penis, I don't want to know or think about what else he is capable of doing. But it's time for me to sit quietly and insure the Defense and State get a fair trial. If the verdict is guilty, there will be something for me to say and do, but the call of 'Guilty' or 'Not Guilty,' that's not my job."

The doctor testified that as he began the initial exam of Star, he was concerned that the injuries were life threatening, so she was immediately taken to surgery. He explained the multiple stitches required to close the tear that extended from Star's vagina to her anus. He showed photos of the lacerations in the vagina under her cervix that were closed by sutures.

And then it was Star's turn. The courtroom was quiet as she walked in. The jury box to her left—empty before—was now filled with twelve jurors and two alternates. They were all women. The Deputy assigned as Court Security picked Star up and put her in *the witness chair. This time she didn't make it swivel, and she didn't touch the mike.*

The prosecutor began, "Can you tell the jury your name?"

She nodded, yes.

"What is your name?"

A tiny voice whispered, "Star."

The Security Officer pulled her chair closer and pulled the mike down lower, thumbing it to be sure it was working. Several more questions were met with that same tiny whisper.

The prosecutor said "Remember to use your outside voice, Star." Then he pointed to the jury and asked, "You want the jury to hear what you have to say, don't you?"

Star looked at the prosecutor, turned her head to the left, and looked at the jury. Then she looked back at the prosecutor and shook her head, "No."

He smiled and kept going. Finally he got to the Big Question. "Did something happen to you the day you went to the hospital?"

The room held its breath. The barrette in the center of Star's forehead swung over one eye and then the other, providing a distraction but no refuge. My refuge is my robe, the state-issued turtle shell under which I pull my soul; the robe is what lets me look like a judge, rather than a mere sentient human.

Into the palpable silence, Star nodded, "Yes."

The prosecutor said, "Let the record reflect that the witness nodded, yes" and I responded, "The record shall so reflect."

"Star, tell the jury what happened."

The tiny voice said, "My daddy hurt me. He stuck his thing in me."

"Would you stand down, Star, and show the jury where you were hurt."

She hopped down before Security could get to her, and there she stood beside the grown-up chair taller than her head.

"Star, point and show the jury where you were hurt."

She glanced at the jury, the barrette swayed, and then she pointed between her legs and whispered, "Down there."

"Let the record reflect that the witness pointed between her legs."

I responded, "The record shall so reflect."

"Between your legs?"

She nodded, yes.

"Let the record reflect that the witness nodded, yes."

I responded, "The record shall so reflect."

Security lifted Star back into her chair, and the Defense began its cross-examination.

"Does your brother have a bike? Did you ride it? Did you have permission? Was the seat missing? Did you fall? What day was that?"

Star answered in her tiny voice or nodded. She began to confuse some time-lines and other facts, giving the defense some things to work with.

After the State rested its case, the Defendant testified that he wasn't sure, but Star must have fallen onto the jagged post of her brother's bike three days earlier. He agreed that he had told the arresting officer several other stories of what happened that early morning while he babysat, and he repeated the story of blacking out and pulling himself off Star, how she had screamed and shook her head, no. He rambled on and on, but forgot to express any concern for his daughter. And on cross-examination, he had to admit to six prior criminal convictions.

Witnesses are not allowed in the courtroom except while testifying so the witness will not be tempted to change a story to match that of others. But once all the evidence is in, witnesses can come back into the courtroom and listen to closing arguments. Witnesses tend to sit where their loyalties lie—like guests at a wedding, the Bride's family on one side of the church and the Groom's on the other. I watched Star's mother (the Defendant's wife) and her grandmother (the Defendant's mother) come in and sit to my left, behind the prosecutor.

After dark on the third day of trial, the all-woman jury deliberated and returned a verdict of Guilty as Charged, Capital Sexual Battery. Under Florida law, there was only one sentence for this verdict—life in prison without parole. Everyone was tired, and the attorneys asked that I schedule the sentencing for another day. Tired or not, I felt that the family and jurors needed closure. So I called the Defendant to the stand, ordered that he serve the rest of his life in prison without parole, and advised him of his right to appeal. I also scheduled his sentencing on the Violation of Probation (VOP), noting that he was on probation for six robberies, a fact the jury could not know before the verdict. It wasn't necessary to say these things in front of the jury; the Defendant would have come up as a matter of routine on the next VOP docket. But my thought was, if a juror woke up some night second-guessing the verdict or my sentence of life without parole, that bit of information about six prior robberies might reduce the angst. Next I thanked the jury for their service and, without adjourning Court, excused them so that Security could escort them out of the now-empty building to their cars. Then I adjourned Court, took off my robe, and left the courthouse through the secured halls and elevator reserved for judges. As the large metal door clanked open above the exit to the judges' parking, I felt shell-shocked, unable to truly comprehend. I drove the dark streets through a light rain and heavy thoughts, "The only part of this week that makes sense is Star screaming and shaking her head, No!"

I thought of other child victims I'd seen and wondered—is more harm done when more blood is drawn? My rage is certainly deeper, wilder, and harder to restrain. But was Star injured more— spiritually, emotionally, or mentally—because so much blood was drawn? What about the child victim of oral sexual battery? Or vaginal penetration by an adult finger? Is the child harmed less—is the Universe harmed less—because no blood was drawn or no scream was heard? Or is it simply easier to look away from the bloodless, silent child, easier to pretend nothing important happened? Easier for the grownups to believe that the child won't remember the horror?

Star didn't quietly accept her father's sadism; she screamed at him and shook her head, "No!" Then as a Lilliputian in the giant world of justice, she communicated to the jury with soft-spoken courage, "My daddy hurt me, down there. He stuck his thing in me." At age five, Star spoke out with courage that many adult sexual battery victims lack. A courage that says she may survive this—a courage that says there are strong women in her life who believe in her and support her.

And what about the child victim no one believes—the child no one supports—the one to whom no refuge is offered? The child whose screams are heard but not acknowledged? The child from whom little or no blood is drawn? The child who quickly learns to scream without making a sound?

Not listening carefully, not believing, not supporting a child—that may be the greatest wrong of all.

❖ ❖ ❖

I watch the water slide by. What a difference it makes. Being heard and believed.

The ferry pulls up to the docks at Orcas Island, and following the pack of wedged vehicles, I drive down the ramp. A friend had come here on a spiritual retreat and spoke of whales, empty beaches, and quiet places. But now that I'm actually here, I'm bewildered rather than enthralled. I feel separate from everything and everyone.

The brochures describe Orcas Island as the largest (57 square miles) and hilliest of the San Juan Islands. Within the Moran State Park is Mt. Constitution; at 2,409 feet it's the highest point in the islands, so that's where I head, away from the rows of cutesy shops and bed and breakfasts. I stop at the stone observation tower at summit for a view of Mt. Baker, still wearing a snowcap in July, and Canada, only a short distance away. The view is spectacular and the air clean, but I feel disoriented, out of sync, and very confused.

At the stone tower there's a group of young kids eight to ten years old, perhaps on a field trip. I smile as I watch them act-out their awkward age. For a photo op, they pile up together like a litter of puppies, then scatter like squawking hens to play an exaggerated game of tag. They're comfortable with one another and very silly. They remind me of large gatherings of my first cousins, and I hope there is no Bluebeard[15] on their bus.

My maternal grandfather had at least 20 grandchildren, and we all "knew" about him. I was in kindergarten when my cousin made me promise not to tell, then whispered horrid details of how Granddaddy had hurt her in a way I didn't understand but knew instinctually was very wrong. When I was older, I learned the words for what she described–sexual abuse, digital penetration, and rape, but as a young child all I learned was fear. The cousin added, in a confused whisper, that Grandmother was right there, watching with a smirk but not saying a word. The grandchildren all understood that he was Bluebeard and that we were not to tell grownups. He was the one about whom we would sometimes whisper, though none of us ever admitted to being afraid. The whispered stories of pain and fear always included the upstairs in our grandparents' house in Jay, a farming community to the north. It was years after my grandparents died before I would drive through Jay, and I still avoid the road that goes by their old house. As a child I knew that Granddaddy would hurt me if I ever let him catch me with no one around but Grandmother. Of course, I had to be around him at routine family gatherings, and I had to be respectful, no matter what. From him, I learned to be afraid in what looked like safe surroundings. From him, I learned that an unnamed danger lurks around the next corner.

Granddaddy lost his left arm and leg just below the elbow and knee when he fell from a mule in front of a disk plow at the farm. Mom was 16 then. But he was evil long before that. Bluebeard was head of the house that my mother grew up in, and their rules were the same as ours–always obey grownups and treat them with respect; never scream; never say "no."

[15]Bluebeard – a fairy tale of a man with a blue beard who thrived on the fear he sparked in women. Bluebeard was an intelligent and violent man who could maintain, for convenience, a facade of respectability. In the basement he had a locked room, full of the bodies of women he had murdered.

My childhood was colored by a pedophile for a grandfather–one who knew he was safely surrounded by grownups who didn't know what to do, so they'd do nothing. My cousins and I were taught as our parents were. We grew up in a world in which it was never OK to scream, or say "No!" to an elder. In our world, it was also not OK to tell. I don't think that the other grownups knew he was sexually abusing children, but surely someone wondered, and maybe they worried. The grownups were confused and unsure; they did not ask nor did they listen. And little girls continued to be cast into a carefully maintained labyrinth of fear, pain, and crime.

I was 12 when my grandparents moved to a cottage next door, bringing with them a black cloud of peril. And for the next 10 years, the dirty old man and his accomplice, our grandmother, lived next door. Only as adults with our grandparents safely dead and buried did my cousins and I share the elaborate plans we devised to stay away from him at family gatherings and to hide if he ever came to our house when our parents were not there. As an adult, I laughed in comic relief as I explained that I knew I'd hear him crossing our wooden floors with his wood leg and walking stick so he couldn't really sneak up on me at my house. I confessed that I practiced hiding under the sink in the upstairs bathroom, "just in case" he came over. And as an adult, I remember that familiar, suppressed panic that he might pick a day when no one else was at home and come thudding up the stairs, looking for me. A visceral fear that can still catapult me backwards when I feel vulnerable.

Family gatherings always included an obligatory visit with my grandparents. After they moved to the cottage next door, Granddaddy Jack would sit reading in his green recliner with his shepherd's hook cane on the floor. Like a spider in his web, he'd quickly attack and retrieve any girl child who strayed within range of his cane. We all knew not to cry out or object once he caught us. We knew no one would listen, that no one would make him stop. We knew the grownups would say he was just playing. He would pull me in fast with his good arm, hold me down with his chin (He always needed a shave. To this day, I recoil at the sight of a gray prickly beard), drop the cane, jerk me hard between his legs and begin to roughly fondle my chest and occasionally between my legs with his left stub wrapped in a wool sock. He pretended he was tickling. This occurred over and over–to me and any other girl child who drifted too close. He'd laugh and rub his beard into the tender neck, while exploring budding puberty with his woolen stub. Often there were other relatives in the room; they either laughed as though we were playing or they ignored us. Grandmother was always there, watching. She was someone we understood to be his aide. And we all knew much worse things would happen if he caught us when no one other than his wife was around.

As I try to shake my uncomfortable memory, I hope none of the kids piling back on the bus at Mt. Constitution understand that dark side of childhood.

"The cure for anything is salt water—sweat, tears, or the ocean."
Isak Dinesen

CHAPTER 11.
LEAVING, AGAIN:
Crabs, do-overs, and horseshoes

A number of bicyclists had trailered up to the lighthouse on Mt. Constitution, to then zoom back to sea level. Shortly after I begin the drive down, I watch in the rear-view mirror as they stack up behind me. There are no turn-outs, and I'm not comfortable driving my big truck down twisting roads as fast as the bikers want to fly. Finally I reach a place where I can pull over, and five bicyclists zing past. They wave as they go by, but I'm not sure which finger they use.

Once out of the State Park, I drive around Orcas Island with a map in hand, but I still manage to spend much of the day lost on the small island. The day is painful and filled with a loneliness that will not be lulled by natural beauty. I take an earlier-than-planned ferry back to Anacortes and drive to the campground at Deception Pass where Bruin and I spend our last night on Whidbey Island.

John and Glenda, my neighbors at the campground here, are full-timers who live in a motor home and pull a Jeep. We've become friends, talking in the evenings and sharing an occasional meal. They're from Fort Walton Beach, Florida, about 50 miles from my home, so I don't have to explain the joy of eating fried mullet and cheese grits. And they don't comment about my strong Southern accent. I explain my plans to go to Blaine in the farthest corner of Washington. Why Blaine? Well, there's an inexpensive campground there. There is a large state fair at nearby Lynden. The fair posters say there will be horses, country cooking, and Willie Nelson. Since John and Glenda have no plans, they decide to follow me to Blaine. RV'ers are like that—sometimes just following the wind, a whim, or another RV'er.

BLAINE, WASHINGTON

The next morning I hook up and pull north to Blaine, a small town that sits on Birch Bay, less than five miles from the Canadian border. This far northwest corner of Washington has a pastoral feel to it with slightly rolling hills sprouting raspberries, corn, and hay. Birch Bay is a quiet, shallow cove off the Pacific; lights of Canadian homes flicker across the waters. There is a significant tidal action in the bay, so at low tide boats wait patiently on their sides while people walk out a quarter of a mile from shore on pebbles and large rocks that will soon be covered again with ocean life.

In the afternoon I walk down to the Bay and just meander. It's low tide and there's almost no sand in the bay; it's not a place to run around barefooted. I watch with curiosity as people bend over to dig for clams, their shovels and rakes clanking unevenly against the rocks. The blue herons and gulls are familiar sights and sounds, reminders that some things are the same in opposite corners of the country. I sit on a driftwood log to admire the blue heron as she sticks her neck out to fly. I pick wild flowers to go with my growing collection of souvenirs hanging on a twig wreath on the wall of my home-on-wheels. I find an empty clamshell, still attached at the hinge and sporting a deep purple on its slick interior wall. I put the shell in my pocket to add to the small basket in my bathroom. As the sun begins to set, I head home and see a young dad with two boys, about five and eight years old, at a picnic table. The dad is squatted down, cleaning large reddish crabs and then dropping them into a pot of boiling water.

I walk to their table and say, "I know Blue crabs in Florida, but I don't know what these are."

He looks up with an easy smile and responds, "Dungeness."

"We don't clean Blue crabs that way," I say as I squat down beside him.

He continues with his rhythm. He picks up a live crab from

the cooler, holds it with a set of legs and pincher in each hand, and then breaks the crab in two by hitting it hard mid-torso on the edge of his plastic cooler. With his finger, he scoops out the black guts (leaving the gills), and drops the halves into the boiling water. Then he picks up another live crab and begins again. The two boys are stuffing themselves with what I understand to be very expensive crabmeat. They have crab all over their faces and dripping from their elbows. I accept the dad's offer of hot crab, and as I eat, I begin my lesson in Dungeness. He explains, "I take the kayak out with both boys and two crab pots. I put chicken in the pots and lower them into about ten feet of water, wait ten minutes, and pull them up. There's a limit of six crabs per day per person. I get to count the boys so I can bring in 18 crabs. It didn't take long to get my limit today."

Growing up, I'd cleaned Blue crabs in Blackwater Bay, in that other northwest corner of that other state, so I had to try my hand at cleaning these large reddish cousins. I pick up a live crab without getting pinched, whack it on the cooler, and it doesn't break. My teacher takes the crab, easily breaks it on the edge of the cooler, and hands it back to me. I pull out black guts with my pointer finger, ignore the gills, and drop the halves into the pot. The youngest wants me to stay and eat more, but I don't want to wear out this delicate welcome. I walk back into the woods with a fistful of wild flowers, a shell in my pocket, and my face and hands sticky with Dungeness crab. I laugh, "Now this is a do-over!"

❊ ❊ ❊

"When I approach a child, he inspires in me two sentiments; tenderness for what he is and respect for what he may become."
Louis Pasteur

Do-overs
When children at play miss a ball or a chance, they call for a "do-

over", and then play on as if they hadn't missed. On a good day, I got to watch do-overs from the Bench.

Jessie, 12-years old, was in Court for her adoption hearing. Her father had sexually abused her, her mother had failed to protect her from him, and finally the State had stepped in. After a convoluted legal process and too long in foster care, Jessie was free to be adopted. This was her day, her do-over, her chance to begin again. Her new mom and dad, in their late 30's, had no other children. After several miscarriages, the new parents decided to begin again— not with an adopted babe-in-arms but with a 12- year-old Jessie. Jessie sat reading a book as the attorney went through the steps to finalize her adoption.

Intrigued, I interrupted the legal business to ask, "Jessie, what are you reading?" She closed her book to show me the title, Greek Mythology.

To my "Wow," she responded, "I also like to read Shakespeare and Edgar Allan Poe."

Then she opened her book and went back to her reading; her new parents beamed. I granted the adoption with a smile. A classic do-over.

David was only 18 months old when he was shipped from Vietnam. His 24 year-old Vietnamese birth mother gave him to one agency that gave him to another that shipped him across the Pacific to another agency that placed him with the proud parents now in my courtroom. On the sixth floor of a courthouse several worlds away from his birthplace, David, now twenty-four months old, stood at the brink of a life his birth mother could not have imagined. The legal documents, some written in Vietnamese, did not speak of his mother's turmoil or sacrifice, yet her presence seemed to fill the room like holy incense. As the attorney spoke in legalese, the toddler squirmed from his dad's lap over the chair arm to his mom. She pulled a ballpoint pen from her purse, and I slid a sheet of paper across the conference table. The attorney continued to question the parents, and I quietly watched David. Mom clicked the point down, wrote on the paper, and handed the pen to David. The little guy *clicked the point up and looked quizzically at his mom when the pen wouldn't write. She clicked the point down, wrote, and handed the pen back to him. Oblivious to the grown-ups and this adoption business, David clicked the point in and out twice. Then he sat up straight with his eyes focused on the pen and his jaw set. "Click"- the point was down, and he began to mark on the paper. "Click" - the point was up. With dancing eyes, the tyke repeated his new trick several times and then was bored. He reached for his mom's purse in pursuit of other magic. An international do-over.*

❧ ❧ ❧

The sun is going down as I walk through the woods in the far northwest corner of the country, with Dungeness crab on my chin and a smile on my face.

I drive to the State Fair at Lynden for a glimpse into the soul of their community. The area has an extensive 4H program, so there are herds of teenagers and herds of horses—kids playing and working hard, focused on horses, rather than on MTV or designer labels. There is an outdoor 4H horse arena and two indoor ones, plus two very large 4H horse barns. Some of the 4H competitions are held in the main arena with a crowd, but the kids go non-stop in their own horse world with or without an audience.

There is such a strong contingency of draft horses in Northwest Washington that the big boys have their separate barn at the State Fair. Draft horses, referred to as gentle giants, are bred for size, strength, and docile nature and historically have been used for heavy tasks such as plowing and hauling. A draft horse is tall (5'4" to 6'4"–or 16 to 19 hands–at the withers), extremely muscular, heavy (typically weighs between 1,400 and 2,000 pounds), with a more upright shoulder and beautiful long hair on its lower legs, referred to as feathering. At one point there are 32 draft horses in the main arena, hitched to wagons and high stepping their enormous hooves, as the handlers work multiple reins through their fingers. As the arena clears, one of the workers sprints out to retrieve a horseshoe dropped by a Clydesdale, the draft horse widely known from Budweiser advertisements. The horseshoe is larger than a dinner plate.

While at the Fair, I fall in love with a 23-year-old real cowboy who does an animal act known as the One-Armed Bandit. Every self-respecting female, regardless of age, shares my response to Lynn Payne. He's tall and looks great in his jeans. He has a strong cowboy accent, and says "Ma'am" and "Boss" a lot. Like me, he drives a Dodge pickup with a Cummins diesel engine.

During the show, Lynn sits astride his Appaloosa horse without holding even the reins as the horse jumps onto the bed of his truck and then climbs a ramp to the roof of his horse trailer. His act includes three Watusi cows, very large animals with horns longer than the Texas Longhorn and beautiful smooth hides like the Brahma but without the hump. Later his dog herds the cows to the roof of the trailer

After the show, I hang around and talk with Lynn as he feeds his animals, and I accept his invitation to join his crew for dinner. I drive over to his motel where we stand out in the parking lot taking turns literally looking under each other's truck hoods. But I quickly fall silent. He's talking about modifying engine parts I can't even locate. For example, he explains how he increased the arc of fuel–either into or out of the injector, I don't remember–and is able to get five more miles per gallon. I am embarrassed by my mechanical ineptitude but in awe of the ease with which Lynn can work machines to his advantage. He's having so much fun explaining it all that he doesn't seem to notice my silence.

Then I go to a steak house with Lynn and several road hands. It's an interesting night, listening to stories about a secluded but rowdy cowboy life on a ranch in Sidler, Oklahoma.

I ask a lot of questions, including "Are you still having fun with the act?"

"Well, ma'am, it stopped being fun when I was about 14.
But the money sure is good."

God, do I understand what that feels like.

TACOMA, WASHINGTON:
Busted knuckles, babies, and tears

Two RV's pull out of Blaine. John and Glenda are heading
east with a flexible destination, perhaps Glacier National Park.
As I turn south, grateful for the freedom to make these spur-
of-the-moment choices, I think of others whose decision to
move became the focus of intense legal battles. One particular
case involved a mother who had remarried and moved to
Virginia to join her new husband. She went with her daughter
but without the father's consent. I stop early that evening, set
up the RV, and have supper. Then I pull out an old journal in
which I had recorded the story of the child with one parent in
Virginia and the other in Florida. As a way of keeping a bit of
sanity, when I came home from the courthouse I often sat
down and wrote some of what I'd seen—in an effort to make
sense of it all, to keep my focus on the humanity I
encountered, and to better understand how I might do justice.

✤ ✤ ✤

Relocating

*Monday morning, I'm scheduled to hear a two-day contested
custody battle that focuses on the right of the mother to move to
Virginia with their daughter, over the objection of the father who
lives here in Florida. In a relocation dispute, there may be no good
answer. In this case, the parents have been divorced for three years;
the mother remarried and moved their seven-year-old daughter
without the father's consent to Virginia where her new husband is
stationed with the military.*

*My spirits are dragging, what with the memory of the nasty divorce
I heard on Friday ricocheting off premonitions of what the next two
days will be like. In this day-to-day world of litigation, light-hearted
spirits have to be tough.*

Monday night. The day was very tense; tomorrow will be similar. I made it through the first day without firing on anyone in Court though I felt my trigger-finger twitch several times. I hope I have a second day of patience and temperance left in me. It is much easier to be short-tempered and aggressive, than patient and open-minded. The intensity of my workday is all the more reason to walk, write, and do yoga before stepping through the doors of the Courthouse.

The attorney for the former husband chose to present his case through hand-to-hand combat, with the intent to sever the mother's emotional jugular; he could, of course, focus on what is best for the child and the need to facilitate communication between the parents. He has a strong case legally and factually; he doesn't need to sully the image of justice to effectively represent his client. But somehow (the result of a heavy-handed marketing, too much TV, and/or not enough introspection?) this attorney does not view an even-handed approach as sexy or effective. I feel both sad and mad as I watch the antagonism the attorney stirs into an already brewing pot of emotions. He knows how—and is too willing—to add fuel to the flame of the parents' strife and to cinch down ever tighter the tension between them. I stand guard over the law as the father's attorney pulls the pin on an emotional hand grenade that he hopes will annihilate the mother and thereby assure a win—for the lawyer.

Regardless of my ruling when the case is over, this attorney will boast of his prowess and his client will believe himself well represented because of the hurt inflicted on his former wife. And me, I just sigh, for part of my job is to insure that such offensive antics do not affect my decision-making.

Tuesday night. The case is over, and I'm numb. Often judges take contested family law cases under advisement, even if they know their decision at the time. If you delay the announcement and send the order later to the attorneys, you don't have to look the parents in the eye, watch them go pale or flushed, see the tears, or listen to the keening. You get to skip the really messy part. But face-to-face gives me the chance to cover unanticipated questions and hopefully offers some closure.

I called the parents into my Chambers late in the afternoon and announced my ruling with the law and facts upon which it was based–the seven-year-old daughter is to return from Virginia to Florida. If the mother chooses to move back to Florida, leaving her new husband at his duty station, she will continue to have primary custody; if she stays in Virginia with her husband, primary custody of the daughter will be with the father. The decision is made, and I'm exhausted. The father's attorney has a condescending, sarcastic tone of voice that reminds me of TV attorneys (as well as other men I've known), a tone intended to stun the female listener into submission. Much of the attorney's focus had nothing to do with the child, and his legal fees exceed $13,000. Because of the facts and law and in spite of his attorney, the father won; because of his attorney, I have a headache.

As part of my job, I'm paid well to cut out hearts and destroy dreams. And the reality is, I'm good at it. But too often, I notice that the stranger's blood is warm on my hands, and I unwillingly wonder how this mother will feel in the middle of the night, impaled on the horns of her choice to live with either her husband or her daughter, knowing she cannot live with both.

❦ ❦ ❦

I have thousands of miles on the road as proof no one is telling me when or where to go, and it's been months since I was paid to make someone cry. Unlike legal issues, mechanical problems are not life altering. But they can be a pain in the butt.

I head south to Camping World in Tacoma for work on the exhaust brake that the mechanic-with-an-attitude disconnected in Montana. At an RV park at Gig Harbor, out of Tacoma, the manager points out my assigned slot and acts as though people park there every day. The layout required that I back my RV up a hill and maneuver it around a tree. I should have been suspicious when he came out to help. As I back up the incline, I know I'm riding the truck's clutch (standard transmission with five forward speeds) but I can't figure out how to avoid it, since the pickup moves too fast with the clutch engaged. As the manager motions me closer and closer to the tree, he folds the mirror on the passenger side against the truck. I back up, clearing the tree by inches. The truck is at a hard angle to the 5th wheel when the manager says, "OK, you're fine," and walks away. I know I'll be in trouble when it's time to hook up again, but I can't figure out how to deal with it. So I just unhook the trailer, following Scarlett O'Hara's conclusion in Gone with the Wind, "I can't think about that now. I'll think about it tomorrow." The 5th wheel is parked, the clutch stinks, and I'm tired.

The next day I'm to meet Bill and Bryan, friends from Lost Prairie, for a jump at their home drop zone, Kapowsin AirSports southeast of Tacoma. I get there a little early, and the other jumpers include me in their easy banter as I wait near the wooden picnic tables. When Bill drives up, he explains, "Bryan bailed on us. Something about having to spend the afternoon with his wife. To hell with him! We'll do a two-way." We put on our gear, and soon I'm gifted with a view of the Snoqualmie National Forest from a higher plane. Mount Rainier quietly supervises as the plane lines up above the DZ for jump run. At 14,200 feet someone yells, "Door!" and a jumper rolls up the plexiglass door. Bill and I go out together, turn a few points, laugh at each other and life, and then land with the skydiving grin that says the world is a good place. I buy a Kapowsin bumper sticker and with a happy heart head back to Bruin, as I watch the sun set on the state of Washington.

The next day I'm to take the truck and rig into Camping World to have the exhaust brake checked. I give myself extra time to get the 5th wheel hooked up because I know it isn't going to be easy. It turns out to be impossible. I almost have it connected once, but the king-pin won't seat into the hitch. I keep talking to myself, "Breathe, be patient, you can do this." The truck is pointing downhill, and for some reason the emergency brake won't hold. There's no one else out in the park, and the office is closed. Twenty minutes later when I get out of the truck for what felt like the 100th time, I see that the front storage compartment of the RV is sprouting a hole where I have backed the edge of the open tailgate of the truck. My pep talks stop, and I put my head on the back of the truck and cry hot, frustrated tears. I-can't-do-it tears. Four-letter-word tears, with exclamation marks. Why-did-I-ever-think-I-could-handle-this-in-the-first-place tears. Followed by you-have-no-choice-you-have-to-handle-it tears. I slam the tailgate shut and mutter, "At least it's just a stupid hole. Nobody got hurt or died because of that stupid hole." I could remember uninvited tears for heartbreak and frustration that were real, that mattered–nothing as simple as this stupid hole in my RV.

❦ ❦ ❦

"Father asked us what was God's noblest work. Anna said men, but I said babies. Men are often bad; babies never are."
Louisa May Alcott

Tears and duty
A series of legal rights trigger judicial hearings within 24 hours of the event, and those hearings must be held 365 days a year. A judge must review probable cause and appoint counsel for each defendant, adult and juvenile, taken into custody and must review each case in which a child has been involuntarily removed from the parents. Judges rotate duty.[16] In Pensacola, it was three to four months between duty assignments.

One February weekend, I had duty so I was at the juvenile detention facility at 8 am on Saturday; from there I would go over to the jail. I was to hear cases for 10 juveniles arrested and detained Friday night, four shelters (children the State wanted to remove from their parents on allegations of abuse or neglect) and 48 adults

---

[16]Duty - the time a Judge works weekends in addition to the regular Monday through Friday dockets to cover those matters which must be heard 365 days a year.

arrested in the last 24 hours who had not bonded out.

On that Saturday morning, I took two newborns away from their mothers—two baby girls, sharing the same birth date and the same experience of having been separated from their moms at birth. One mother wasn't at the hearing; she was on the psych ward. The report said the nurse was showing her how to bottle-feed the baby. Mom got mad at the baby because she squirmed and spit up the formula. Mom reared back and threw the baby. The baby landed safely on the mother's bed, and Mom landed safely in the psych ward. I appointed an attorney for the mother and set a review hearing. Mom wasn't doing well and her prognosis was unknown. Today her baby would go "home" from the hospital to foster parents.

Mom Number Two was seated at the long conference table. According to the reports, Alabama had removed her three young daughters a couple of years before. Last year Alabama TPR'd the kids [Termination of Parental Rights is a very complex legal process available only in cases of extreme abuse or neglect. The result of a TPR is to sever all parental rights and free the child for adoption.] The report also explained that Alabama had temporarily held the TPR order and allowed the children to go back to the mother for yet another try. Mom refused to follow through with the Court's orders or her promises to the Court, and she then ran with the kids to Florida. Alabama issued an order that the children be picked up and returned. Working from a tip, DCF [Department of Children and Family, the Florida agency that handles cases of abused and neglected children] found the three kids with their very pregnant mother; DCF picked up the kids and sent them back to Alabama, leaving Mom here in Florida. The mother gave birth to her fourth child, another little girl; somehow DCF didn't notice, and she took the baby home. When DCF realized the mother was no longer pregnant, they came to Court asking for custody of the newborn.

Mom sobbed, "My milk's come in! I'm breast-feeding my baby! For God's sake, don't take this one, too. I ain't done nothin' wrong. I'll do anything you tell me. I still have the stitches from my baby, for God's sake! I ain't even healed yet! But the State wants to rip my baby from me."

The mother's emotions were as raw as her body. Though I didn't have the Alabama file for their TPR, certain facts were clear. A mother must do something terribly wrong for the slow-moving System to request permanent removal of children. It is technically difficult, from a legal standpoint, to prove permanent termination, yet Alabama had done that. And the mother had run from the Alabama Court with three daughters and a belly full of another baby. I ordered the newborn into shelter, and the mother laid her head on the table as her body jerked with sobs.

She looked up at me and said, "Can I at least see my baby, please? Can I hold her?"

The case worker from DCF said, "I'm sorry, Your Honor, but we can't accommodate visitation until Monday and then only during regular business hours."

I wondered if the caseworker really believed you could put babies and other important issues of humanity on an eight-to-five, five-day-a-week schedule. If I'd had the energy or if I'd thought it would help, I would have screamed at this bureaucratically-tightened sphincter muscle. But I said nothing, except "The mother may visit her baby daily at the office of DCF." I stood up and walked out of the room. I had finished the four shelter hearings as well as the detention hearings for the 10 delinquents, so I walked over to the jail for First Appearances. It was 55 degrees outside with clear blue skies. A nice change, since the temperatures had been in the 30's

As I walked into the jail and picked up my bright orange clip-on pass at the glass reception window, I noticed a crowd waiting in the rows of seats now to my back - family and friends of those I would soon meet.

I spoke to the officer behind the glass, "Long docket?"

He made a face and said, "48."

I smiled, "Whoa, business was good last night." I walked the few steps to my right and the first large door of metal bars clanged open. I moved through and the door slid shut with a groan, sandwiching me between it and another just like it a couple of feet away. I looked through a tinted plate glass window at the Officer overseeing the bank of TV monitors and held up my orange card. She smiled at me and flipped a switch.

The second door slid open, and I walked through into a long hall. I turned left and was met by a different officer who explained, "They're bringing the inmates up, Judge. They'll be here in a minute. I'll unlock the room for you."

I walked into a windowless and empty room thick with the smell of an industrial-strength antiseptic. I sat in the tall-backed chair behind a table at the front of the room; in front of me were a wooden podium and about 20 gray metal folding chairs. The floors were a nondescript linoleum that matched the gray walls. The doors to this room were not barred but a solid metal that clanged when opened or closed. I sat alone in the empty room for a few minutes, reading from the large stack of arrest warrants as doors banged open or shut in the halls. Soon, the inmates filed in and sat in alphabetical order. Everyone wore orange plastic shower shoes and a green cotton jump suit that buttoned up the front. I introduced myself, explained their legal rights and told them how I would handle the docket.

I called the first case. A man with permanently dirty skin, tattoos, red matted hair, and a humble attitude came to the podium. The police report said he was charged with Disorderly Intoxication - that he had screamed and cussed at everyone at a church's bingo parlor and then went to another church across the street, one without bingo, and continued screaming and cussing until the police arrested him. I had to smile; I knew this M.O. from my days in the Public Defender's Office. On a night with temperatures in the low 30's, he did what it took to get a warm bed, some food, and time to sober up. Now he was sober, it was warmer outside, and he was ready to go home, which I suspected meant back to the woods along the Interstate. I offered and he accepted. He pled guilty to Disorderly Intoxication for two days in jail.

As he turned to leave, he looked me in the eye, nodded his head, and said gently, "Thank you, ma'am."

I responded softly, "Good luck." And since he had come in two nights before (they didn't bring him to First Appearances on

Friday morning because he was still drunk), I thought with a smile "You may be on the street quicker than I am, with such a long docket ahead."

When I called the next case, an older gray-headed man with a scant beard came to the podium. He seemed very comfortable, almost confident as I quietly read the police report that described multiple acts of sexual battery on a four-year-old girl.

The investigating officer reported that when he asked the four-year-old to describe the Defendant's penis, she said, "It's a mean one. And white yucky stuff comes out of it. "

As I read, I had to work hard to hide my horror and my rage. Then I had to speak politely, even respectfully to him, and to get on with the judge-business of appointing counsel and setting bond. But I did not have to leave the bond at the officer's suggestion of $20,000. I said, "Sir, your bond is set at $500,000." We both knew what that meant. He could pay a bondsman 10% and be bonded out. But the price of his get-out-of-jail ticket had just jumped from $2,000 to $50,000. His mouth jerked open as though to speak his surprise and displeasure, but he took a breath and tightened his lips without making a sound. His eyes hardened, he turned his back to me, and began walking to his chair before I finished what I had to say. "Sir, I'm not through yet. Return to the podium, please." He glared over his shoulder, but as the officers moved closer he returned. I appointed the Public Defender to represent him and set his court dates. Then I said, "You may take your seat now, sir." I could feel the electricity of his anger as he plopped down on the front row. He sat and glared at me. His eyes didn't waiver from me nor did his body relax as I called each of the other 20 men in the room. I ignored him and those mean eyes.

When I had called the last of that group, the officers took them back to their cells and a second group of 20 filed into the room.

I finished the docket and left the jail at noon; from there I went to the Village Inn for a late breakfast. Then I went across the street to Target and looked at things for new-borns. My daughter-in-law, Joan, was pregnant and due in September. As I fondled soft receiving

191

blankets and bibs, I found myself crying. I took off my glasses and wiped my eyes and nose, but they filled again with long hot tears as I stood alone in the baby aisle at Target's. A four-year-old who describes an old man's penis as a "mean one." A mother who throws her newborn. A pregnant mother who runs with her three children to get Alabama out of her hair, only to get caught here in Florida, where the system slowly adds three plus one and realizes—she has four children now. A mother sobbing those sounds many mother animals make when separated from their babies—cows, elephants, horses, whales—other females who have been programmed to give birth and then to mother. But some women are wired only for birthing and not for mothering.

Yet my son and daughter-in-law were walking around on clouds, patting her barely growing stomach, moving with joy into a life that will never be the same. And I stood in the baby aisle at Target's and cried because there was nothing else I could do about it all.

❖ ❖ ❖

I straighten up and look through tears at my home on wheels. In the midst of a long paragraph of four-letter words, I decide to give up and go ask a man, any man, to be my second set of eyes to help me line up the truck and trailer. As I walk across the parking lot, a neighbor comes outside and offers to help. Instead of giving me directions, he gets in the driver's seat; I don't object and give him hand signals as he begins to back. Finally he manages to align the truck and 5th wheel at the proper weird angle. Then he rams the truck hitch into the trailer hitch with a force that could have bent the front legs of my RV, but didn't. I thank him with a tired smile, get in the truck, snake the 5th wheel around the pine tree, and drive away.

Less than five miles later, a car pulls up beside me on the freeway, and the driver waves frantically. (I'm learning to hate it when they do that. It's never a sign of good things to come.) At about that point, I'm realizing something isn't working right with my truck (that's about as mechanical as I get) for it won't accelerate or change gears. I pull over into the emergency lane. I can't open the driver's door because the traffic is insane, but I can see black smoke in the side mirror. I crawl out the passenger door and am surprised to find I don't have a flat tire. I don't have any idea what's wrong. The smoke is fading away, but something sure stinks. I decide I need to pull onto the grass shoulder because the traffic is so scary, but the truck won't move. That makes no sense. It was working fine a minute ago.

Back in the truck and wondering what to do next, I see two heads pop up outside the passenger door–two highway patrolmen, my personal icon of safety. "Ma'am, are you OK? We had a report of vehicle on fire. There's a fire truck in route."

Talking with them, all of my tension and fear melt away. I'm thinking, "Hey, I'm not on fire! How important is this unnamed mechanical problem? I'm not on fire! I'm not watching everything I own go up in flames; I don't have to be afraid for Bruin."

When I suggest that I move the truck and rig further onto the shoulder, they respond, "No, ma'am! Do not try to start the engine again! You could catch on fire! And we've already called off the fire truck." They offer to call a wrecker on their radio but I decline for that is too much detail to process through a 3rd party.

The officers turn off their flashing lights and drive away as Bruin and I climb high onto the shoulder of the road, away from the screaming traffic. From there, I use my cell phone to call emergency road-side service, and they dispatch two tow vehicles, one for the truck and the second to move the 5th wheel. Then I start calling Dodge dealerships. The first dealer said it would be two weeks before they could even look at my truck. Three calls later I find a dealer who will check the truck tomorrow.

Sitting in the tall grass, I go through my Parks Directory and find a campground near the Dodge dealer; I call them and make reservations for the 5th wheel. Then I run my hand through Bruin's fur and brag to him about the marvels of cell phones. I also tell him how much braver I am with him around. I'm not scared, but I would be without him. As I sit on the grass shoulder above the screaming traffic, stranded but with two tow trucks in route, I laugh at myself. I had been in tears less than an hour before simply because I punched a not-so-large hole in the front storage compartment of the RV. Nothing like a little smoke, two highway patrolmen, flashing blue lights, and a fire truck to put things in perspective.

The tow trucks arrive; one tows my truck to the dealer (Bruin and I ride in the cab with the mechanic) and the other takes the 5th wheel to the RV Park, backs it in and levels it. When I finish the paperwork at the Dodge dealer, they give me a ride to the campground. All I have to do is unlock the door, fold down the steps, and I'm home again with everything I own. When Bruin and I explore this unscheduled stop, we find blackberry vines everywhere, heavy with fruit and still ripening in August. In Northwest Florida, those thorny vines are as thin as spaghetti and produce an early summer treat, but in Washington, the vines are thick as my fingers and run 20 feet in the air, climbing over an old fence, a rusty car, and anything else that doesn't outrun them. Brier Rabbit lives in this briar patch.

Four days after sitting on the shoulder of the road watching traffic whiz by, I pick up my truck and the $1,900 bill. I had burned out the clutch, and, of course, there were a few other things that needed to be adjusted, including the emergency brake. They checked out the exhaust brake, declared it fine and reconnected it. They didn't know what was causing the truck to lurch. I mumble as I walk back to the truck "Just what I need. Another AFGE!" Though crass, that acronym (Another Fucking Growth Experience) sums up much of my life and certainly this latest hard knock in the world of mechanical things. And I'm getting tired of growing. The routine stuff is one thing–blowing a clutch, crunching the RV, but the lurch is an on-going hazard, a risk no one has been able to help me with. Just improving my attitude doesn't fix the lurch. I don't have any other choice: I've paid the bill, and it's time to get back on the road, lurch and all.

"A ship in a harbor is safe, but that's not what ships are built for."
William Shedd

CHAPTER 12.
SAN JUAN ISLANDS:
Falcons, faces, and screams

I leave the Dodge dealer in Tacoma at 6 p.m., and by 7:30 I'm hooked up and pulling my RV down the freeway. Before blowing out the clutch, I accepted an invitation to park my 5th wheel on San Juan Island near the home of Ken and Suzanne, friends of a skydiving friend I'd met while jumping in Mexico, so now I'm heading north to Anacortes to catch a ferry.

It's 10:00 p.m. when I join the short line of vehicles at the dock. I'm nervous about pulling my large RV onto the ferry, but it's the only way to get it to the island. There's no bridge; you either go by boat or plane, or don't go. I understood the schedule to say that a San Juan ferry would depart at 12:40 a.m.; I decide the almost three-hour wait would at least get me over to the island, and this part of the trip would be done. Bruin and I wait in the truck and doze. I wake with a start at 2:00 a.m.; what happened to my 12:40 ferry? Nothing is moving in the damp glow of street lamps, though the line of vehicles has grown. I find my glasses and turn on a light to reread the schedule. The 12:40 a.m. ferry runs only on Saturday and Sunday; not, as I had assumed, each day except Saturday and Sunday. And the next ferry is at 4:30 a.m.! I put the leash on Bruin, and we walk across the eerie-quiet of the parking lot to a patch of grass and then crawl back into the cab of the truck. And there we sit, sleepy and grumpy for another two and a half hours.

Six hours after I pulled into the line, a ferry worker walks down the now long rows of vehicles banging on doors and windows, his version of a wake-up call. Engines rev' and headlights come on, and we're all herded into the belly of the ferry. I exhale a nervous sigh and then with a smile compare myself to Jonah who suddenly found himself in the belly of a whale. Large vehicles are sandwiched into the center of the ferry, with passenger cars and pick-ups stuffed together along the sides and up the ramps. Because I'd gotten in line early, I'm the first large vehicle shepherded into the center, and I'm parked at water level at the front of the ferry. There is a semi behind me, a twenty-foot van truck to my left, and a steel wall to my right. I watch in amazement as the ferryman pulls a mere rope between my truck and the front ramp of the ferry. "Bruin," I stammered, "What is he thinking? A little rope is supposed to keep us out of that cold water?" When he puts only one chock under my wheel, I explain to Bruin, "He has more faith than I do in my emergency brake and the mechanics who just worked on it." As the ferry pulls out from the docks, I have a great view of the water from the driver's seat, but I feel uncomfortable sitting in my truck as it bolts across the dark San Juan Straits. I figure there's no reason to try to sleep now, so I go up to the passenger portion of the ferry, drink reheated coffee and eat prepackaged bagels. Three semi-truck drivers are in the café joking and flirting with the waitress, giving me a sleepy-eyed view of yet another world, one that for these truckers includes a routine of long waits and ferry rides shortened by good-natured jokes shared with other night owls. When the sun comes up, they'll deliver staples to the island and return to the ferry for their maritime commute.

During the hour and 15 minute ride over to San Juan Island, it's too dark to see much and too cold for a true Floridian to stand outside very long. Finally, as we approach Friday Harbor, the loud speaker barks, "Please return to your vehicles." When I get to the truck, Bruin pops his head up from the rear seat, curious. I sit behind the steering wheel watching the waves and then the piling and cement of the dock heading straight for the hood of my truck. As the ferry noses up to the pilings, I realize I'm pushing on the brake.

I drive over to Ken and Suzanne's. Their directions

included, "Once you're out of town, go about three miles 'til you see a sneaker hanging from the power lines on your left. Just past the shoe, turn left on a dirt road. There's no mailbox or sign, but you'll see our airplane after you round the first bend in the dirt road." Ken and Suzanne live among rolling hills and open pastures; their home sits beside their private grass runway, one of many on the island. Ken is a master falconer and skydiver who is training peregrine falcons to dive out of an airplane with him and then come to him in free fall. The Parachutist magazine featured an incredible cover photo of Ken in free fall at sunset over San Juan Island with his falcon coming straight down at him in a dive for food known as a "stoop."

The sky has begun to glow in early morning pinks and purples as I park at the edge of a runway owned by people I have not yet met. I have to laugh at the pleasant absurdity of it all, for I had left the legal world to travel and see what life could be without structure. And here I am walking with Bruin down a dirt road on San Juan Island where I'll stay for a few days to watch a stranger jump out of an airplane with a bird.

I spend eight days parked beside Ken and Suzanne's house, watching. Watching for two days as low clouds cancelled Ken's work with the falcons. Later watching him work the birds using both his ultra-light and Cessna airplane. Watching Suzanne feed, whether the birds had flown or not. Watching Ken and Suzanne interact with their two kids–Cole, 11-years old, and Rhiana, six-years old–at family dinners with classical music in the background, rather than the noise of a TV. Watching Ken and Suzanne as they listen and talk with their children, consistently and intentionally involved as a family.

Rhiana, wearing shorts and pink cowgirl boots, rides her wooden pony through a world of magic and imagination. Watching Rhiana move with boundless energy, I'm fascinated by the kaleidoscope of emotions that play across her face– mad, glad, sad, confused, convinced. She holds nothing back;

she's as uninhibited by the display of her in-the-moment emotions as she is about walking naked from the bathroom to get her PJ's. As she scoots to her bedroom, her face is transparent, her body is bare. She is the antithesis of all of my professional training.

❦ ❦ ❦

My mask

My professional life is one of covering up. I'm paid to guard my thoughts, feelings, and humanity. I wear a robe to cloak me from the neck down. That black armor covers my clothes, my gender, and my physical size, and it deflects questions about such human things. The face—that is my job. If you can tell what I'm thinking or feeling, I'm not doing a good job; I'm not being judicial.

At all times, a judge is to be inscrutable, so I tighten up and readjust this professional mask of nothingness. I am to be only a face with two eyes, a nose, and a mouth, none of which are to move; there is to be only a slight nod at the close of testimony or legal argument to indicate that the mask was listening. I am to listen but not feel, listen but withhold judgment.

Dealing with children's issues in Family Law, the Judge seldom gets to call a simple "Ball" or "Strike" for there is often no clear right and wrong. Rarely is there is an obvious solution, and both parents are generally good people. The Law leaves much to the discretion of the Court, and there are no burning bushes, crystal balls, flaming chariots, or lightning strikes on which the Judge can rely for the right answer.

My best judgment is only that. My judgment. My judgment is simply the best I can come up with, based on the law and the facts, both of which may be open to multiple interpretations. It's a judgment I'm paid to make in Family Law because at least one side is so invested in the negative energy that he or she won't or can't accept responsibility for resolving their own problems. So they bring their negativity to me, funnel it through legal terms and postures, and then they watch my rigid mask closely, hoping to guess what I'm thinking and how to sway me.

After hours or days of poker-faced listening, the professional mask speaks without feeling of ultimate conclusions of law and fact. The mask is often required by Law to announce judgments that are deeply hurtful: "The Court rejects the testimony of the mother" (a legal way of saying I think she lied); "The Court finds that the father's negative attitude toward the mother is detrimental to the child" (legalese for you're being an asshole and your spite is poisoning your son's spirit); "The child will move to Maine with the mother" (unspoken: Dad, you're going to miss out on coaching Little League for a few years); "The child will not move to D.C. with the mom" (implying: Mom, you have to choose between your new husband stationed in D.C. and your son who is going to live here in Florida.)

I listen, from deep behind my mask, and then finally I speak. I'm not paid to speak of hope, beauty, and life. No, I speak of findings of fact and conclusions of law. Then I move on to the next case feeling a little more cynical and much older.

❈ ❈ ❈

Suzanne does all the routine day-to-day work with the birds, including feeding. Feeding falcons is a very earthy process and not for the squeamish. Late in the day Suzanne takes them one at a time onto her gloved left hand and feeds them each half a quail. Suzanne buys the quail frozen–feathers, guts and all–two dozen to a box. She also feeds rabbit to the birds, and she keeps a coop of live pigeons, like TV dinners to be used when she's in a hurry or forgets to go to the store. In case you've ever wondered, falcons don't like quail gizzard, liver, or intestines, so they spit those right out. They love quail brain, though, so Suzanne breaks the quail's neck at the base of the skull and holds the head back with the brain exposed so the birds can get to it easier. Not surprisingly, the birds fling small pieces of flesh around as they eat, and some gets stuck on their beaks. Suzanne, like the mom she is, uses her thumb and forefinger to wipe their noses clean. It's not long before I have quail guts, brains, and feathers on me. I don't actually feed the birds; I'm just Suzanne's "go-fer" and butcher.

Their new falcon, Piggy, is what they call an imprinted bird, meaning that when she sees a person she thinks and squawks "Food!" She has an ear-piercing shriek that doesn't stop as long as she can see a human. Ignoring Piggy's ruckus, Cole goes about his busy life as the oldest son in a close-knit family. My thoughts tumble inward to children I've met in court, children whose lives are the converse of the noisy normalcy of this household. One of those children is Dan, a child stored in various foster homes, a child who could hear nothing but learned ways to make himself noticed.

❧ ❧ ❧

Dan

When Dan was two years old, his mother brought him to the doctor with a ruptured left eardrum—suspiciously ruptured from a medical standpoint. Dan left with his mom, permanently deaf in that ear and eligible for a Social Security disability check. Several months later Dan came back to the doctor with his right eardrum permanently damaged. Mom asked too many questions about how to get the increased disability (two deaf ears pay more than one, of course), and she answered too few questions about how this happened. Dan was taken away from his mom and put in foster care. Indications are that Mom stuck an ice pick through each of her baby's eardrums, but there was insufficient evidence to pursue criminal charges.

I first met Dan when he was about ten-years old, a special-needs child, totally deaf, very intelligent, and floundering in foster care. At our first hearing, it was easy to see that one thing Dan had going for him was a set of grandparents who deeply loved him, though they couldn't take another child into their home. The grandparents spent time with Dan, were at each hearing, and were active in all phases of his life. Dan's life in foster care was typical; he had been moved

201

several times; he'd been in some good homes and some not-so-good homes. Watching Dan, it was obvious he was pretty good at reading body language and he could read lips some, but he didn't sign. I asked the caseworker, and she explained that locally there was no one to teach signing.

"What about the school for the deaf in St. Petersburg?" I asked.

"Well, Your Honor, we asked the mom for permission to send him, but she said, 'No.'"

I was puzzled and asked, "Am I missing something here? Apparently the mom hasn't been to court in years, though she always gets notice of the hearings. She visits him sporadically but refuses to be involved in his life. The Department has custody of Dan with full authority to authorize any needed medical treatment, place him in schools, and change his residence....?"

"Yes, ma'am."

"So, is there any reason, other than the mom saying' no,' that the Department has not sent Dan to school to learn how to sign?"

"No, Your Honor."

As I quietly pondered the mother's resistance, I wondered if she was afraid for Dan to learn to communicate, afraid of what he might tell law enforcement. But I had no idea why the Department gave a damn—legally or morally—what the icepick mom thought.

I ordered the Department to send Dan to school in St. Petersburg. His grandparents were delighted and volunteered to drive him down. At later hearings the grandparents gave me status reports. Dan had quickly learned to sign and was doing extremely well academically. I hoped for the best.

I saw Dan one more time. When he finished his schooling in St. Pete, he returned to foster care and attended the next hearing. He was a good looking and physically fit 12 year-old with blond hair, light blue eyes, and a scrappy attitude.

I learned at later hearings that as Dan increased in stature, he also increased in rage. He became progressively more violent and as a teenager was locked up in a program for delinquents. His violence grew into manhood, and he was promoted to the adult prison.

I can't image how angry I'd be if two times my own mother had held me down and stuck ice picks through my ear-drums and then for years drifted in and out of my life, pretending that she loved me. What if I couldn't cuss or yell my rage, what if the only thing that people seemed to respond to was violence. Violence: a way to roar in sign language, a way to scream at a world that never gave a damn anyway.

So, in our land of opportunity, Dan matured from a blue-eyed toddler, to a deaf victim of child abuse, to a child stashed in serial foster homes, to a youngster alone in a residential school hundreds of miles from the world he knew. He ripened, learning violence as his means of communication; then he was locked up, and his rage continued to smolder. For Dan, the love of grandparents and the occasional intervention of others were just not enough. What would I say to him if he could hear me? Is there anything I should have done differently? Dan is one of the children who has painted my soul with the sounds and colors of his life.

❧ ❧ ❧

I'm grateful that Cole knows nothing of the world of silent violence. But he knows falcons and explains that their second bird, Pete, is always the gentleman. Because of a difference in his early training, Pete is not a squawker. One-third smaller than the female Piggy, Pete (known as a tercel) is a petite, sleek bird. Cole explains, "This is just the way guys are built in the falcon world."

I guess there are people who wonder, "Why would you jump out of a perfectly good airplane with a falcon?" Aside from the simple fun factor, Ken wants to document the vertical rate of descent of a falcon and prove that the falcon, a wild and free spirit, would agree to a merged venture with man.

Ken flies his ultra-light to exercise the birds; someone else pilots the airplane when he and Piggy ride up together so that he can jump and Piggy follow. The first time I watch Ken work Piggy, he taxis the ultra-light down the runway while

Piggy waits, untethered, on a fence post. With quiet majesty, she stretches her wings and takes off in free flight, following Ken as he ascends into the open blue skies. I plop down on the grass with tears of wonder. As Ken circles higher, Piggy follows. When Ken releases the lure (a small but sturdy bag garnished with bloody quail and trailing on a long rope attached to the rear of the ultra-light), Piggy pauses mid-air, tucks her wings, drops her head, and goes into a stoop. She easily catches the falling lure and flies with it to the runway where she lands. While Piggy plucks at the lure, Suzanne mindfully walks up to her and slips the jess, or leather strap, on Piggy's leg. Using a second piece of quail, Suzanne entices Piggy to step from the lure onto her fist where Piggy finishes her meal.

"It is not the path which is the difficulty; rather it is the difficulty which is the path."
Soren Kierkegaard

CHAPTER 13.
FROM NORTHWEST WASHINGTON TO
NORTHWEST FLORIDA:
A broken heart and a new life

While on San Juan Island, I buy a round trip plane ticket from Seattle to Pensacola in anticipation of my grandchild's birth. When it's time to go, I leave my 5th wheel parked at Ken and Suzanne's. Bruin and I sit in the truck waiting for the ferry and I explain to him that I really don't want to leave and yet I can't wait to meet my grandson. Back on the mainland, I take Bruin to my skydiving friends from the Montana boogie. Bill and Amy live south of Tacoma and insist Bruin stay with them rather than going to "jail" (their word for the kennel). So I leave my 100-pound four-legged friend to sleep on their couch, hang out with their two dogs, and play in their yard until I return three weeks later. Bill sees to it that Bruin e-mails me. Generally Bruin complains about how snotty their small dog is, but he also sends photos of himself in the wading pool to prove he's just fine without me.

Flying back to Florida triggers many responses. It feels eerie, like I've crossed a time warp. It also feels like I've never left. It feels like I belong here and like I'm a stranger, maybe even an alien.

Al invited me to stay with him though he'd be going out of town for work in a week. Being with Al again—in his arms, in his home, in his life—is a huge piece of being back in Northwest Florida. We laugh a lot; life is good. Although the relationship has not been exclusive during my travels, it is far from casual. The affection we share is deep and wide.

On Monday, Al declined the invitation to join me for dinner with friends at Pensacola Beach but said that he'd meet me back at the house. After dinner, I go back to his home. He doesn't. I wait ... and wait. I leave messages on his cell phone. As the hours crawl by, sleeping is not an option so I read all of Anne Lamott's *Traveling Mercies*. I call the local hospitals; he's not been in a wreck. I call the Highway Patrol; he's not been arrested for DUI. I move through the hours like a zombie. As the sun comes up, I pack up.

As I look around to be sure I've not left anything, the phone rings, "Hi," he says.

I sputter in relief, "Are you OK!??"

"Sure," he mumbles.

My words tumble, "Where have you been?!?"

After too long of a pause, he answers, "Well, I.... I had supper with this woman I know. We had too much to drink. So I just spent the night with her. I'm heading home now."

My mind isn't working. Nothing is working. Nothing makes sense. I'm too hurt to be mad, and I don't seem to have enough air to speak above a whisper. I hang up the phone and put my suitcase in the rental car. Then I wait because I need to talk with him face-to-face; I need to make some sense of this. I need to leave with some understanding. We agreed we would not be in an exclusive relationship while I was gone. Yet, for me, a non-exclusive relationship with someone I love never meant that on my short trip home he could leave me in his bed to go sleep with another woman.

Two hours later Al is still not home. I feel betrayed and lost. It seems as though he's cut the last major cord binding my life to Northwest Florida, and I'm in danger of floating off into a black hole. How am I supposed to launch my far-flung plans without his push; how am I to dream without him laughing and telling me to go for it? Who can I call when I'm lonely? Who will notice when I get lost? Without his home, what will I call home? I drive away, bleary eyed and stunned. I look back at Al's home through the rearview mirror of the rental car, and I hear the words of a defendant, a young man who taught me that I have a choice in how I respond to Al.

❦ ❦ ❦

"The weak can never forgive. Forgiveness is the attribute of the strong."
Mahatma Gandhi

A lesson in forgiveness
    The State and Defense had agreed to a sentence of three years straight probation with a $2,000 fine on the charge of driving while license suspended and causing an accident resulting in death; I accepted the negotiated plea. Anthony Hill was a young black male in his early 20's with a driver's license suspended for failure to pay a traffic fine; he was arrested because he ran a stop sign and hit the victim who was traveling at a high speed. In Civil Court there would be issues of comparative negligence—what percentage of responsibility did each driver bear for the accident (running a stop sign vs. excessive speeding)—and the verdict would be measured in dollars, not issues of freedom. In Criminal Court it is a felony to combine Driving While License Suspended with an accident involving death, though the suspended driver's license certainly did not cause the crash.
    The victim was a 19-year-old white male, a Marine whose parents drove over from Louisiana to address the Court before sentence was imposed. As I called the case, they asked Security to move the Defendant farther away from them. Then as they walked toward the wooden podium to speak, they visibly recoiled from the Defendant, as though he were a water moccasin. The mother read a lengthy, gut-wrenching account of her pain and grief. I listened, hoping that somehow giving them these minutes would help with their healing. When the mother finished speaking to me, she turned toward the Defendant and in a tone that suddenly changed to cold steel, she avenged, "Each morning and each evening, when I think of my son, I wish it was Anthony Hill who was dead instead."
    The father then read his lengthy testimonial of loss, grief, and pain. He, too, choked up, and then stopped to wipe tears. It was hard watching their deep grief six days after my mother's funeral. I had to back away, emotionally and mentally, so I could keep my

*voice strong and do my job. As he finished, the father glared at me
and said, "Judge, how would you feel if it was your son who had
been killed? Then what would you want as justice?"*

*Though I spoke not a word, my mind was flashing, "Look buddy,
you know this is a negotiated plea. Don't try to put that on me. Plus,
the Defendant's suspended driver's license didn't kill your son—that
was caused by the Defendant running a stop sign and your son's
excessive speed. If the license had not been suspended for an old ticket,
your son would still be dead but the case would not be in Criminal
Court. And what does 'justice' mean, anyway?" Aloud I said
only, "Thank you for your comments, sir."*

*I asked, "Does the Defendant care to be heard before sentence is
imposed?"*

Anthony said, "Judge, I want to speak to the parents."

*Though I had no idea what would happen next, I responded,
"You need to look at them, not me, if there is something you want to
say to them."*

*Anthony turned, looked directly at the parents sitting on the front
row, and apologized, said he thought of the accident every day, and
that if he had one wish it would not be for money or success, but to
bring their son back. Then he added, "If it had been reversed, if I
had been killed and your son was standing here, my mother would
never say, never wish your son was dead instead of me. I'm sure of
that. She would never wish such pain for you. And I forgive you for
saying that about me."*

❈ ❈ ❈

As I drive away from Al's, I call Carolyne, one of my
skydiving friends. "Can I come and stay with you? For a couple
of weeks?"

"Sure, girlfriend! I'll leave ya a key."

I spend the day in her backyard, watching the herons feed
on the sandbars of the bayou, watching the tide come in and
go out, watching the live oaks sway gently in the wind.
Watching without words, without understanding. That night I

sleep, or rather lay, on her couch, moving gingerly to guard the large hole in the center of my chest and the broken pieces of my heart that are now clanking around on the outside of me, utterly unprotected.

About midnight, Clay calls on my cell phone to say Joan is in labor.

"Can I come, son?"

"Not yet, Mom. Her parents aren't here. We're doing this on our own. I'll call you."

Then shortly after sunrise, Clay calls again, "Mom. The baby's here. It's a little boy, just like they said. He and Joan are both fine. You can come now if you like."

I walk back to the edge of the bayou; I'm crying again but these are happy tears. "A new life. A new beginning." Rather than dance a jig, I turn a cartwheel on the damp grass, under the massive maternal live oaks. I leave Carolyne a quick note and draw on it a series of stick figures of the new grandma with a big smile, doing a cartwheel.

All the confusion and pain of the last two nights are blown off the page when I walk into the recovery room and see Clay holding his son, my grandson. Clay holds that tiny bundle like a pro. He pulls the blanket away from Will's face, and we talk. But he doesn't offer to let me hold him, not right away. He acts like this is his son. I smile and think, "Your point is well made, son." And I silently pray that I can keep my enthusiasm under control while honoring and supporting Clay and Joan as THE parents, the directors of this new life. Because of some serious last minute complications, Joan had a Caesarean, but she and Will are doing great.

This new grandmother, on the other hand, has been blind-sided by an enormous bolt of pure, unfiltered love energy, the intensity of which is almost embarrassing. I've always adored Clay (and the ground he walks on), and I have a huge place in my heart for children. But this is different. A few grandmother friends had tried to warn me, but no warning could have prepared me, not really. I spend hours outside the hospital nursery window watching Will with tears of hope and wonder running down my face–amazed that this love could peacefully co-exist with my broken heart, astonished that such awe and promise were possible when I also felt that so much of my world had come to an end.

On their second night home, Clay and Joan accept my offer of help. Clay hands Will to me with detailed instructions, goes to their bedroom, closes the door, and falls into an exhausted sleep. I rock Will, astonished by the gift my son has given; he trust me enough to hand me his son and then to go to sleep. Will doesn't do much sleeping during our first night together. Unlike his mom, I haven't had my stomach cut open; unlike his dad, I haven't been awake for most of the last 72 hours. So I rock and smile; Will's tiny fussing is an echo of my wonder.

The Saturday before I fly back to Washington, I'm to meet skydiving friends at the drop zone in Elberta, Alabama. I explain it all to Will the night before, "Granny's going skydiving tomorrow. Then she'll come back and see you. Jumping is one of those things grannies do."

Going to the DZ is like going home–the plane, the people, and the area I know so well. The spot[17] on the first jump was bad, so only two on the load of 18 jumpers made it back to the DZ. I was not one of those two. Elberta is a farming community, so when you land off-DZ, there are many safe options. With an off-DZ landing at a metropolitan drop zone, you may be at risk of being impaled on a tree, becoming road kill on the Interstate, or landing on a rooftop like a crippled reindeer. At Elberta it's generally a question of which crop you land in, while avoiding Farmer McNasty.[18] I land in an empty pasture. Michelle, the Gypsy Trash girlfriend who is young enough to be my daughter, opened her parachute lower

---

[17]Spot - the point at which you exit the plane for your skydive. The spot is determined based on the speed and direction of the winds. With a good spot, you land back at the DZ.
[18]Farmer McNasty - a farmer who is not skydiver-friendly. The neighbors are generally kind and intrigued by our skydiving, but avoiding Farmer McNasty is a universal joke among jumpers.

and would land farther from the DZ. To avoid power lines Michelle choses to land in a soybean field. When jumpers land out, someone from the DZ will usually drive to you so you don't have to walk long distances (sometimes miles), while carrying your parachute in your arms.

Paige picks me up in her car, and I tell her how to find Michelle: go south about a quarter of a mile to a field I'd landed in the year before. By the time we arrive, Michelle has walked to the edge of the field near the road. I help pass the 210 square feet of her canopy under the barbed wire without snagging it. Then I hold the bottom wire up as she squirms under and crawls between my legs into the wet drainage ditch, muttering the whole time about how I need to be careful so I don't snag her new nylon jump suit on the barbs. Home! Familiar smells–fresh plowed earth, soybeans with knee-high weeds in the wet ditch and the playfulness of friends. Michelle is covered in mud. She explains that she had to choose between landing crosswind or cross-row; unfortunately she chose cross-row. The rows of soybeans were deeper than she thought and the soybean plants higher. Her foot caught on a row, and she did a face-plant, baptizing her brand new jump suit. She isn't hurt, but she has to put up with a lot of ribbing there and back at the DZ.

Late that afternoon we make a beach jump over the Gulf of Mexico, landing at the Flora-Bama Bar. The setting sun has painted the water gold, orange, pink, and purple; the sugar-white sand squeaks as I land. Holding our parachutes, we maneuver through the crowd of tourists to the bar to pick up the pitcher of beer the manager gives to each jumper. Later we eat fried mullet, hushpuppies, and coleslaw. A perfect day. Home. Gravity. Laughter. Friends.

I'm here for three weeks, long enough to cross the emotional warp from Northwest Washington to Northwest Florida. Long enough to touch and remember some of the reasons Northwest Florida can feel like home. Time to toast my girlfriends with raw oysters piled onto saltine crackers, nailed down with the exact alchemy of horseradish and catsup. Time to walk along the edge of the Gulf with waves rolling, soothing my mind. Time to watch the sun rise and set, playing hide and go seek with pines and oaks but not with mountains. In spite of my wanderlust, I settle in, feel comfortable, feel loved, and feel alive. And then it's time to go.

The day before my flight back to Seattle, I get to keep Will for the afternoon. We walk outside to talk to Mr. Squirrel and to watch the clouds scurry by. Inside we rock. I sing, remembering more and more of the countless songs my mom and Katie, our beloved housekeeper, sang to me. "Sure as the vine grows 'round the stump, you are my darlin' sugar lump!" Will is restless, and I stretch out across the bed with him on my chest as he catnaps. With his miniature heart beating through my sternum, my heart, shattered the day before his birth by a big guy, is being wrapped and protected by a love as resilient as a spider-web. The rhythm of this new life works a gentle magic, making the world "all better." Then Joan comes home. She works in sales, is ambitious, and very good at her job. She has a quick humor and a good eye for design. Tears come easy for Joan, and I don't want this to be difficult. I make silly jokes as I leave, hoping my heart will survive, hoping I won't embarrass both of us with a flood of tears.

The next morning I have last-minute chores to do. Then I meet Clay, Joan, and Will in the mall parking lot for a few minutes of goodbyes. After a round of hugs and a kiss on Will's tiny forehead, we retreat to our separate vehicles. I sit quietly and watch as they drive away through a parking lot blurred by tears. Tears so deep, so overwhelming, so confusing. How can I belong, truly belong, in both Northwests? I know I could live in the Pacific Northwest; Washington personifies my new life–a life of writing, traveling, indulging my curiosities. This is the first time in my 53 years that I've left home, expectations, and roles. It's my turn to eat the whole box of Whitman's Samplers, without sharing with a large family. My turn. My choice. Take a bite, and if it's not what I really want, put it back for later or for never. I love the freedom and the anonymity. But then there's this delicate bundle in my son's arms, that diminutive heart that beat against my chest the day before.

It's time to go; Bruin is waiting for me in Washington.

I have one more commitment before I catch my afternoon flight. The retirement party for Nancy Gilliam, the only other female Circuit Judge, is at 1 p.m. at the Courthouse, and for that I have to get my judge's face back in place, but I refuse to put on pantyhose. Through my years on the Bench I shared a close friendship with two judges–Nancy and Terry Terrell. We trusted one another and would toss around ideas or problems and share inside jokes and anguish. Terry and I sat together in Juvenile for three years and then again at the main courthouse in Pensacola. Nancy and I had offices on the same floor for several years, so it was easier to catch one another in the midst of hectic dockets.

I've not been back to the courthouse since my own retirement, and I come in through the public entrance. A law enforcement officer recognizes me, waves me around the metal detector, and gives me a hug before returning to his duties. I ride the crowded public elevator to visit friends on the 5th floor. Then I take the elevator down to the main floor. Nancy's reception, like mine, would be in Courtroom 101, the one designated for Domestic Violence hearings and retirement receptions. Back in a courtroom, I feel awkward, like I've come to school late, like everyone else is in class working and has been since the first bell at 8 a.m. But then I notice several attorneys standing where I'd packed my parachute four months before, and I smile.

One of the judges asks, "Has it been hard to make the transition?"

I laugh, "No, it's been embarrassingly easy!"

My first visit to the courthouse since my retirement is a

brief whirlwind. There are many hands to shake, a few necks to hug, and, of course, I have to flash pictures of the new grandbaby. Soon it's time to leave that familiar world of rules, schedules, wooden benches, attorneys dressed in business suits, and friendly law enforcement officers, for I have a 3 p.m. plane to catch.

I leave the Courthouse, as I had come in, through the public entrance. I leave to go back to my first name, Laura, back to the San Juan Islands, to open days and open roads. I leave, to fly back to Seattle, to Bruin, to my home on wheels. I will go from familiar heat and humidity to damp cold. From being known, to being unknown; from being a visible power figure to being anonymous; from being recognized by strangers to being a stranger with a strange accent. From one northwest to another. I go, leaving my heart in the palm of Will's tiny hand.

FROM NORTHWEST FLORIDA TO NORTHWEST WASHINGTON

I arrive in Washington late so I spend the night in a motel. The next morning I drive over to get Bruin at Bill and Amy's, my skydiving friends on whose couch Bruin has slept these last three weeks. It's so good to see my dog again, though I'm not sure he missed me. After a short visit, it's time to go. Bill interrupts our light-hearted leave-taking to go to his office; he comes out with a small green wooden plaque with an Irish blessing printed on it. He says, "OK, this is weird. I've had this thing for years, but suddenly thought you might like it." To Bill's surprise and my embarrassment, I begin crying as he hands me a duplicate of the plaque that had hung in my parents' room, familiar words often quoted by my dad;

May the road rise up to meet you
May the wind be always at your back
May the sun shine warm upon your face
And rains fall soft upon your fields

214

And until we meet again
May God hold you in the hollow of His Hand.

I've been at their home less than an hour, a familiar place with friends I love. But it's time for me to leave. I don't know whether I'll see Bill and Amy again; I know I'll never see my dad again. This leaving is poignantly familiar.

Bruin and I drive back to Anacortes to catch the ferry to San Juan Island where my 5th wheel is parked.

I love being back on the island but soon I have to admit that the days are growing short, and there's much to see before I cross the mountains ahead of the first snow. So early in October, I say good-bye to Ken and Suzanne, hook up the RV, and return to the docks. With quiet tears of confusion I wait in line for the ferry. It's time to go, to point the truck south toward my grandson, but I also don't want to leave the peace of these islands. As that old saying goes, "More than one thing can be true."

After months on the road, I continue to charge out across the country in confidence–only to round a corner and screech to a halt, white-knuckled and teetering on the edge of this over-sized dream that is both a blessing and a curse.

Waiting for the ferry, I watch the water swirl around the dock and remember other leave-takings, particularly my recent farewell to everything I'd worked for and all I knew–a leaving that felt like both death and life.

✦ ✦ ✦

My opening farewell

I plan to retire in May of 2000 but I haven't made the official announcement. First I'll send a letter to Chief Judge Kuder and copy the other judges in our Circuit. But I'll probably wait until December of 1999 to send my formal resignation to the Governor–still hedging my bets in case I wake up filled with reason or contract a fast-moving terminal disease.

My opening farewell to the legal world will begin without fanfare when I submit my resignation to the Governor, to say quietly, "Excuse me, but I'm leaving now." Do I expect those in the legal profession to understand and support me? No, I expect responses like sniper bullets, "What? What! What!!!! You can't do that!!" Then the eyes of the hardcore, those judges and attorneys gleefully entrenched in The System, will quickly glass over with total detachment. Or is it disdain? Disdain for anyone who could leave this world of law and order; a world of power—the power of enforcing rules—a world in which we as judges force people to do as we say and even be polite to us in the process. And as I've been taught too well, to leave is often viewed by those left behind as an act of betrayal.

There's not much I can say, not much that would be heard by that crowd who has no real interest in understanding me, those comfortable with their prepared security, those who value assets but not adventures, those who do not need to seek because they believe they already have all the answers. Gratefully, there are also those who will listen deeply, ask good questions, and care what I do, whether or not they understand.

But what do I say in farewell to my dad, the one who truly tugs at my soul? Perhaps the person I've loved most deeply. How do I explain? Will I ever get him to accept my farewell, my leaving his love, the Law? Will he see this as an act of betrayal? He's been dead for five years, yet he colors my thoughts and actions as though he were waiting in the next room. And so I struggle for his understanding and doubt that I will ever earn his approval.

Dad didn't do farewells. He never left his first love, the Law. He never left Mom though for long periods they were both miserable. He died in the small town he was born in. Dad believed in sticking it out.

I was raised Southern Baptist, in the forever mode, as in "til death you do part." I was taught there were no excuses, so I was to shut up and try harder. After 13 years of trying harder, I screwed up the courage to divorce my husband, the father of my only child. Now, I can see that relationship was wrong for me, the real me. But at the

216

time it was all I could do to leave, without explanation.

It was my second year of law school; Clay was eight and in the second grade. As Clay and I rode from Tallahassee to my parents' home in Milton, I explained that his dad and I were getting divorced, that it was not his fault or about him, that we both loved him and would never divorce or leave him. I pointed out that I'd told him before anyone else, including his grandparents, because he was the most important. As soon as we got into my parents' house, Clay asked, "When are you going to tell Grandmamma and Granddaddy what you told me?"

So much for picking my time. I sat on their couch with Clay and stumbled through my explanation. Though I knew the rules ("What God has joined together, let no man set asunder"), though it was blasphemy, I was going to give up. They listened quietly and said nothing to encourage or discourage my decision.

Two days later my sister-in-law and I were waiting in the emergency room of a hospital in St. Augustine, Florida, where Dad had been delivered by ambulance from the Circuit Judges' Conference. Dad had a history of heart problems and once again had chest pains while unwinding with a bottle of scotch on a business trip. After Jackie and I talked of Dad and his needs, I told her of the divorce.

She asked, "How did your dad take it?"

I looked around, laughed nervously, and said "Not too well."

Now 20 years after telling Dad I was leaving my marriage, I'm nervous about telling him I'm leaving the Bench. I don't have to leave, of course. I have two years left on this six-year term, and I doubt I'd draw opposition after that. But if I stay? I'll need more prescriptions for the migraines, waves of stomach acids, chronic cough, and serial sinus infections. I'll need to drink more and feel less. I'll need something to calm me down so I can sleep without thinking. If I don't leave, I need to say farewell to Laura. I'll have to watch her slip below the waters again and again, until at some point she stops fighting and then stops breathing.

But would Dad understand? I don't think so. I'm walking away from his life, what he lived for and did so well until he ran out of energy, until he had nothing left to give to his love, the Law. He really wanted me to follow through, to fight the good fight, his fight. Sharing his profession was a unique way to get him to talk with me, to love me, and it worked. I have no regrets about the connection we shared through law. But now, at age 53, it feels like time to move on, to say farewell to what I have known so well and worked so hard to get.

No, I don't believe Dad would ever understand, and that's the hardest, saddest part of my leave-taking. After some time, some messy time, I also believe he'd accept it; he'd never like it, but he'd accept it, with an "OK, baby." And he would worry.

So, for my farewell I look and feel like a five-year-old on a bike that's too tall. I push off from the fence - teetering - determined - scared - no training wheels - no dad around to catch me or even to watch. The whole family - everyone - is in the house doing something else

✦ ✦ ✦

"Experience is one thing you can't get for nothing."
Oscar Wilde

CHAPTER 14.
OREGON:
Errant teeth and other things I can't fix

My heart feels tender as the ferry begins its tack from San Juan Island to the mainland, but outside on the deck I feel buoyed by the salt air and gentle edges of this world. I look up to see a single-engine airplane homing in on a stretch of land ahead, and smile as I remember another adventure these islands offered me.

Ken had an appointment for his flight physical in Arlington, about 45 minutes away by air, and I tagged along for the flight, for the view. From the air, the water has a clear blue quality; you can see gulls and seals (no whales around), sailboats and fishing boats. I'm fascinated with the islands; the more remote, the better I like them. As we flew, I played games with myself, picking out where I'd live. Of course, I'd own and fly a plane. We flew across Whidbey Island near Deception Pass Bridge where Bruin and I had stayed, then across Skagit Valley where gazillions of tulips are grown, and across the mud flats at the mouth of the Skagit River, red with silt from upstream. We fly low—between 800 and 1,500 feet. My kind of ride. My heart sung with questions of learning to fly, buying a Cessna 180, traveling by plane rather than RV. A bush pilot with a smile.

The next afternoon Ken started some charcoal for steaks and asked, "Do you wanna make a jump?" (Meaning skydive from his plane and land on his property). I'd refused similar invitations back in Alabama for a private jump onto a private landing strip, because I was afraid, afraid of becoming bug splatter.

"I'm ready," I responded.

A few minutes later I stood by the BBQ grill with my parachute and a smile. Ken banked the fire, and we walked over to his plane. While the coals got hot, we taxied down the long grass runway and lifted off. As we climbed to altitude, I began to orient from the air, locating Ken's house and runway, noting how it's situated in relation to the highway and the shores of the island, distinguishing it from other grass runways - watching for more landmarks, a lake here, a building with a red roof there. I knew that when I opened my canopy, it could spin me 180 degrees, so I'd suddenly be looking at what had been behind me. I'm easily disoriented even on the ground; I didn't want the embarrassment of landing on the wrong grass runway or a long walk back. I took deep breaths to help ease my fear. There was no radio control tower for the island, and another plane wouldn't be expecting a bright-colored falling object—me. It was up to Ken and me to keep an eye out for air traffic, and I didn't want to end my trip as a splatter on the windshield of an unsuspecting airplane. As we flew out over the San Juan straits, the sun was beginning to lay down blankets of gold across the water.

Ken said, "I'll take you to Ten-five."[19]

"No, Five's fine." (I'm thinking, "I want to jump, play a little, open high, and enjoy the parachute ride. But the longer I'm in free fall, the greater my chance of becoming a hood ornament on a surprised plane.")

Ken added, "I don't mind."

"No, line me up at about Five."

Soon he gave me a nod and yelled, "Door!"

A quick glance at my altimeter showed we were at 5,700 feet. I opened the top-hinged passenger door, leaned my head out and looked straight down. My 5th wheel was directly below us, and there were no planes in sight. I smiled at Ken, waved, and dove out the door. As I fell away from the plane I turned my head to watch Ken; he tipped the wing to slam the door shut and flew away. I turned a couple of 360's, and after about 15 seconds opened my parachute at 3,500 feet. In spite of my pre-planning, I could not find their property in free fall. Under canopy, things began to look familiar again, and I land on my butt on their runway, adding San Juan grass stains to the Alabama soybeans, red Colorado dirt, and brown Montana dust smeared on the rear

---

[19]Ten-five - 10,500 feet, the typical altitude for jumping from a Cessna.

of my jump suit. I land happy and proud of myself, though Ken gives me grief for the butt landing.

Too soon, the ferry reaches the mainland; I maneuver my truck and RV out of the metal belly and begin the trip south. I plan to spend a couple of days on the coast, make a few skydives in Southern California, and then meet a friend in Phoenix on October 31. I've signed up for nine days of skydive training with Arizona Airspeed over Thanksgiving; then I'll drive back to Florida for Christmas.

Portions of the Oregon coast are postcard scenes with waves crashing onto high, rocky cliffs; other stretches are wide, sandy, and rock-less. Some of the beaches at low tide are a quarter of a mile wide, flat with an eastern bookend of knobby and treeless brown sand dunes. In the less populated areas, it's assumed you're there to drive on the hard beach sand, and the roads lead directly onto the beach, with no parking options other than the sand. The moods and rhythms of the ocean set the tempo for daily life on the coast; local stores hand out tidal charts.

Late one afternoon Bruin and I drive north on Highway101 and then turn left on a side road that dead-ends at the sunset. I turn north on the beach into a heavy ground fog and encounter only seagulls. I can get disoriented coming out of the Wal-Mart parking lot, and I don't relish the idea of making a turn back to the south to then drive to the Mexican border looking for that one cut in the sameness of sand dunes that would return us to the 5th wheel. So I set my odometer to mark our beginning, for fear of getting lost in the beautiful haze. The surf is rough, skidding up to the shore from faraway fantasy places like China and Japan. The odometer trick works—three miles north and then three miles south—and we're back at our beginning.

But the simple tricks don't work in my search for justice, and sometimes I fear getting lost in the haze of uncertainty. The worst day on the road may be less complicated than a good day on the Bench.

The next morning I hook up and move further south. It's late afternoon when I approach my assigned site at the next RV park. I swing the truck wide to the left, but quickly have to turn right to avoid a light pole and dumpster. As I turn hard I tell Bruin, "Oops, the rear end of the rig may hit that bush." I don't want to take the time and energy to back out of that maze, so I decide it'll be OK if the 5th wheel just brushes against that little bitty bush. Wrong! I forgot that the truck has the power to pull down a bridge if the RV could hold together as the battering ram; I forgot that I can't count on the truck to give even a hint that the 5th wheel is in trouble. As I pull forward, I watch the bush easily slide down the side of the RV. When I get out of the truck, my heart leaks out through my shoes. Mt. Rainier was hiding under that squatty rhododendron bush. It looks as though the vengeful god of RV's has taken a king-size can opener and cut off the rear quarter panel of the 5th wheel. The side is covered in nasty looking scratches, parts are lying on the ground, and other pieces are dangling like loose teeth. Errant teeth, calling me back to the mouth of a murder victim and an inopportune appointment I had with the dentist. A murder trial I was asked to decide without a jury–a judge trial that was a graphic reminder that there may be no easy answers in this business of seeking justice and that justice can be messy, especially when the State has no case without granting immunity to someone involved in the crime.

❖ ❖ ❖

The dentist

It was Tuesday, and I had a dentist appointment at noon for a crown. But first I needed to handle this trial, a first-degree capital murder case that the State described as a drug deal–or drug party– gone bad. Glenn, the victim, was found suffocated, face down in a small puddle with mud packed down to his vocal cords. He had been stabbed repeatedly with a cheap steak knife that was too flimsy to penetrate his chest cavity.

The State had a dead body but no suspects until Victor came in with an offer to turn State's evidence. The State made a deal that Victor would not be prosecuted and he would testify against the others. Based on Victor' testimony, the Grand Jury indicted three men (Timmy, Cliff, and Hank). Tuesday was Timmy's trial.

Because of some unique legal twists, I had heard Victor testify several times, and he'd not told the same story twice. I listened as he swore to at least four totally convincing though exceptionally inconsistent versions of the murder, and I thought, "He's really good. He should go to Hollywood." Though Victor's testimony left many questions unanswered, one thing was clear from the physical evidence: this was a brutal murder.

Several months before this trial, in response to a defense motion, Victor admitted under oath that his varying statements were inconsistent with his first testimony to the Grand Jury, and in the process of explaining himself, Victor gave yet another convincing version of what happened the night Glenn died. He offered a lengthy, rambling explanation for the various changes in his story—why he was mistaken when he testified before the Grand Jury and how he was right now. The legal reality remained that the Grand Jury relied on one version of "facts" when issuing its indictment and the stories Victor told later were simply not the same. So after listening carefully to the arguments of the State and Defense and doing additional research on my own, I dismissed the Grand Jury's indictment. I was silently amazed, for I'd never heard of a judge dismissing a murder indictment. I thought with a smile, "It's a good thing I'm not up for re-election this year." I released Cliff and Hank from jail but held Timmy because the State announced they would take only his case back to the Grand Jury.

Based on Victor's most recent testimony, the Grand Jury re-indicted Timmy. The State did not pursue Cliff and Hank because of weaknesses in their cases, and the two of them remained on the street with Victor. The week before his trial, Timmy asked to waive his right to a jury trial and have me sit as both judge and jury, and the Prosecutor agreed. Timmy, about five feet, seven inches and maybe 160 pounds, with a scruffy beard and unkempt hair, came into Court in the jail-house-issue green jump suit and orange plastic shower shoes. As he had been during each of the other hearings, he was polite, soft spoken, and reserved. His lawyer explained his preference for a judge trial, and I asked, "Sir, do you understand you have the absolute right to a trial by a jury of twelve people? The jurors are coming in, and we've scheduled your trial for next Tuesday." Timmy looked me straight in the eye and said, "I don't wont no jury. I knows I can have one - I've had 'em before. I jest wanna fair trial. So I want you to do it, Judge." I looked down and took a deep breath. After many legal steps, I began the trial on Tuesday, without a jury to back me up, without twelve people to assume responsibility on the question of guilt.

And my dentist appointment? I had broken off a quarter of a rear molar and was scheduled for a crown, at noon, on Tuesday.

We started the trial very early on Tuesday, and without a jury, we moved fast. Soon I was sitting in the courtroom listening to the Medical Examiner while looking at eight-by-ten color photos of this dead, mutilated thing that only vaguely, but too much, resembled a man. His two front teeth were sticking straight out. I couldn't decide how they got at that angle, and why they hadn't fallen out. As if reading my mind, the Medical Examiner said, "The front teeth were totally dislodged but soft tissue has held them in the mouth." I thought, "I guess if he'd have stood up, his teeth would have fallen out." Then I stuck my tongue in the hole where my tooth had been and looked at my watch. The attorneys had assured me they'd be through by 11:45, but it didn't look like they were going to make it.

I'd never wanted to witness the changes a human body makes as it passes beyond the ordinary and moves into another state. Yet spread out before me were yet more photos from the autopsy. I looked at the eight-by-ten color glossies of something where a mouth would belong, but this looked more like a posthole recently packed with dark dirt, with white shovel-like things scattered around the opening at weird angles. Again, I wondered how the teeth got at those angles. One eye was open; it didn't look particularly dead. The other eye was partially covered with mud, and there were a couple of maggots on the eyeball.

That eye looked very dead. And then there were those front teeth. I wondered, "What did Glenn want to say?"

The Medical Examiner explained, "The cause of death was asphyxiation. State's Exhibit 12, the knife found at the scene, is a cheap steak knife with a thin blade and a plastic handle. So it bent rather than penetrate the heavy cartilage around the heart and lungs. These random blows do not qualify as the cause of death. Most of the 14 knife blows struck bone. You'll notice, though, these wounds in the palms of the hands and on the backside of the forearms. Those are referred to as defensive wounds, consistent with the victim trying to block the knife with his hands and forearms."

And while I still had all of the crime scene and autopsy photos spread out on the bench, the State's star witness took the stand. Victor's story was somewhat like the other stories he'd told, and in almost all of them, he said he saw Timmy holding Glenn while either Cliff, or Hank, or Cliff and Hank, or Hank and an unknown male, beat Glenn up. Victor always said he never touched Glenn.

Victor looked so ordinary, sitting there in his creased jeans and blue plaid shirt. He sounded believable, though the story of the day was yet another new one. He peppered his speech with otherwise innocuous phrases, "I swear... God help me... I'll tell you what ..."

The one thing he said that I believed was–he was there and saw what happened. Was he actively involved in the murder? My gut said that was very likely; my head said Victor wasn't the one on trial and the State had nothing without him except a decaying body and an open case. I watched Victor as he testified and pulled back inside my robe, inside myself, knowing this is not a perfect world, knowing Victor was a free man, regardless of my decision in Timmy's case.

Victor described a party with everybody on crack, how he and Glenn were smoking marijuana with crack powdered through it. It was not a nice party. But, Glenn certainly didn't agree to die; in fact he was damn stubborn about it.

The defense attorney was impeaching Victor when I called the attorneys to the bench at 11:30. I reminded them I had a 12:00 dentist appointment and said we'd have to reschedule the balance of the trial. They didn't want to quit, so they assured me they could finish in 20 minutes or so. I stuck my tongue in the hole in my tooth and glanced down at the photo of Glenn and his two front teeth. Twenty minutes more and I'd miss my dentist appointment.

"Counsel, you have only five minutes left."

"Judge, could we just wait for you? Could you be back in two hours?"

I thought, "I don't want to sit in the dentist chair for two hours and then hurry back here without lunch to look at autopsy photos and errant, dead teeth as my drooping face comes back to life. I don't have a jury to accommodate today; I'll accommodate myself for a change." I said simply, "No, Counsel. I'll hear the rest of the case at noon on Thursday." I sighed, knowing that Thursday would be a crazy, too-full day of divorce cases, and that I'd just penciled in the balance of a murder trial for lunch. But they could finish this trial in two hours, Thursday was another day, and by then my tooth would be fixed.

I adjourned court and was only a few minutes late to the dentist. I lay back in the chair, and the dentist pulled down the glaring round light. Then she put the long-handled cotton swab of bitter medicine on my gums. I thought of Glenn's teeth as I caught a glimpse of the long needle going into the back of my opened mouth. The procedure took a long time but it wasn't too bad. As I stood up to leave, the dentist said, "I've never seen a tooth with so many fractures. The remaining three-fourths were on the verge of falling out, too." I replied, "I grind my teeth." She asked, "Are you under any pressure?" I mumbled and hurried back to the courthouse with half of my face numb and sagging. I had a stack of warrants to sign, and I needed to work on a custody case I'd taken under advisement.

On Thursday rather than eating lunch, I heard the rest of the testimony in the murder trial. As I considered my verdict, I knew that if I said not guilty, Timmy went home; if I said guilty, he would spend the rest of his life in prison. I knew that no matter what I said, Victor was free and Glenn was dead. I knew that even though Victor sounded truthful, he had the ability to tell multiple versions of "truth" with equal sincerity and commitment. I knew that I couldn't believe Victor.

The State did not prove its case, and I entered a verdict of not guilty. I felt alone and humbled, there at the end of the line of justice. The next day I mentioned the case briefly to a fellow judge over coffee, and he laughed, "That's why they pay us the big bucks."

✦ ✦ ✦

Frustrated with myself and my memories, I yank off the dangling tooth-like pieces from the side of my RV, pick up torn RV body parts from the ground, and throw them all in the bed of the truck, thoroughly embarrassed. The metal steps fold out only after I hit them with a hammer. Then I use the same hammer to unfold the metal lip that is holding the door closed. Then, of course, it starts raining, so I give up for the night. The next morning, my mood has improved, the rain has stopped, and the 5th wheel doesn't look as bad, though it's still not pretty. The damage is cosmetic and limited to one panel and the fender. I decide to order replacement parts, and while I'm at it, I'll get a new door for the front storage compartment I punched out at Gig Harbor, just before I blew the clutch.

In the legal world on the Gulf Coast I'd been paid to fix things, even those beyond repair. It was my job to make things right, to straighten out problems, to make life fair and just. I felt like the Wizard of Oz, hiding behind my robe as I pushed levers and made impressive noises–sounds designed to spark awe, obedience and, as needed, fear so that I could get on with my job of doing justice. My voice would ring out and a man would disappear behind a clanging metal door, to stay as long as the voice decreed, for years or even life. The same voice spoke, and the next person walked out the door he came in, returning to daylight, freedom, family, and home. Later the voice set asunder marriages and other solemn commitments made before God, gave babies to one parent but not the other, and ordered visitation and child support that were often viewed as patently unfair. I understood there were wrongs I couldn't right and problems I couldn't solve, but people continued to line up, hopeful, perhaps even convinced that I would work a unique magic for them. Some were certain that I would put Humpty Dumpty back together again; others were sure I would, at the very least, grant them a pound of flesh in retribution for the wrongs they'd suffered. But, hell, I couldn't even straighten a fold in the side of my trailer!

Four days later I'm ready to get back on the road. I hook up and pull out of the RV park without a route planned, yet the stop sign at Highway 101, only 50 yards away, demands a decision. I laugh and turn north. At Newport I head east and am soon pulling through rolling hills wrapped in bright orange and red foliage. I'd like to check out Lassen National Park, described by a friend as "a great place to hike." All I remember is that it's somewhere in Northern California, east of Interstate 5.

Too soon I'm back on the boring but efficient Interstate. The slab is a good way to cover a lot of miles but its monotony frees up a part of my brain. As I drive on, a memory slips into my new world, like choking smoke creeping through a small hole, the memory of three young girls whose years of horror were recorded in a family album of porn. I'm tempted to open a window, turn up the radio and do whatever it takes to stay here on the road, in the sunshine, but I exhale loudly and refuse to slam the door of my mind to those young girls. I remind myself that like thunderstorms, their horrors don't have to last forever. I bury my hand in the deep fur of Bruin's neck and explain, "Their story matters, Bruin. It's important that they're heard and believed. And as crazy as it sounds, somehow, I'm to be their scribe."

✦ ✦ ✦

"Honor thy father."
Exodus 20:12

The Fifth Commandment.
  *After another long day in court, I sat at my dining room table,
with a plate of nachos and a glass of wine, hoping to wipe my rage
onto a blank piece of paper.*
  *That afternoon a deputy brought me arrest warrants charging
Harry with multiple counts of Capital Sexual Battery. Thank God
I didn't sit down beside the deputy to read over his paper work.
Instead I took the warrants and large brown manila envelope into
my office and shut the door. The report said the three victims were
now 24, 25, and 26. They were 9, 10, and 11 when Harry, the
father of one of the girls, performed multiple sex acts on those three
best friends.*
  *The manila envelope contained 70 black-and-white Polaroid
photos, 15 years old. Each photo was in a separate plastic bag and
marked in the familiar style for evidence with a fine-point marker,
showing the case number, date, exhibit number, and the officer's
initials. A catalog of the objective, concrete evidence that had lurched
to my hands straight from the sewers of hell.*
  *The photos showed Harry with the girls—sometimes all three girls,
sometimes just him and his daughter. In each photo Harry and the
girls were naked. Harry, with sideburns and a full head of Beatles-
hair, posed with an air of arrogance. He wore a practiced expression
as he puffed out his chest and photographed himself with an erect
penis in his daughter's mouth while he fondled the hairless genitals
of her best friend. He had taught the three girls to look at the camera
and assume facial and body positions you might see in a porno
magazine, but not in a family album.*
  *The arrest report contained the necessary facts. The now-grown
women had identified the photos and themselves. As I read, I recoiled
for I couldn't even imagine their shame and embarrassment in being
flashed back 15 years, riding on cheap Polaroid paper, as they looked*

at their skinny tomboy bodies still far from puberty, bodies not photographed in a ballet class or playing with friends on a swing set but bodies of little girls, best friends, entwined in hard-core porn. I picked up another photo. The only things that protruded from the little naked fronts were the bones in their shoulders. The officer made no mention of overt force in his report. I thought, "None was needed. The girls were totally naive and trusting. He taught them, much too early, about raw sex. But he left out the lessons of respect, trust, and love. What did he say to the face in his bathroom mirror? Because they didn't bleed, they weren't hurt? Because they didn't scream, they were not afraid? Because they didn't run from him, they wanted him to steal their childhood? Could he look himself in the eye? Babies, jerked from their rightful place of innocence by the same person the Bible said they were to honor.

The report stated that Harry repeatedly ejaculated onto the girls, telling them it was "love juice." The affidavit asserted that Harry never could get "in" in spite of many attempts because the girls were simply too tiny, but he repeatedly penetrated them with his tongue and finger. As I read, I thought, "And the son of a bitch was so egotistical that he photographed his 'conquests'! And having made the photos, he was vain enough to keep them for 15 years!"

As I sat in my office with the paperwork, my soul slammed around in my rib cage until my chest and stomach were sore. I wanted to scream; instead I made a calculated decision: "Probable cause to arrest, Capital Sexual Battery, hold without bond." I was supposed to set a dollar amount of bond, but I didn't. I couldn't, not if I wanted to sleep that night.

I signed the warrant after looking at only three of the 70 photos. I didn't want to see any more, and those three were enough for probable cause. I took off my glasses and stared at the wall, wordless. Then I got up and walked out to my assistant's office where the deputy was waiting. I handed him the paperwork and he asked, "Is it OK?" I wanted to scream "Hell no! It's not OK!" Instead I said quietly, "The affidavit was well done. I signed the warrant and set No Bond." I quickly went back to my office and shut the door. I sat down behind the desk and put my face in my hands so my anger *wouldn't leak across the rest of my workday and sabotage my ability to be intellectually impartial. And there I sat–objective and impartial–with my soul pinging off my rib cage.*

❖ ❖ ❖

Having grown up with a father who was a judge, I realized that my job would be hard in ways most people could not imagine. Watching colleagues and experiencing my own humanity, I understood the temptation to become arrogant, dismissive, and callous. I realized how easy it was to develop hard edges to protect myself from the relentless onslaught of humanity; I experienced the difficulty of facing that parade of pain and confusion, seasoned heavily with mean-spiritedness; I knew how tiring it can be to deal with a long line of litigants asking (or demanding) justice as they define that ethereal term. I accepted that people bring to court the fantasy that there are clear answers to every problem, that judges "know" what to do, and that we will simply make a clear call–Ball or Strike–in their favor. But unlike the court programs on TV, it's just not that simple, though the degree of messiness varies according to the division the judge is assigned to. The judges with the most seniority are generally found in the Civil Division, where they work with well-prepared attorneys on big-money cases that are intellectually challenging but not life altering. In Civil, the litigants are only arguing about money and "stuff," the law is straight-forward, and the impact of a judicial error can be measured in mere dollars, rather than the life-long fallout of misjudging a custody case or the case of an abused child. The Criminal division can be almost as easy from the judges' perspective and is the second most popular assignment. The Legislature has removed much of the discretion from the Criminal Judge, creating a computerized application of justice. Plug in the numbers, and out comes the sentence; judges joke that a monkey could impose the sentencing guidelines. Of course, judges in Criminal see the evidence of a lot of violence, but it is something like coming

231

onto the scene after a train wreck; though it may be a gory one, the judge is not responsible for the wreck, just dealing with its aftermath from a safe and intellectual distance. However, few judges will volunteer for Family Law and fewer still for Juvenile. Juvenile tends to be the bottom of the heap, the place the new judge is sent because no one else wants to be there, or the assignment to which you are banished if you offend your chief judge. The problem with Juvenile cases is that very little is clear and the stakes couldn't be higher; when you're assessing an abuse case, there are few unambiguous options and virtually nothing is as simple as calling a ball or strike. It's only slightly better in Family Law, where the judge deals with issues of children in the divorce arena. In Family and Juvenile, you try to sound like you know; but you know that you don't, not really. You're just there, doing the best you can to protect kids and families as you work to do justice, while dealing with an impossibly long list of cases. To continue the train wreck metaphor, in Family and Juvenile, the judge works with on-going train wrecks; it's not a matter of assessing the completed damage of a criminal or civil case but rather how to best minimize this wreck of humanity that is evolving before your eyes.

I remember one young lady who simply wouldn't let me get away with pretending I had the answers

✦ ✦ ✦

"Grown-ups never understand anything for themselves and it is tiresome for children to be always and forever explaining things to them."
Antoine de Saint-Exupery

A nine-year-old's view of the judiciary
This was the first day of a two-day custody battle. I spent about an hour with the three kids; they came into my Chambers one at a time As often happened, the attorneys and parents had agreed that

I would spend this time alone with the children, without the attorneys, parents, or a court reporter to help me get a better sense of each individual child.

As each came in and sat down, I asked some general questions to help them relax. "What grade are you in, who is your teacher, what's your favorite class/color...."

Then I went into the hard part, "We're here because your mom and dad both love you very much. They can't agree what's best for you, but because you are so very important, they're here asking for help. You don't get to make the decision of where you will live, because that's my job. There is only one robe in the room and it's mine. But even though you don't get to choose, what you think and what you feel are very important to me. So, first, is there something you want to ask me or something you want to say to me?"

I listened, asked questions, and tried to answer their questions.

As Jennifer spoke of living with her mom here or her father in Alabama, she explained, "Either way I lose. Because either way I won't get to be with my friends in the other place." At 13, friends were all that she talked about.

Wes, age 11, came in next. He worked hard at being cool and knowing everything. He had little to say, and I talked into a vacuum as I described some of what went on in the hearing–practical, boy-stuff like explaining the stenograph machine the court reporter had left in the corner of the room.

Finally I repeated my earlier request, "Is there anything you want to ask me, or that you want to tell me?"

He grinned a little and asked, "Do you think it'd hurt if you got drop-kicked in the mouth?"

"Well, yes," I responded, curious.

"Nope. It only stung me a minute, and I just kept playing."

I walked Wes to the door, trying to keep my judge-face in place, and asked the Bailiff to send in Stephanie.

Stephanie, at the age of nine, was a quiet, deep little soul. When she didn't respond to my opening lines, I kept talking, "I might not be able to make a decision when the hearing is over tomorrow. You guys are too important for me to hurry my decision. It might be next week before I can decide."

She looked me straight in the eye and asked, "How do you make up your mind? How do you do that?"

I felt like a deer caught in the headlights of a nine-year-old driver. It didn't seem right to tell her the truth–that I listen, look at the law, weigh the competing facts, worry for hours or days, pray, try on different answers, and then finally rule, often with no idea that I'm right. I didn't want to confess to a nine-year-old that making a decision in Family Law is particularly tough, that the answer is seldom obvious, that I don't get messages from On High, that I don't hear voices or see burning bushes, that the choices are not simple Balls and Strikes, that there isn't always a right and wrong. Most grownups don't know all of that, and I didn't want her to know, just yet, how messy this elevated decision-making process really is. Rather than tell her that I was not omnipotent, magical, or clairvoyant–rather than confess how often I question my own wisdom and judgment, I muttered something about the law and facts, hoping to sound like an adult.

She ignored my response, looked out a low-slung window, and asked "How high up are we?"

"We're on the sixth floor."

She responded, "Being up this high would scare some kids."

"Are you afraid of heights, Stephanie?"

"Some," she replied.

Part of me wanted to tell her about my fear of heights and my skydiving; another part said, "Keep a lid on it. You're supposed to act judge-like here!" To fill the awkward silence, I muttered, "My dad was a judge."

She turned her swivel chair away from me and looked through the wall of windows across rooftops. Then she harrumphed, "I don't know why anybody would be a judge!"

I responded to her nine-year-old back, "'cause then I get to talk with neat kids like you."

She spoke to the window, "Hmmp! But you could have been a

teacher! Then you'd see kids happy and playing. Now you only see them when they're sad and scared."

"Stephanie, if you have to be here, would you rather have a judge that likes kids?"

The back of her head nodded, "Yes." Then she got up and walked to the window that hit her mid-calf. Looking down she said, "This isn't so high."

❧ ❧ ❧

"When we get out of the glass bottles of our egos ... and get into the forest again, we shall shiver with cold and fright but things will happen to us so that we do not know ourselves ... we shall laugh and institutions will curl up like burnt paper."
D.H. Lawrence

CHAPTER 15.
CALIFORNIA:
Mud pots, aging gypsies, and real criminals

Shingletown is a tiny village about 15 miles west of Lassen National Park, and I decide to stay there, rather than chance snow at the higher elevations. I stop at a pleasant mobile home park with a few RV sites at one end. I'm the only RV'er there. Bruin and I find a trail that leads away from the park, through the woods, and down to a fast-moving stream where the tree-tops canopy out the sky. Bruin was checking out the stream with his nose when his hind end slipped on the muddy bank, and he fell in. I laughed, "That's just your karma for drenching me in the dinosaur graveyard back in Kentucky." He pulled himself up the bank, dropped his head, shook with disgust, and walked away without even glancing in my direction.

When Bruin and I drive up to Lassen National Park, we find that all the campgrounds but one have closed for the winter. At the higher elevations, I watch snow fall, fill the ditches, and blanket the rocks.

Lassen Volcano National Park is beautiful, complex, and varied. The wind bends stubby brown grass on the meadow floor, tall timber with scant undergrowth surrounds the lakes, and jagged grey mountain peaks push against the winter sky. There are a number of volcanoes in the park; one is active and last erupted in 1917, blowing rock and pumice 30,000 feet into the air. Fumaroles or mud pots (openings in the planet's crust) spout steam and gases.

I drive toward Lassen Peak, intending to hike to Bumpass Hell, a field of bubbling mud pots named for Kendall V.

Bumpass, an explorer whose leg was amputated after he stepped through the unstable crust into a thermal pool of mud and water at temperatures that reach 240 degrees. At the trailhead parking lot, it's 27 degrees with winds of at least 40 MPH. Bruin is fidgeting and anxious to get out of the truck, but after drawing quick yellow lines in the snow, he's pulling on the leash, leaning back to the truck. I won't let him in the pickup until he poses for the camera, sitting in the snow with mountains as a backdrop. He's compliant but not happy; I can tell from the expression on his face that he doesn't like the snow, the cold, the wind, or my absurd idea of a photo op. He clearly has no interest in my collection of photos. After I put Bruin in the truck, I bundle up and hike off. By the outer edge of the pavement, I realize I'll be satisfied with a hike around the Bumpass Hell parking lot. I turn back toward the truck and wonder if a tourist ever froze to death on the pavement and, if I were the first, would they name the parking lot after me? At the truck, the wind jerks the door from my hand and pins it open. I'm not strong enough to pull the door closed against the gust, so I get out, push the door into the wind and beyond the catch on the hinge, squeeze through while holding the door open, and then slam it shut. I drive to Shingletown through wet snow and fix a pot of chili.

There are mountain roads between me and Southern California that could soon be closed by snow. I need to move on. I hook up the 5th wheel and then go to pay my bill and say goodbye. I knock at the door of the lady who manages the mobile home park, and she calls out, "Come on in. It's not locked." Her husband is sitting in the living room watching TV; he looks up with a quick "Hello." I follow the Mrs. back to the kitchen and explain, "Well, I'm hooked up and heading out. I owe you for two nights." She responds, "Oh! I know you have to go but I wish someone were with you. At least you have Bruin." Then she adds with a laugh, "Let me show you what I'm making for my granddaughter."

We step into her sewing room and she holds up a pink gingham sun dress. She laughs, "I guess this wouldn't work too well for your grandson." I give her my check and hug her neck. I feel a sharp sad as I turn and walk down the sidewalk to my truck. As I drive away, she's standing at her bay window, waving.

The truck begins again the not-very-funny trick of surging or lurching at about 1800 rpms or 40 MPH, jerking as though I were trying to start out in fourth gear. As I stumble through that jerk-your-head-off range, I think, "So much for the exhaust brake being the problem!" The truck begins the dance with a lurch forward, and the 5th wheel joins in but about half a beat off. The 5th wheel jumps forward to catch up, just as the truck jams backwards; then as the truck lunges forward, the 5th wheel recoils. As the two buckle and slam into each other with ever-increasing violence, my heart races, my eyes get big, my hands go clammy, and my vocabulary goes to the gutter. The answer seems simple–stay out of the 1800 RPM range; in other words, either don't go faster than 30 MPH or slower than 50 MPH. Driving at less than 30 MPH on the freeway in Southern California isn't an option, so the trick is to get above 40 MPH with my head still attached and then not slow down. But the heavy traffic won't honor my new plan. Through trial and error, I learn to lessen the crescendo by taking my foot off the fuel pedal when the lurching starts. The traffic is getting progressively heavier and slower as I drive south, and the bump-and-grind dance of the mechanical monsters is wearing me down.

When pulling the 5th wheel, I'm alert and fine, until without warning, I'm not. It's like a Large Hand unplugs me, and I simply and suddenly have nothing left. I hate it when I get that stupid tired, so I make a conscious effort to stop before it's too late. But this is a very desolate stretch of Interstate 5 with lots of agriculture and no secure spot to stop for the night. Much too tired, I finally park at a Wal-Mart in Fresno, the closest safe place.

"And the day came when the risk it took to remain tight inside the bud was more painful than the risk it took to blossom."
Anaiis Nin

I'm walking Bruin across the Wal-Mart parking lot just before it's too dark for us to be out, when I see a small-built, elderly lady, obviously tidying up her car, getting ready to sleep in it. She opens the rear driver-side door, climbs in, and adjusts a curtain over the window. I wonder what kind of sad emergency would force her to be out on her own, sleeping in her car.

I see her again the next morning; it's obvious we're both traveling alone. I walk over to her car and say, "Good morning. I'm Laura, your neighbor" as I motion with my thumb toward my RV. She looks up with a gentle smile, and we drop quickly into an easy conversation.

Naomi, a 73-year-old retired architect and graduate of MIT, doesn't weight 100 pounds sopping wet, and she moves with the happy energy of an aging Jack Russell terrier. As she speaks, she looks me straight in the eye, and she doesn't waste time on cocktail talk. Standing there in the parking lot, we laugh and give each other high fives and hugs as we learn we're two wandering women, out to see the country.

She explains, "I've taken only two two-week vacations in my life. I've always wanted to see this country, and I decided I'd better get on with it while I can. A friend was going to come with me, but she backed out."

Naomi unfolds a U.S. map on the trunk of her car; the heavy green line makes loops and circles all across the country–west, south, east, and then north. She left Massachusetts three months ago and would be home by (perhaps) Christmas. To travel within a very tight budget, she stays at campgrounds, cooks on her small stove, and stores food in a tiny refrigerator that cools only while her car is running. She removed the rear seat of her older compact car

239

and put down a board and air mattress that butts up to the rear of the driver's seat. She climbs in the rear door, puts her feet in the trunk, and lies down to sleep. She assures me it's very comfortable and that since her doors lock, she feels safe. She carries a tent but hasn't slept in it yet. There are no campgrounds nearby, so she'd asked the manager of the Fresno Wal-Mart for permission to sleep over in their parking lot.

This was her first night at a Wal-Mart, and she's pleased. "I parked over here, close to the bus stop. I figured that if I had to yell for help, somebody waiting on a bus would come. Plus, look at me!" she says with a laugh. "Who wants to mess with a little old lady? One that sleeps in her car!"

She comes over to my RV for a cup of tea; to drink tea at her place, I would have had to lie down in the back seat with my feet in her trunk. Without the need to be "nice" or meet the expectations of the other, Naomi and I speak candidly, like two strangers talking late at night on a train as it crosses wide, empty spaces. We talk of death and family, ambition and inner peace, loves and losses. We speak of nature (the need to walk in the Pacific and Atlantic; the poignant joy of hearing coyotes in the desert; the smells–the Redwoods, the desert, mountain sage, and an approaching thunderstorm); the joy of moving across the country alone with no fixed schedule as we respond to tugs of curiosity. Naomi and I giggle like six-year-olds as we repeat in gentle but mocking tones words we often hear, "Aren't you afraid? Don't you get lonely? I'd never do that–not alone." We share road stories and laugh a lot. She shows me the space-tech silver socks she wears while in bed to keep her feet warm and reduce the number of times she has to get up in the middle of the night, go outside, and open the trunk to retrieve her sliding blanket. In her eyes, milky with years but lit with curiosity and openness, I catch a hopeful glimpse of my future. In the parking lot of a Wal-Mart, I meet my role model for how to live, old and wide open–how to go on, even when others suggest that is not safe, appropriate, or wise–how to be adventuresome when others say that I'm just too old.

We swap addresses, and then it's time to go. We're both heading to the Sequoia National Park. The last time I saw Naomi, she was bent over, moving her kitchen from the front seat to the rear, so she could sit behind the wheel and drive on. I wave, but she doesn't look up.

❅ ❅ ❅

A real criminal

Dick's advertised specialty was law for the elderly, and he handled estate planning, probate, and trusts. He had a turbulent extramarital affair with his legal secretary, Diane, during which they stole hundreds of thousands of dollars from his aged clients. Dick and Diane each pled no contest to a string of charges involving those thefts and then argued to me at sentencing that the other was the only bad guy and he/she was also a victim. The evidence showed that they used the stolen money for drugs and otherwise wasted the life's work and savings of many old folks who came to Dick, trusting him as the attorney who helped people who were past their prime. Dick and Diane would set up trusts for his clients, naming either of them as sole trustee and waiving bond. They then withdrew and spent all the monies; because there was no bond, there was no insurance available to reimburse the people. A complicated, sophisticated crime that involved misleading timeworn folks and stealing their money.

I listened for half a day to evidence and argument at Dick's sentencing hearing. There was no plea agreement; the sentence was to be my decision. When sentencing a defendant, a judge may adjudicate that person guilty (a formal finding that the individual is, in fact, guilty) or under some circumstances withhold adjudication. The issue of adjudication was particularly important to Dick because if I adjudicated him, he would lose his license to practice law. The sentencing guidelines set by the Legislature said Dick would receive no more than a year in the county jail and

241

probation and that to exceed such a sentence, I would have to make certain legal findings. His attorney argued that the blame was primarily the secretary's and that I should place Dick on probation and withhold adjudication to enable him to continue to practice law so he could support his family and begin to repay the huge sums of money they'd stolen.

The sentencing hearing was the third hearing I'd had in his case. I'd read the Pre-sentence Investigation Report and carefully reviewed the sentencing guidelines, including the criteria required for imposing a sentence greater or lesser than that recommended by the guidelines. I struggled with the question of sentencing an attorney. I looked at the facts and the law. I listened to Dick's explanations, as well as testimony from several of his venerable victims who spoke of facing failing health and increased financial demands, without the benefit of their life-long savings.

Plato spoke of the capacity to know what differences make a difference; the Legislature spoke of facts that can support a sentence that is greater than recommended by the guidelines. At the sentencing, I listened for several hours but heard no reason that Dick's case was the general rule, heard no reason to impose the guideline sentence of county jail and probation. After hours of listening, it seemed clear that this case was the exception—a difference that made a difference—and that it was one recognized by the Legislature.

"The Court adjudicates you guilty and sentences you to five years in prison on Count Twelve. As to the other counts, you will complete a total of ten years probation; the probation will run consecutive to your prison sentence. It is a condition of your probation that you repay all sums stolen. It is further a condition of your probation that you may not practice law in any state, nor may you work as a law clerk or in any other position associated with the legal field." I then meticulously spelled out the facts to support the statutory basis for the upward departure in the sentence—the victims were especially vulnerable due to age, the offense resulted in substantial economic hardship to the victims, there were multiple victims, and the Defendant used a position of trust, confidence, or fiduciary relationship in committing the crime. The room was heavy with quiet. As I went through the litany to impose sentence, Dick's wife began to cry. I continued on. I finished the sentencing and advised Dick of his right to appeal; then the Security Officer fingerprinted him. I adjourned court, stepped down from the Bench, and went out the back door to the hall. I took off my robe and waited. In a moment, Andy, my Security Officer, handed me the card on which he'd put Dick's fingerprints. I leaned over a cart of files to sign the card, and Andy also bent down. As I finished and while still bent over the files, I looked into Andy's face, uncommonly close to mine, and said quietly, "You don't fuck with old folks." Andy maintained a professional, expressionless face and said nothing. I stood up and walked down the long empty hall to my office, slowly embarrassed by what I'd said. But I also knew that the same rule applies to harming children and animals.

A month later Dick was back in Court on a Motion to Reduce the five-year prison sentence. His attorney argued, "Your Honor, there are real criminals out there on the streets on probation." Dick was sitting at the defense table in Courtroom 501 dressed in a jail-house-issue green jump suit and orange plastic shower shoes.

Before this hearing, Dick had sent me a letter in which he continued to blame Diane, saying he, too, was a victim. He spoke of his "vain hope" for a "miracle" of my "expressing a modicum of compassion" or "dispensing justice." I was being criticized for my sense of justice by a man with a juris doctorate, so he used bigger words.

During the hearing on the Motion to Reduce Sentence, Dick sat indignant in his jailhouse jumpsuit, as his attorney repeated, "Judge, there are lots of real criminals out there on the street on probation." The phrase stuck on the side of my brain like a wet dirt ball. Real criminals? I wondered, "How do you know a real criminal?" Thirty minutes earlier, I'd sent a twenty-something-year-old kid to prison for 12 years on technical violations of his probation (failure to pay restitution and failure to stay in touch with his probation officer), not because I thought he was a real criminal, or because I thought society would be better for his long incarceration, or because I thought that 12 years was what Justice required. I did it because that's what *the guidelines called for and there was no legal reason not to. On the same docket was a 18-year-old, to be sentenced for armed robbery, but his attorney rescheduled it for the next day. I'd read all the kid's reports—he probably was a real criminal. But the guidelines said three years in prison; his attorney said the three years should be in Boot Camp in the Youthful Offender Program. And I knew if he went to Boot Camp, he'd be out on parole before the three years were up. There was something cold and unblinking about that kid. He committed an armed robbery with determined calculation. Was three years in prison a band-aid? If I could find a legal reason to exceed the guideline and thus survive the inevitable appeal of a 15-year sentence—let's see, he'd be 33 and commit no robberies in public for 15 years. Would he then have his PhD in crime and be a godfather, a mother fucking son of a bitch, instead of a mere "real criminal"? But, it doesn't matter because I'd looked closely at the law in his case; if I exceed the guidelines, I know I'd be reversed on appeal, and that's an enormous waste of time and money.*

I denied Dick's Motion to Reduce Sentence, and he filed an appeal. I felt pretty sure the five-year prison term would "stick" (a non-technical legal term meaning that on review the appellate court will not find an abuse of discretion or a failure to follow the law and will affirm the lower court's decision).[20]

❖ ❖ ❖

It's a short drive to an RV park in Kingsburg, California. I unhook the 5th wheel and drive the truck up to the Sequoia National Park, to be totally knocked out by those gentle giants. General Sherman, 313 feet high and about 2,500 years old, is the largest living thing on Earth; the tree now stands behind a short fence designed to keep tourists at bay. I wonder, "If the

---

[20]Following Florida law, I authorized the defendant's release on bail pending appeal. On May 4, 2000, the First District Court of Appeal affirmed the sentence (in other words, said I had made no legal errors nor abused my discretion), and on June 8, 2000, the defendant began to serve his five-year prison sentence. After I retired, on April 15, 2002, a subsequent judge, granting a motion, modified his sentence of imprisonment to time served, thereby releasing him from prison to begin his probation. All other conditions of the sentence were left in effect. On March 17, 2005, that same judge granted the defendant's motion to terminate his probation.

congestion and pollution continue, will we need fences to keep the Sequoias from leaving us, in disgust?"

My neighbors at the RV park are Gwen and her two daughters, ages four and six. Bruin and I walk while the girls ride their bikes, showing me their favorite places - a tree with a hidden nest, a grassy trail down to a creek. The girls are relaxed and thriving; I relish the glimpse through their young eyes of the wonder and excitement of being alive in nature. I listen closely, but they didn't mention their dad. Hopefully that omission means nothing.

❀ ❀ ❀

Children are human, too

As a judge, I heard hundreds, even thousands of divorce cases; some are hard to forget, others are hard to remember. The contested divorce cases often included custody battles. In one, the grandmother told the parents that she had walked into the room to see a 14-year-old cousin licking the vagina of their 18-month-old giggling daughter. The parents, now embroiled in an emotionally charged divorce, each blamed the other for the way they jointly responded to that situation. One of the attorneys began a line of questions intending to demonstrate that no expert had determined that the 18-month-old was affected by such an early introduction to oral sex.

I erupted. "Counsel! That's like asking if an expert has determined that when walking in the rain, the person got wet!"

It was obvious he was frustrated with me and confused by my intensity. Somehow he did not understand that giving oral sex to an 18-month-old was a problem. How do you teach in law school or in society that children are human too, with memories, feelings, and souls?

The next day I handled an adoption, the favorite case of all judges, I imagine. The couple was in their mid-40's, without any other children. Their black-eyed, dark-haired angel was five months old. Rachel was petite and calm. As I watched the new parents quietly interact with their little one, I felt a large, holy silence. The attorney's words, legal and proper, sounded heavy and frivolous. It seemed more appropriate to make the sign of the cross, or bow Namaste. Instead, I granted the adoption and then, of course, held Rachel. She grabbed my necklace; when I rubbed the center of her back, she leaned against my chest and became very still.

After the hearing, I walked out of my Chambers and into my office, basking in the energy of Rachel, as well as the love and hope of her new family. I can't schedule much time for basking, so as I sat there quietly with my doors closed, I began to read and sign arrest warrants. As I read, I felt like I had been jerked backwards through a knothole in a pine board.

In the stack was a warrant for the arrest of a man for Lewd and Lascivious Assault on a Child. His wife had gotten up in the middle of the night to go to the bathroom and discovered her husband masturbating while fingering the vagina of their four-month old daughter. The baby in the police report was one month younger than Rachel. Rachel, that very real angel that just left my arms and my office. I sat in an office that was quiet but in a soul that was screaming. It was as though I found myself by the side of the road, stunned and confused, watching Christmas lights blink and reflect off a horrific wreck.

❖ ❖ ❖

Gwen loans me books. She and I pile up with her two little girls to watch skydiving videos on my TV. Gwen cooks dinner, and I join them in their travel trailer; my contribution is to bake Congo bars, a family recipe that's something of a cross between brownies and chocolate chip cookies. The girls give me hand-made cards, and then it's time for me to go. I hook up and pull away, pleasantly aware that the only signs of my presence are bent blades of grass, grass that will soon straighten.

Heading south on Interstate 5, the traffic is heavy and fast, and the truck continues its surging trick, especially going over the mountains. As I get closer to Los Angeles, the traffic thickens, slows, and then stops in jerks. It's late, and I'm exhausted when I pull into Skydive Perris, a drop zone outside Ontario, California. Though bleary-eyed and road-weary, I'm comfortable here in the dark, deserted parking lot of a strange drop zone. Four months earlier when Sara and I stopped at Front Range Skydiving east of Colorado Springs, I was nervous and uncomfortable with the unknown. Thousands of miles later, my confidence has grown.

The next morning it's raining as I unhook the 5th wheel. I have an appointment at the Banks factory near Ontario to address the lurching and banging problem. I leave Bruin in the RV and drive the truck through the hellacious traffic of Southern California. I'm a nervous wreck, not because of the traffic or the rain but because I'm certain that my own mechanical incompetence is the cause of all my woes and that I will soon be found out and severely reprimanded. I go to the Banks factory ("The surge is not your Banks, ma'am"), and then to the diesel mechanic that Banks suggested, ("Go to a Dodge dealer ma'am. It's in your fuel pump, and if I fix it, it'll cost you $1,800. But it should be covered by warranty. And driving's not gonna hurt it.") Not one of the large, hairy diesel mechanics criticizes me or laughs; no one says it's simply my imagination, incompetence, or gender. I leave without an answer, but I feel much better. I go back to Skydive Perris and stay a second night in their parking lot.

I wake up to more rain, and that means no jumping. I don't want to wait a few days for the weather to break; I'm ready to leave. The Los Angeles area is my idea of Hell - the traffic, the hordes of people, the smog. Whenever I leave the drop zone, I'm caught up in six lanes of traffic that lurches like jack-rabbits; I pass under banks of traffic lights and wait beside cars filled with anxious people blowing horns. There are shards of natural beauty that have not yet been paved over, but those scarce, lonely fragments of nature feel sad and are not enough to keep me grounded. I feel lonely and assailed by the clamor of development, concrete, and crowds. I'm tired of it all, and I just don't have the energy to make friends yet again at a new drop zone; There are too many people, everywhere I turn. With a wet cloud cover over both my plans to jump at Perris and my spirit, I hook up and pull out. There's a rule of honor among skydivers–you can't wear the T-shirt unless you've made the jump; the rule seemed to apply to bumper stickers as well. So I leave Skydive Perris without either.

I drive hard, hoping to out-run this newest devil on my coat tail, those negative voices in my head that castigate me for leaving Perris early, leaving without jumping. Leaving when I said I wanted to jump there, and I certainly had the time to hang out, make friends, and wait for the weather to break. With the truck lurching, I bump right past Hell, driving east on Interstate 10. Interstate 10 sounds like home; its eastern leg runs right through the county in which I grew up, where my family and friends still live. When I cross the state line into Arizona, the traffic drops off, Mother Nature reappears, and I am comfortable again.

"If you have a notion of where you are going, you will never get anywhere."
Joan Miro', Spanish artist

CHAPTER 16.
ARIZONA:
Margaritas, coyotes, and hiccups

I don't stop until I get to Eloy, Arizona, 400 miles of pavement away from Los Angeles. Now what am I going to do? I don't pick up my friend, Liz, at the Phoenix airport for a week. Liz is a judge in Guam, and we met when she came to Pensacola to observe the juvenile drug court. She was excited to learn of my upcoming trip, and we figured out how to meet on the road. She's going to travel with me to Sedona, then catch a flight to Reno, Nevada, where she'll take some courses at the National Judicial College. After she leaves, I'm scheduled for training with Skydive Arizona, an Olympic-level team.

I find an RV park in Casa Grande, New Mexico, maybe 15 miles from the drop zone and an hour from the Phoenix airport. The lots are wide and level, and there are no obstacle courses (trees, mail boxes, flower gardens) to back around. The laundry is clean, and it's not close to highway noise. I sign in for four nights, which is a long-term commitment for me. The next day I leave Bruin in the 5th wheel and drive to SkyDive Arizona. I know no one there; I feel alone and lonely–the kid with her nose pressed to the window, watching everyone else have fun. It's hard for me to ask strangers to let me play with them; it's easy to hide in my RV and eat worms while ruminating on the nasty string of mechanical challenges thrown at me. But I take a deep breath and walk up to Manifest and asked if anyone is organizing. The guy at Manifest promptly introduces me to their organizer, and within the hour I'm geared up and on a plane to altitude with a group of new playmates. I do three quality skydives (including a four point eleven-way, meaning that eleven jumpers come together and make four predetermined slot-perfect formations in free-fall). I boost my confidence, meet new friends, and most of all relax and have fun. Typical of skydivers, we talk about jumping—cool gear, where we've jumped, and a few "there I was, thought I would die" stories told with a laugh. We don't talk about jobs or career goals. After a sunset jump, I hang around in the Bent Prop, the local watering hole and enjoy spending time with people I've just met yet who share certain traits common among skydivers—fierce independence, a sense of adventure, a willingness to play hard, and good sense of humor. I leave tired and deeply happy. The next morning I buy a Skydive Arizona T-shirt and put my fourth bumper sticker on the spare tire cover of the 5th wheel.

I take the truck in for an oil change at a local Dodge dealer; the mechanic won't even talk about the lurching problem. At his suggestion, I call the Dodge dealer in Chandler outside of Phoenix and make an appointment for the following week.

I spend a good part of Wednesday at the Phoenix airport waiting for Liz and writing; she spends the day learning about delays to her flight. Liz finally arrives, six hours late.

Thursday we drive to Sedona and find a tiny RV park, tucked between a hill and a creek. There are not many RVs on Guam, and she's intrigued with my turtle house. We read a brochure about hot air balloons at sunrise above the red cliffs and make a phone call.

Friday we're up at 4:30 a.m. to meet the crew and are soon gently swinging in a waist-high basket that continues to rise to 3,000 feet. It's different, beautiful, and scary. I get very quiet; I don't like heights unless I'm safely wrapped in a parachute with at least 1,000 feet of altitude below me so I can make good use of the rig. I don't know the guy flying the hot air balloon, and I don't have a clue what my options would be in an emergency. I grip the edge of the gondola and practice taking deep breaths. The height doesn't make Liz uncomfortable, but the cold does. She keeps muttering things like, "Island girls aren't meant to be out in the cold."

We land somewhere in the rolling desert hills of cacti and rock with the chase vehicle waiting. By then our feet are so cold they hurt as we walk. The crew serves what they described as breakfast–tart orange juice mixed with champagne, strawberries with artificial whipped cream in a can, and cold sugary donuts. We drink a little of the champagne orange juice, throw the rest on a rock, and are the first ones in the truck. That afternoon we drive up to the red cliffs and sit on the back of my truck with a good bottle of wine, blue cheese in olive oil, and a loaf of crusty bread. We toast the sunset and Liz gives me some island lessons: Guam has typhoons rather than hurricanes; pretty much everything is made of cement to resist damage from flood surges, and that includes her house and kitchen counters; generators are as necessary as refrigerators. The size of a court docket is determined by population, so hers is much lighter than ours. She explains with a laugh, "Guam is so small it would fit in Lake Tahoe."

Liz has a too-early flight from Phoenix; after the hustle and bustle of getting her to the airport, she waves and is gone. This is the fourth time a friend has visited in my home-on-wheels and then flown away. With the passenger seat empty and my heart a bit heavy, I drive back to Casa Grande

That evening I pour a glass of wine to grease the too-familiar path from companionship to solitude. As I start on my second glass, I am aware of the lure of that elixir. I've watched the pain of too many children who depend upon and deeply love grownups who drink too much, grownups who use their position of authority and the cunning of alcohol to deny their drunkenness and to prove the child is mistaken if she dare suggest something is wrong. Children may become adults before learning the facts about alcoholism, but from a young age a child can experience its ability to distort reality. I pour the wine down the drain and sit in my recliner, remembering Laurel, a child whose name is similar to mine, a child who shares my birthday–a little girl who needed someone to say "no" to the destruction of alcohol early in her life.

❖ ❖ ❖

Laurel

It was a routine Tuesday in Juvenile Court–a long day with many hearings. I had read the reports for Tuesday's docket the night before. One of the cases was a routine 15-minute Shelter Review Hearing for a child named Laurel. Laurel's mother was arrested over the weekend on a DUI; Laurel, seven-months old, was in the backseat of the car. I knew the mother because she had been involved in Juvenile Court for years; she already had two dead babies–two toddlers who on separate death dates had waddled into separate swimming pools to drown while Mom slept, in a vain effort to drown out the world in alcohol. Five years earlier I placed her three older children with various relatives and various degrees of hope and success. This was an extended family of upper middle-class, educated people, willing to help and often frustrated by Mom's unwillingness to accept responsibility. Laurel was her mother's sixth child.

Several months before this routine Tuesday in Juvenile Court, I'd learned of Laurel's birth during a standard review of the three older children, and I silently panicked as I noticed that none of the other players in the courtroom were concerned. In response to my questions about the newborn, everyone glowed, assuring me that Mom is sober, working, and in a new stable marriage with a recovering alcoholic. As their eternal optimism gushed, I looked over at Mom. She sat demurely with her eyes downcast. I swallowed a bitter lump of fear and prayed– prayed that I was wrong, that I was cynical, that the mother would remain sober, that this baby would be treated differently.

This most recent report stated that the new husband had gone fishing Saturday morning, and Mom went out drunk for a mid-morning drive with the seven-month-old baby in the backseat of her car. Another judge saw the case for Laurel's first shelter hearing over the weekend; he gave custody to the father who was to supervise the mother's contact with the baby.

On Tuesday I called the mother's name, looked at her, and said, "Good morning." She didn't respond, smile, or make eye contact with me. When everyone was seated and sworn in, the attorneys went through the preliminaries but failed to address many of the questions that had been haunting me since I read the report over supper the night before.

So I began, "Where is the mother living?"

The attorney for DCF explained, "Oh, yes, Judge, she's living in the home with her husband and Laurel."

"Has she gone to treatment, detox, or AA?"

"Well, Judge, not yet."

"And who takes care of Laurel while her dad is at work?"

After a brief huddle, the attorney explained, "Dad told us he's signed Laurel up for day care, starting tomorrow."

I listened, swallowing the anger that wanted to speak only in four-letter words. All of the other players—the attorney and case worker for DCF, the Guardian ad Litem director and guardian, the attorneys for the mother and father—everyone else was convinced that all was well, and they each spoke of "ensuring Mother's close contact with her baby." Mom and Dad were holding hands, sitting deep in their chairs at the large round oak table.

Though four-letter words tried to burp out, I managed to say, "Given her history, I'm not comfortable with the mother sleeping in the home with the child. My concern is for the child's safety. If the mom gets drunk again in the middle of the night, when Dad is asleep, he wouldn't know that she had left again with the baby." (Note that I managed to NOT say that I thought two dead babies were enough for any one mother. I also managed to not say, "You dumb shit, Mom has relapsed. She hasn't gone to AA, detox or treatment. She's a Roman candle between rounds!!") Instead, I ordered "Custody remains exclusively with the father, subject to protective services supervision. The mother may have contact with the baby only from 6 p.m. to 9 p.m. each day, with Dad present. The child must be in daycare while Dad is working. Under no circumstances may the mother have unsupervised contact with the baby. She will give urine for a drug screen today, and DCF will take regular drug tests thereafter."

The mother's face, earlier bland and evasive, hardened as she glared at me. Her body tensed and her nostrils flared as she interrupted, "You're putting me out on the street! Why can't I stay in my own house?" Then, as an exclamation mark, she bolted from the hearing room. We concluded the hearing without her, and I scheduled it for another routine review in 30 days.

Three days later Laurel's case was back on my docket for, by then, even the Department was worried. The pleadings DCF submitted stated that after the hearing on Tuesday, the mother had refused a drug screen because, as she explained, she had a cold so she'd just drunk a bottle of cough medicine. Thus the bureaucracy scheduled a 15-minute hearing on Friday to suggest to me "some additional steps that should be required of the mother." As on Tuesday, the same players were seated at the large round table in my Hearing Room. The Department's testimony showed that the mother was staying at the house during the day while the baby was in daycare, but that the mother couldn't remember the name of the people she was staying with at night or their address. The caseworker testified that Dad was being very defensive of Mom and would cut off questions by the caseworker and Guardian ad Litem.

Then the caseworker noted, in an off-handed way, "And the parents' house has a swimming pool in the back yard. An old pool choked with green slime. That causes me some concern."

The bitter lump of anger was harder to swallow this time. I managed keep my response short: "Is there any reason why the Court should not, on its own motion, order the Department to pick up the child and place her in a shelter home?" Leaving unsaid–a shelter home without a drunken mom who has two drowned babies, who is drinking as we speak, and who has a third pool waiting at home.

Into the surprised silence, the Department's attorney said, "We would welcome the order."

I quietly wondered if there is some buried regulation that keeps the Department from using common sense or four-letter words; is there a rule against calling danger by its true name?

The room remained awkwardly still, and I ordered, "The child is removed from the dad and placed in the temporary custody of the Department. The mother may have no contact with the child until she demonstrates to the Court some effort toward sobriety. That may take the form of detox, treatment, AA meetings, and/or negative drug tests. All contact by the father is to be supervised by the Department until further order. At this point the Court has concerns over the father's priorities. He will have to demonstrate a willingness and ability to choose, if need be, the safety of the child over his relationship with his wife." Tensions were high and my sermons would not be heard, so I left unsaid that I was also concerned that Dad was too much "in love" with Mom, with not enough focus on the baby; I left unvoiced my concern that through all this craziness, Dad, a recovering alcoholic, hadn't seen the need to get back to AA, so it looked like he was at major risk of relapse himself.

And so I adjourned the hearing, without answers or solutions, but with yet another hearing waiting in the wings.

❧ ❧ ❧

When I take the truck to the Dodge dealer in Chandler, the tech explains the work may require several days, and I find myself having to rent a car to return to Bruin and my rig. Four days later the dealer calls to say my truck is ready, except that there is no repair available for the lurching problem. A brand new phrase for me—"no repair available." I hang up the phone with a growing fire of anger. By the time I've made the hour drive to pick up my unrepaired-after-four-days-of-paying-for-a-rental-car truck, I've calmed down some. The tech explains that though he confirmed my problem and had seen it in other trucks, there are no service bulletins or recalls from Dodge, so there was "No repair available." He even wrote that magic phrase on my invoice.

I know too much about problems for which there is no answer, no fix. I thought I'd left those behind me.

✦ ✦ ✦

"Where did we ever get the crazy idea that in order to make children do better, first we have to make them feel worse? Think of the last time you felt humiliated or treated unfairly. Did you feel like cooperating or doing better?"
Dr. Jane Nelson

A margarita for Heather
After work, I would often set the kitchen timer and write without stopping until the 20-minute buzzer sounded. But this particular evening I decided to write until I finished my margarita.
So I drank a margarita for Heather, the budding 11-year-old who was the subject of the custody battle I'd heard that day. Heather had curly, shoulder-length brown hair, a pale complexion, and bright brown eyes, full of life. She was artistic, soft spoken, a good student—an all-around good kid.
Heather had lived with her father since she was about six months old, and she now wanted to live with her mother. Her mother had hired an attorney who filed papers requesting a change of custody, arguing that because the mother was now settled into a new home and working, Heather's best interest would be served by changing custody from the father to the mother. I was intrigued as I read the pleadings and listened to the mother's attorney. In Florida a judge cannot change custody simply because that is the preference of the child and the situation of the non-custodial parent has improved; yet that was all the mother's attorney was focusing on.
Heather's mother was hearing impaired and spoke through an interpreter. Mom seemed pleased to have an audience. She signed fast and non-stop. It looked like speed signing. She wouldn't stay on the subject, and I was amazed by how hard it was to interrupt her to bring her back to the matters at hand. She wore me out. But I was even more frustrated by the mother's attorney who presented and

256

argued only irrelevant trivia that could not legally support the change of custody. And he did so with an air of arrogance.

At the end of three hours, I talked with Heather alone—no parents, no attorneys, and no court reporter. And as a child will do, she made a simple, strong case.

She explained, "I love my daddy, but I'm really scared of him. I want to live with my mama. Please let me. I'm not scared of her."

"What's going on with your dad, Heather?"

"Lots of times when he gets really mad, he hits things. He sticks his fist through the wall 'cause he's mad."

"How many is lots?"

"Oh, at least five times, that's how many holes there are. He doesn't fix 'em. He mostly hits the wall around the door. He keeps saying it's better to punch a wall than a person. And he yells a lot. Mama never yells. She gets mad at me sometimes, but we talk it out. I get on restriction sometimes with Mama, but only when I need to. Mama would never hurt me. When Daddy gets to yelling, he swings his arms around a lot, I guess to make a point."

"Has your daddy ever hurt you?"

"Not in a long time, but when he spanked Rob, he's my half-brother, he left a big-ol' bruise. Daddy said he missed and that's why Rob got the bruise."

"How long ago was that?"

"A couple of months ago. This year."

"I know your mother doesn't hear. So, how do you guys talk?"

"Oh, she can talk some, and I can understand her. I can sign good, too, and she reads my lips. Talking's not a problem. She asks me questions, and she listens to me. She doesn't get loud or stomp around the house. This summer when I was at my mama's, I asked her if I could please come live with her. I can talk with my mama, but not Daddy. If I told Daddy I was scared of him, he'd just get mad, and he might hurt me like he did Rob."

"You're in the sixth grade, right?"

"Yes, ma'am."

"Well, if you go live with your mom, you'll have to change schools.

You're doing great where you are. Wouldn't you miss your school and your friends?"

"I can make more friends. I wanna be with my mama. I want to see my daddy, but it's just too scary living with him all the time." I watch her belly bounce with mini-sobs. Through tears, she adds, "I hardly ever talk at Daddy's, and he doesn't even notice."

As I listened to Heather, I was silently screaming in frustration. This was important testimony for it had the potential of demonstrating a substantial change in circumstances. Yet, the only significant legal issue that was raised was in private, by a child.

After Heather left, I called the adults back into my Chambers and gave them a summary of Heather's concerns, with a positive spin designed to stave off Dad's anger.

Then I said, "I don't know what I'm going to do, but I'm not going to rule today. I'll send you an Order. The Order may take the motion for change of custody under advisement and reschedule this matter for further hearing."

This was not my typical ruling. The parents were there for an answer; I was to grant or deny the motion. But I wouldn't give them a pat answer, not now. Even as I spoke, I knew I was hoping for something. What? That at another hearing, the mother's attorney would present some pleadings and testimony on which I could base a change of custody?

I looked down into my emptying glass of margarita and thought, "OK, lots of kids are scared of physically large, bullying fathers. If I had changed Heather's custody based on the pleadings and testimony of record today, the District Court would reverse me and send her back to her dad. It's not my job to fix things, unless the attorneys and witnesses say the right things in the right way." But I had sat there, knee to knee, with a real child—not a legal theory—and that child said, "I'm scared of my daddy. Please, let me go live with my mama." Though a child, her fears seemed well based and genuine.

My indigestion burned as I thought of the impact of the mother's attorney. But what could I do? I could finish this margarita and know I had listened to Heather.

Where is it written that the child loses and remains in a scary household because of the way the attorney handled the case? Is this really the way we want to define justice? Even if the attorney had presented evidence that Heather had not been afraid of her dad earlier but was now and that her fear is well based, I'm not certain the District Court would affirm a custody change. Why? There are limits to how much discretion the law gives to the trial judge, the one sitting knee-to-knee with Heather. See, it takes lots of minute rules to keep us all the same, to keep us all between the white lines. The line of salt around the edge of this margarita is more flexible and forgiving than the rules made by grownups.

I'm sorry, Heather.

❋ ❋ ❋

Back at the RV park in Arizona with the truck tagged "no repair available," I decide to have a margarita and drink to mechanical problems that cannot be fixed. As I work my way around the line of salt, I count without amusement, "Montana, Washington, California, and Arizona. Great! Arizona is the fourth state that didn't fix the lurch!"

I'm comfortable at this RV park and decide to stay put while waiting for the first of my courses at SkyDive Arizona.

Bruin and I prefer nature to pavement and manicured palm trees, so we're pleased to find a deserted desert that butts up to the RV park. Bruin insists on his morning excursion at 5:30 am, before even the sun wants to get up. He makes his point by standing quietly beside my bed, staring but not touching me–wagging his thick tail and whacking the wall. It's easier to get up and walk with him than to ignore his drumming. We often hear coyotes in those wee hours. At times, we'll be within 25 yards of their singing, pleased and surprised they let us get so close. Our desert is mostly flat with cacti and crusty animal burrows scattered about at the base of larger prickly bushes. The ground is coarse sand with a heavy coat of small rocks. At the far edge of the desert is a large irrigated field of cotton, cotton that seems out of place, a transplant like Bruin and me. A cotton field that reminds me of other walks and a face of nature more familiar than the desert.

❦ ❦ ❦

Balance

I had an early docket so I walked Bruin at 5:15 in the morning. There was no moon; the world was so delightfully dark, we could barely see our feet. After being out awhile our eyes adjusted some but never enough to see as the owl and bat do. As we walked, the sun slipped up on the backside of waist-high weeds and grasses, their heads wet with dew, their feet blanketed in the low ground fog. A young bat, who had stayed out too late, took one more dive before running from the dawn. I wondered if she was hurrying to avoid the curse of being turned into a human.

When I've seen too much in my work-a-day man-made world, when things seem too broken, when I face fundamental wrongs that can't be made right, I have to go outside. I have to look up at the stars or down in the grass. I need to listen to the owl and wonder about other bird sounds. I need to again find Wonder—those things that make me stop with a smile and say, "Wow!"

Later that morning, six-year-old Milian came into my Chambers for her adoption. Her parents were in their mid-30's; she was their only child. Milian was dressed neatly in beige bib coveralls with a matching T-shirt. Her hair was pulled back into a ponytail. The pink ribbon in her hair looked like a concession to her mom. She smiled gaping holes where baby teeth had been. The one permanent tooth on the top looked too large for her mouth. After the introductions, she sat down and opened her book.

She caught my eye and explained, "My book doesn't have pictures in it." She read quietly while the grownups took care of the legal details.

I asked her if she had any questions, and she responded, "No. I picked out my mama and daddy, and now they're mine forever and ever."

After the hearing she said, "Daddy, hold me up so I can see that picture."

He smiled, "Sure, Milian," and picked her up though with her lanky legs and arms, she was almost too big to hold. She and I talked briefly about the photo on my wall of a lighthouse on a tiny island during a heavy storm. Then she buried her head into the shoulder of her forever-and-ever dad. He held her, as though she were a shy six-month-old, and continued to talk with me about the photo and another one hanging nearby. Then he carried his quiet armload of love from my Chambers.

In the afternoon I had a particularly difficult sentencing in a criminal case. The month before, the Defendant, Sam, had pled guilty to Burglary of a Dwelling.

He and his wife were separated and their divorce was pending; the wife lived with their three-month old daughter. Sam had a long history of domestic violence, and the wife had recently gotten a restraining order prohibiting all contact. In the middle of the night, the Defendant had gone to his wife's home, cut the phone wires, kicked in a window and went inside.

The investigative report contained the wife's version of that night. She had run hysterical and naked to the neighbors to call the police. She said she was able to get away only because he'd gone to the bathroom. She said he had repeatedly raped her. She had red marks on her wrists and a bruise on her left shoulder. The pelvic exam showed other bruises and the Defendant's semen.

Originally Sam had been charged with rape but, with the consent of his wife, he had negotiated a plea to a lesser charge of Burglary. There was no agreement as to the sentence; the State and Defense would each make their argument but the decision would be mine. The Defendant had been in jail since his arrest.

The wife had unstable diabetes, and after the Defendant pled guilty but before his sentencing, she became critically ill and died. The Defendant filed an emergency motion that he be allowed to go to his wife's funeral to say his farewells and to comfort their baby. I denied the motion.

During the two-hour sentencing hearing, the wife's family asked that I sentence the Defendant to the max. Her mother cried as she described the terror in which her daughter had lived and talked about the granddaughter who was now living with her. The wife's family painted the picture of a manipulative, violent man.

Next the Defendant and his witnesses testified. Sam spoke at length, often rambling. "Judge, I love my wife, and I always will. We were going to get back together as soon as I got out of jail. She couldn't work; she needed me. I'm a good worker. If she were here, she'd tell you she doesn't want me to go to prison. She was going to testify for me, Judge. She told me that she trusted me and that if anything happened to her she wanted to be sure I raised the baby. She knew how iffy her diabetes was. She didn't want her mama to raise the baby. She knew I'd raise her right and in the church. A lot was going on in my life–uncontrollable events. I went over to our home and, yes, I made love with my wife. But, Judge, that's all it was. And now, I have to get out of jail, for the baby. I've learned many things in the last four months. I couldn't be there when the baby was born but, Judge, I can be there for her now."

I listened carefully. He never called his child by name. He never accepted any responsibility for his actions. It was clear he felt remorse—for being in jail and for having a complicated life.

And then the jail minister spoke for the Defendant. He wore a black suit, a white shirt and a burgundy tie. He had preacher hair–a full head of gray hair carefully coiffured. The preacher explained, "Judge, I don't come to court for inmates. I've seen too many fail to keep their promises to God. But I've prayed with Sam a lot, and he made such a dramatic and positive change when he accepted Jesus into his life, that I felt led to speak for him, Your Honor."

And with that, he turned to the audience. With his back to me, he began preaching, using his arms to punctuate his sermon with grandiose preacher-like gestures. He made scattered references to the Defendant, and occasionally made a passing turn back to me. I halfway expected him to give an altar call–an invitation to step forward to accept Jesus as Lord and Savior and be baptized as Christian.

After about ten minutes, I'd listened as long as I could bear, so I said, "Thank you, Reverend. I must move on. In quick summary, is there anything else you think I should know about this Defendant before I impose sentence?" He seemed startled; perhaps he viewed my interruption as rude and an interference with God's work. He started preaching again, and as he turned back to the audience with yet another exaggerated arm gesture, I cut him off. "Thank you, Sir. I'm sure there's much more you and others would like to say. But my reality is limited by the clock, and I must move on. I appreciate your taking the time to be here. Does the State or Defense have any other witnesses?"

And so after listening for two hours, it was my turn. I gave Sam a long prison sentence, followed by probation. When I asked him to step over to a side table for fingerprinting, he remained at the podium, glaring at me.

The officer put his hand on the Defendant's arm, and the Defendant's anger bristled, "Judge! You don't understand!"

In response, I called for the next case.

He was certain he would be released to follow through on his newest commitment to Jesus. He was certain a woman judge would understand. He was still angry that I had not allowed him to attend his wife's funeral. He was still blaming everything and everyone, except himself. He was still out of balance with the world as I believe it to exist. A world of nature, low fog, slow sun rises, bats who stay out too late. A world where a woman can be safe in her own home, and a daddy will call his child by name. A world where a little girl can bury her head into her daddy's shoulder. A world of gentleness, cotton, and coyotes.

❖ ❖ ❖

For the first time on the road, I wake up sick. Sick. By myself. All alone. And I don't like it, not even a little bit. No one knows or cares that I have a sinus infection, a sore throat, and a fever, or that my stomach feels like I've been hit with a board. I tell the secretary at the RV park I'm not feeling well, but that's just not the same. Skydiving, the reason I'm in the deserts of Arizona in the first place, is out of the question for now. The planes aren't pressurized, and the jumpers often open the door in route to altitude. And then, of course, falling 10,000 feet in 60 seconds can blow infected sinuses and ears up or out. So I wait, hoping to get over the worse of this malady before the first skydiving course, which begins in a week.

While I'm feeling miserable, Clay calls and we talk about things that are going on in Milton, 1700 miles away, with a focus on my three-month-old grandson. I ask about a tiny staccato sound in the background, and Clay explains, "Oh, that's Will. He has the hiccups."

As I hang up, the earth quietly shifts on its axis. I explain to Bruin, "Will has the hiccups. It's time to go home."

My heart has often been bullied by reason and rational analysis. But sometimes "the heart has reasons that reason does not understand." (Blaise Pascal, 1623–1662). And now my heart makes a firm decision without discussing it with my head. I sit alone in the RV with the cell phone in my hand; I can hear the echo of those tiny sounds, faint but too real to deny. Nor will I deny that something is changing in me at a visceral level. There have been other times my heart has said I need to make an abrupt U turn; thus I went to law school, rappelled down a fire tower, skydived, and left the Bench. Perhaps it's that's prayer again: "Creator, please don't be subtle." Perhaps it's time to trust nebulous things like tiny hiccups.

Later I call my friend, Cherry, and explain my abrupt change of plans. She listens deeply, then laughs, "It's all OK, Laura. And I look forward to seeing you soon."

I cancel the long-awaited skydiving classes, and I give myself a couple of days to feel better before beginning the drive to Florida. Being miserable alone while sitting still is bad enough; misery in motion with a long rig tagging behind a lurching truck would be worse. Plus, the secretary at the RV park (the one I silently designated as my concerned other) said, "Ya don't wanna be sick on the road."

*"I have a compulsion to wander and a compulsion to return–
a homing instinct like a migrating bird."*
Bruce Chatwin

CHAPTER 17.
RETURNING:
Hot coffee, cookies, and busted knuckles

My fever breaks, the stomach cramps lessen, and I leave
Arizona on a new mission. "It's time to go home, Bruin. Will
has the hiccups." And so I head east on Interstate 10; I'm
ready to go back.

Later in the morning, I stop at McDonald's for a cup of
coffee. When the young kid behind the counter smiles,
memories stronger and hotter than the coffee take me back to
the courtroom and my last jury trial before retiring.

*"Nobody has ever measured, not even poets, how much a heart can
hold."*
Zelda Fitzgerald

McDonald's
   *I'm sitting at a picnic table at the edge of Pensacola Bay, at the
end of a long day and yet another murder trial. There's a stiff cold
wind blowing in my face, but the bench and thus my butt are
comfortably warm in the sun.*
   *Last week it was a stabbing death; this week it was one shot to
the back of the head. Last week as I listened to the medical examiner
explain the knife wound through the sternum to the heart, I thought,
"I know too much about autopsies. I've learned more than I care to
know about the myriad ways the human body can violently die."
But this week, I've had more lessons about brutal deaths. Perhaps
this last class in man's inhumanity to man is the Universe's way of
confirming my decision to leave the Bench, while also reminding me
of the love and kindness in the world.*
   *I sit by the water, surrounded by natural beauty but distracted by
a man-made world of violence. The sun is warming my back. There's*

a monarch butterfly dancing to the tune of crows; a sprinkling of pigeons flash their purple necks to the sun as they plod around in burgundy house slippers.

Crow. That's what I'd like to do, make a loud, dissonant sound, while flying–flying above the world of human meanness and pettiness–a world at times salted with real danger, genuine threats, and evil personified.

But here I sit with only one assignment–keep my hand moving. Today, it's just me, with a warming butt, sitting at a picnic table painted in white bird poop, listening to snippets of birdcalls.

Wednesday of last week, I ruled on a Motion to Suppress the confession of Justin, a 17-year-old accused of the First Degree Murder of a 16-year-old co-worker at a local McDonald's. Both boys were in the 10th grade. The cops deeply offended my personal sense of justice and fairness when they took the confession.

I was angry for days; I delayed ruling while I screamed inside, "There is no fucking excuse for this! Cops can do their job AND be fair. Cops can't lean on 17-year-olds, even those who shoot people in the head. My mama always said, 'Two wrongs don't make a right.' The cops were wrong, and they're not entitled to such errors."

I did a great deal of legal research, as well as soul-searching. From a legal standpoint, it appeared I could call it either way. Ball or strike. Suppress or admit the confession. But night after night, I felt no peace, saw no burning bush, felt no assurance. I was inclined to grant the suppression, but ...

My question became, "Do I want to suppress the confession because law enforcement offended my personal morals, or because they violated the law?"

And it certainly didn't help to know that it was a close call, legally.

When Justin's case was called in the crowded courtroom, I was still unsure how I would rule. I took a deep breath and announced I was denying the motion to suppress and would provide the factual basis on the record before we selected the jury. Afterwards, I felt deeply satisfied, with no more intellectual turning or soul twisting, because once I backed out my personal, moral outrage, I understood that the confession should go to the jury so that they could decide a verdict based on all the facts, including the confession and how it was obtained. If I'm wrong and should have suppressed the confession, the kid can appeal me if found guilty, with the benefit of all the facts I gave on the record to show how close the call was. But if I'd suppressed the confession and the kid was then found not guilty, the State could not appeal. The case was a good, messy reminder that this job is not about how I feel; it's about the Law and the facts. I've let the Motion to Suppress go into that huge pile of "I've done the best I know how," a pile subtitled "And I may be wrong."

Friday of last week I also had a hearing on a Motion for Post Conviction Relief in State vs. Suggs. Suggs is one of two men I've sentenced to death– one of two men whose life turns on a decision in which I take no pride. We did the hearing via video teleconferencing; the Defendant was brought from Death Row at Raiford prison to the District Court of Appeal in Tallahassee, a distance of about 100 miles. The Assistant Attorney General and Defense Attorney were with Suggs in a conference room; I was in a courtroom in Pensacola, about 200 miles away, with the Assistant State Attorney.

Convicted of two separate, sophisticated murders, the record describes Suggs as an incredibly dangerous man who presents a real threat to others. In private, I don't pretend to have the moral or ethical answers to cases like this. Yet I'm the one whose job description requires I do battle into the night, night after night, struggling to understand what it means "to do justice." It's my job to separate my own morals from the laws written by the Legislature; I have to remember that I'm only paid to maintain my focus on the law and to follow its dictates.

Suggs has changed a lot in these seven years. He's gained weight and aged. His skin, long caged without sunlight, is the color of a white moth. I would not have recognized him; he probably said the same thing about me.

We discussed finite legal issues that must be resolved before the State can legally kill Suggs for having illegally killed a woman. The *arguments were interesting and the attorneys well prepared, so the hearing was intellectually challenging and satisfying.*

During the hearing Suggs sat at the end of the conference table. He wasn't wearing handcuffs but his ankles were encased in leg irons. After the hearing, the officers asked Suggs to stand, and they began the ritual of getting him ready to transport. I watched as they clamped his wrists into the handcuffs attached to the heavy chain around his waist. Then they ran a second chain from his belly chain down to his leg irons, so he couldn't kick, run, or swing his legs. Shackled like a wild elephant, Suggs shuffled out of the building to the squad car to be returned to Death Row—that inner sanctuary in the bowels of our prison in which people, mostly men and mostly black, wait while their attorneys do battle with the bureaucracy that wants to kill them—legally, of course. In his brief pass through the free world, I hope Suggs caught a glimpse of a monarch butterfly in a patch of sun light and that he heard the high, clear "kaaw" of a gull and the hoarse "caar" of a crow; I wish for him a glimpse of the iridescent neck of a pigeon.

And then this week I handled the jury trial for Justin, the 17-year-old accused of shooting to death Geraldo, a coworker at McDonald's. The prosecutor did not ask for the death penalty, so a verdict of guilty as charged would result in a mandatory sentence of life in prison without parole.

The second day of testimony, I tried to back away from the emotional toll of yet another murder trial. I took a blank legal pad to the courtroom, and as the witnesses testified, I made a list of personal items I wanted specifically distributed on my death. (I wasn't planning on dying soon, but I decided to get myself organized before I quit the daytime job.) As I listened to a teenage McDonald employee testify that the Defendant said, "I shot him. And the mother-fucker died in his uniform," I wrote, "The large porcelain horse figurine titled Black Beauty goes to my friend Sara." I learned the trick from other judges who have sent me personal e-mails from the Bench while in the middle of a trial. It looked for the world like I was taking trial notes.

It was interesting how short my list is, the list of things I value enough to give away. It wasn't interesting to watch the deceased's very young mother on the stand. She had one of those voices that spoke with quiet strength though she was barely able to breathe. When the Prosecutor asked her to ID her son's glasses, her face melted in incalculable sorrow.

I asked if she needed a moment; she stood and spoke from a place deep down inside, "I have to leave now."

I replied, "You may leave, but we'll need to call you back later to finish the questioning." Then I gave both attorneys a look that clearly said, "Don't you dare object!" She walked out of the courtroom, unaware of anything except her shattered soul.

The Prosecutor crisply called the next witness, and I resumed my list making. "My dad's desk lamp to my brother, Mac." So how could I be so distant? I don't know. I just thought I'd try it this way to see if it helped, helped the trial time pass by and helped lessen the emotional impact of another violent death.

But it didn't.

The Medical Examiner explained the autopsy and described the path of the bullet. The State introduced the X-ray of Geraldo's 16-year-old skull showing what looked like a white marker behind his right eye, a marker that went in as a .25 caliber bullet and then stopped. A bullet that stopped Geraldo, stopped him from going back to school or work, and stopped his 17th birthday. It also stopped the hope of his mother; it blew her dreams into shards as unrecognizable as that white "thing" on his X-ray. And there were color photos of his dead hands. Geraldo's fingers were long and thin; his hands were clearly dead. Hands no longer able to hold or be held. I didn't want this advanced study in dead hands or the graduate degree in the depth of grief of a young mother. I didn't want to watch another young man alive in the courtroom mocking responsibility.

Making that list of personal items in Court didn't change a thing, except that I felt guilty and callous. I was technically correct and alert, but I tried repeatedly to hit the mute button on the humanity of the day. I tried to watch the action without acknowledging its reality.

But the reality remained; Geraldo was still dead. His mother's grief was still too vast and heavy to contain in a mere courtroom. Justin slept again in the county jail, and the next day we'd tee up and go again. And I promised myself I wouldn't hit the mute button.

After the close of the evidence in the McDonald murder trial and while the jury was deliberating, the State handed me a warrant for a new charge on Justin, alleging a crime committed while in jail (which is not easy to do). He was charged with an Unnatural Act in Public; the warrant alleges that he jacked off while in the van in route back to the jail from my last docket day (when his attorney argued why I should suppress his confession to this murder) and that he then reached through the cage at the front of the bus to smear his semen on a female inmate. He laughed and thought it was a great joke. After his semen-smearing escapade, he wrote me a Jesus-letter, explaining he'd been saved and therefore didn't need to go to prison; he didn't explain the murder or the semen smearing.

At 6:45 p.m., after five and a half hours, the jury found Justin guilty of First Degree Premeditated Murder. I read the verdict to the crowd in the Courtroom that included the victim's mother, the victim's girlfriend, the Defendant's parents, the Defendant's girlfriend, 30 to 40 people, a TV camera, a still camera, and a newscaster. The facts were certainly there to support the verdict, but because of the Defendant's age, I was a little surprised that the jury came back with First Degree Murder.

Though he was only 17, Justin didn't elicit a lot of sympathy. As the clerk polled the jury (asked them one at a time "Is this your verdict?"), he glared at them with a steely look subject to various interpretations, none of them gentle or humble.

Generally, a convicted defendant is not sentenced immediately upon the return of the verdict because there are reports to be filed, testimony taken from both the State and Defense, and arguments presented on the nature of the sentence. Because the jurors are not involved with the sentencing decision, it is a common practice to schedule sentencing for a later day and excuse the jury. But for several years, when the reports are not required and only one sentence is possible—for Justin, life in prison—I have imposed sentence while the jury was still in the courtroom on the theory they've been here this long, they might as well know the final score.

With the jurors still in the jury box, I asked the Defense attorney "Is there any legal reason why sentence should not now be imposed?"

The attorneys requested to approach the Bench, and the Prosecutor quietly asked me to excuse the jury before sentencing. I scowled at him, and he added, "They'll read it in the paper tomorrow anyway."

I snapped, "They might as well know the rest of the story."

I was in my all-business mode. I was ready to finish this case; I was ready to go home. I glanced at my watch and hoped to make my yoga class. But I didn't look at this unique jury before making the decision to have them observe the sentencing.

I said, "Will the Defendant approach the Bench." The State Attorney sat down, and Justin stood beside his lawyer. To educate the jury—for Justin knew this all too well—I talked about the fact that the State could have requested the death penalty for First Degree Murder but had chosen not to, and that the Legislature had set the punishment for First Degree Murder at Life in Prison. I noted that he had an outstanding warrant, appointed the Public Defender to represent him on that case, and scheduled it for arraignment. This wasn't necessary either, for the new charge would have been automatically assigned to a docket, but now that the jury had reached a verdict, I wanted them to know he had other charges pending. Then I sentenced Justin to life in prison without parole for First Degree Murder. The Defendant acted as though I had placed an order for French fries at his drive-up window.

As the Bailiff began to fingerprint Justin, I finally looked over at the jury. A man on the front row was trying to bite back tears from his now very red face; and a woman on the second row sobbed quietly as her shoulders gently shook. So much for my Civics lesson, so much for providing some closure for the jury.

Justin's sentence would have been the same if I had first excused the jury. Did I lean too hard on this unique group by requiring that they see the legal results of their verdict?

I was satisfied with the verdict for the facts were definitely here. I also knew that though we "did justice," Geraldo is still dead.

I adjourned court and stepped into the back hall. There I took off my robe and handed it to Andy, the deputy assigned to me for this trial. We walked to my office and then down to my car in the judges' parking lot. He checked the sidewalks, stood in the road to stop traffic, and motioned for me to pull out. I smiled, "That's a nice touch, on a bad day." So I came home alone, late to a dark house. And I didn't make it to my yoga class.

I've sentenced my youngest, a 17-year-old, to life in prison without parole. Do I notch the handle of my gun? Fall down on my knees in prayer? Act like the sentence—or Geraldo's death—is no big deal, just another day at work?

In the midst of this ordinary day of dealing with extraordinary problems, I agreed to an interview by a reporter from the local paper about my retirement plans. When the jury began its deliberations in Justin's trial, my assistant called and the reporter came over to the office. I was a little nervous and wondered, "After many years of being politically correct while holding my cards close to my chest, dare I speak openly now?" I took a deep breath and a huge risk as I disclosed to the reporter my humanity and my hopes. On this routine day of heightened judicial demeanor and tough calls in the courtroom, I made sure the reporter spelled my dog's name right. At the same time, I felt awkward about such personal disclosures, disclosures always scorned by my colleagues because they show humanity, that which the robe is designed to hide. Disclosures that might also increase my visibility and vulnerability to those who would harm me if they had the chance.

I got to work early the morning after Justin's sentencing and went down to the snack bar to pick up coffee and the newspaper. I was both anxious and curious to see how I fared with my public disclosure to the reporter about my retirement plans.

On the front page was an article about my retirement that included my interview. The reporter obviously had fun, and she made me shine! She even included a large pleasant photo of me in my robe, and the caption under it read "When Judge Melvin retires in May, she says she looks forward to traveling 'in the coolest pickup ever'" I laughed. I had passed another challenge without being blown to bits.

And how did they handle the news of the verdict in the murder trial? There was a lengthy article on the first page of the local section that included a second photo of me, this time as the bad-ass-in-the-robe. I guess the Universe wanted to be sure that anyone who read the front page article of my retirement with criticism of my skydiving, writing, and traveling would see I could also be tough.

I couldn't buy that much or that kind of publicity. Ever. Much less on my way out the door.

Back in the office I had a phone call from the Victim's Advocate, relaying a message from Geraldo's mother and extended family from Illinois. The message was—"Thank you for correctly pronouncing Geraldo's name. Thank you for the respect you showed our culture. It meant a lot to our family." I listened with my mouth open. Such a tiny thing, calling him by his true name. I felt awkward with the attention, like being told thank you for ... breathing.

The following week a super-sized tin box of cookies was delivered to my office; this was not an ordinary cookie tin for it contained shapes, colors, and flavors that were mysterious to me. Attached to the tin box was a card from Geraldo's mother, "Thank you for correctly pronouncing my son's name. Now that the trial and sentencing are over, perhaps the hole in our hearts can begin to heal." A family dealing with such deep, impossible issues taking the time to send cookies?

Of course, Judges aren't supposed to accept gifts from litigants (a gift can also be called a bribe). But how could I return cookies to a grieving mother? At the end of the day, I stood behind closed doors in the quiet courthouse and opened the box, took a cookie, and with my mouth full, examined my judicial dilemma.

As I munched, I pondered, "OK, would eating a gift from a litigant be prosecuted as the felony, 'Tampering with or Destroying Evidence?' Would the case law be that which we apply to defendants *who chew and swallow their crack cocaine when cornered?" I ate several more cookies and continued the debate of those complex legal issues. Then, with the cookie tin under my arm, I left for the day. Later, to scatter the evidence, magic, and calories, I divided the cookies, put them in plastic bags, and gave them away, without explanation.*

In the New Testament story of the birth of Christ, after the shepherds left and the hullabaloo had begun to die down, Luke says, "Mary kept all these things, and pondered them in her heart." (Luke 2:19)

I don't have a clue what these things mean, but I'm pondering them.

❅ ❅ ❅

The coffee is cold; I look down at the floor and shake my head. I return to the counter for fresh coffee and add chocolate chip cookies to my order. With the first bite, I wish for another exotic cookie from Geraldo's mother.

I continue my push eastward on Interstate 10, toward Will and his hiccups. I'm in Texas, driving through heavy ground fog with a temperature of 34 degrees. There are patches of snow and ice in the ditches. I'm amazed (this cold on Interstate 10?!?) and a little scared. Being born and raised in LA (that part of Northwest Florida known as Lower Alabama), I know nothing about pulling a heavy trailer through that white, slippery stuff. I didn't mind getting delayed in Northern California by the winds, but I don't want to get pinned down in Texas for God-knows-how-long by snow and ice on I-10, not when Will has the hiccups. When it begins to sleet, I turn off the radio and sit up straight, with both hands on the steering wheel. I take a deep breath and decide to push on, hoping to outrun the ice storm. I figure I'll drive to San Antonio before stopping, though that means I'll be on the road for maybe an hour after dark. Around 4 p.m. I stop at an authentic truck stop; this is not a stop favored by the owner-operated rigs that look like rolling Christmas trees at night, the purple semi's pulling trailers decorated with elaborate designs, or the meticulously cleaned ones pulling trailers with curtain sides of soft canvas to hide the top-dollar sports cars. No, this is an uneven cement parking lot with stripped-down, dirty tractor-trailers pulling fertilizer, heavy equipment, and other sturdy stuff. I pump my diesel and go inside where it's warm and small. The two truckers waiting to pay for fuel include me in their banter.

I say, "It's sleeting out there." One guy laughs and replies, "It don't count if I can still see the hood of my truck." He's heading to San Antonio to unload and then drive home to Lake Wales, Florida, for Thanksgiving. He smiles, "I'll be in San Antonio in about three hours."

My heart sinks; I thought I had only an hour left in this weather. I buy a large coffee and a hot cinnamon roll, a personal bribe to keep moving. As I walk back to Bruin and my rig, I begin working on my attitude, telling myself that I can drive another three hours in the sleet.

Back on the road, I finish off the coffee and cinnamon roll. The cruise control is holding our speed at 75 MPH, and I have my left foot propped on the door. Suddenly, the truck slows down and the tach shows that the RPM's have dropped from 2,100 to 1,000. I sit up, put both feet on the floor, and mutter, "What in the hell is wrong now?!?" as I shift from 5th to 4th gear. The RPM's go back up to 2,000 and the truck begins pulling. I shift to 5th, the RPM's drop, and the truck slows. "Shit! Now what?" I pull out my handy-dandy index of all the Interstate exits, lay it across the console, and find an exit not so far down the road that has a truck stop, RV park, and a motel. I drive on in 4th gear. It's dark when I pull in to find the RV park closed and deserted. Though the park is a little spooky, I decide I'll stay there for the night, locked in my 5th wheel, if I can just get power. So I pull into a slot, yank the hood of my jacket over my head, step out into the sleet, and plug the 5th wheel into an outlet. There's no electricity.

"Shit! Just what I need. Another AFGE!" I mumble. "Why do I only meet Another Fucking Growth Experience when I'm too damn tired to grow!" I don't want to stay in that deserted RV park without electricity; I'm exhausted, cold, and fantasizing about my electric blanket. I don't want to run the generator in the bed of the pickup because I'm not willing to go outside in the middle of the night in this desolate spot and miserable weather if something goes awry. I pull out of the RV park and explain to Bruin, "If they take dogs in this motel, we're sleeping inside tonight. I want a long hot tub bath. And if not, we'll park with the truckers next door." The motel takes us both for $68. This is the first night we've stayed in a motel since leaving Florida, and we're only here now because of the weather and that #@&* transmission. I park the truck and 5th wheel near our room, which is on the deserted, dark side of the motel–a place my parents would tell me I have no business being. Before going to our room, I take Bruin for a walk. He keeps pulling on his leash to get into the truck or the RV. He makes it clear he doesn't want to be out here.

I say softly, "It's going to be OK, buddy." Then with a catch in my voice, I add, "Now, it's your turn to tell me, 'It's going to be OK.'" I move toward a dark grassy area and suddenly I'm looking into the face of a deer maybe 50 feet away. She and I stare quietly at each other. I feel my shoulders relax and my heart smile. I exhale a murmur, "OK, it's going to be OK." She moves into the shadows, and I see four more deer grazing in the open field between the motel and deserted RV park. I laugh out loud, "I get the message. It's really going to be OK."

Bruin and I go into a motel room larger than the 5th wheel. I soak in a hot tub of water and play on the Internet. I put Bruin's food and water in the bathroom and lay his bed down at the foot of mine. He won't eat, but paces between the bowls and the front door making small questioning sounds as he looks at me. When I get in bed, he lays down against the door for the night.

Staring at the ceiling, I consider my options. Tomorrow is Sunday, and Thanksgiving is on Thursday. I know I have to have the transmission repairs done by a Dodge dealer to have them covered by warranty. I also know I could wait at the motel until Monday, try to schedule an appointment with Dodge in San Antonio, to then be told they have to order a part. Factor in the holidays, and it could be ten days or more before I get back on the road.

Though we had major problems when I was in Florida for the birth of my grandson, Sunday morning I decide to call Al. I'd read an anonymous definition of forgiveness that helped: "Forgiveness is me giving up my right to hurt you for hurting me." I no longer thought of Al in hurtful terms, and I trust his mechanical judgment. This is the first time we've talked since I left; it feels good. He listens as I explain the problem with the truck.

Then I ask, "So now what? I don't want to get stuck here forever, while they order parts. What if I just drive it like it is?"

He replies, "You must have blown fifth gear but don't worry. You won't hurt the truck by driving it in fourth. You could drive it across the country in first gear if you wanted to, but it'd take a little longer. Just keep an eye on the tach, don't strain the engine, and take your time. You'll be fine." I hang up with a smile and a plan.

Bruin and I check out of the motel and start home. Driving the truck at 2,000 RPMS in fourth gear produces a top speed of 52 MPH, but being stuck in West Texas would be worse. The truck still lurches and jumps each time I accelerate through 40 MPH, but by now I'm pretty good at minimizing the bump and grind of the behemoths.

Stoked with coffee, donuts, and aspirin, I just keep driving for 900 miles. Al calls several times to check on us, and, as he predicted, the transmission pulls fine in 4th gear. Slowing down to 50 MPH adds a new dimension to the trip. As we plod along, I laugh and tell Bruin "It's all OK. We need to get home. Will has the hiccups."

I have plenty of time to think as I plod east on the boring, endless stretch of cement that crosses Texas. I lumber down Interstate 10 with lots of questions and memories that make me smile, but with few answers or certainties.

In honor of my Rule of Fours, I've off-loaded items in route and have managed to keep the number of coffee cups and blue jeans in line. The truck could best be described using four-letter words, and I've had four major mechanical problems with it–I blew the clutch in Washington, crunched the side in Oregon, lurched from Montana to Texas where I am now driving without fifth gear. Four states have worked on but failed to fix its lurching–Montana, Washington, California, and Arizona. On a lighter note, I've made skydives in Colorado, Montana, Washington, and Arizona, and have the bumper stickers on the rear of the RV to prove it.

Moving in and out of time zones, I've finally gotten my eye off the clock. It's become easy to lose track of the day of the week and the week of the month. Alone much of the time, I've faced the great demon of loneliness. I think that skirmish is a draw.

I've learned something about listening, hope, courage, and stubbornness. Perhaps the most important and difficult thing we can do is to truly listen. If you bump into Melissa Fox in New York, ask her about the importance of someone listening and believing you. Ask the recently adopted twelve-year-old about hope. You could ask the five-year-old witness about courage though she may not know what the word means. But watch how she handled herself on the witness stand, and you'll see a lot of courage in a small container. Sometimes stubborn pays off; ask Jewel's foster mom about stubborn and she'll tell you about love.

Trudging down Interstate 10, I admit I've busted my

knuckles on a long list of mechanical problems. I guess I'd
have to describe myself as stubborn, but that's not necessarily
a bad thing. Some friends suggested, "Why don't you just park
that damn truck and fly home?" But there's no way I'll leave
the truck–quit, give up–not until I get it figured out and prove
to myself I can handle it. If I quit, I won't have my tail
between my legs. And then there's this other problem–I can't
fly home because I don't know where home is. Feels like it's
everywhere and nowhere. Feels like I need to go back to
Florida, not to Be Home, but to spend precious time with Will.

"You can't step in the same river twice."
Heraclitus

NORTHWEST FLORIDA:
Back at the beginning?

After dark on Tuesday before Thanksgiving, I pull into
Milton 10,000 miles and 174 days after I drove away. I stay
at an RV park on Interstate 10, about five miles from my
parents' home. It feels weird being back. I'm home, and I'm
not. My parents are dead. After more than 20 years, I'm no
longer part of the legal circle. An important personal
relationship has ended. This world of live oaks and Spanish
moss looks the same, but everything is different.

The next morning I make an appointment with Hill Kelley
Dodge in Pensacola to repair fifth gear. When I drop the truck
off, I explain to yet another mechanic the problem with the
truck lurching.

He nods, takes a few notes, and says, "We'll fix you up,
ma'am. And I think I know what's causing that lurch." The
truck is ready early the next day. With little hope I ask about
the lurching problem.

The mechanic responds, "You're good to go, ma'am. Don't
think you'll have any more problems."

I sputter, "You mean you fixed the lurch?!?"

"Yes, ma'am. It was just a $26 spring on the fuel injector pump, and it's covered by warranty. Just like you thought, the 5th gear cog broke off. But you're good to go now. No charge today 'cause it's all under warranty."

I drive my finally-repaired truck to Clay's house, and I stay with Will while his parents work. Will snuggles up against my chest as we rock. I smile. I still have lots of questions and few answers. I don't know where my home is, but my heart is right here with my grandson. Today, I'll enjoy the view through his eyes.

"It is unwise to be too sure of one's own wisdom. It is healthy to be reminded that the strongest might weaken and the wisest might err."
Mohandas K. Gandhi

POSTSCRIPT:

Years have passed since I left the Bench yet I still ponder what it means to do justice. Throughout the history of the United States, laws have defined justice in various ways, and today we recognize many of those earlier definitions as fundamentally unfair, immoral, and unjust. In the late 1600's women were legally hanged as convicted witches in Salem, Massachusetts. 150 years ago a black person in the South could be legally killed for the crime of striking a white person, regardless of the circumstance. At the same time, it was legal for a white person to chain, beat, rape, or kill a black person for any reason or no reason at all; under the law, justice required that you pay the owner for damages to his property if the black person wasn't your own slave. Blacks were not allowed to vote until the 15th Amendment was ratified in 1870; women were denied the right to vote until the 19th Amendment in 1920.

The Legislature continues to define justice–somewhat in response to the voters but with an ear closely tuned to the changing demands of special interest groups who benefit financially from certain laws and provide significant contributions to the Legislators. Many of our criminal laws seem to view people as intrinsically evil and violent and therefore the State is justified in doing whatever it takes to punish them. Yet history tends to repeat itself, so I predict that many of the crimes of today will become obsolete and viewed in the future as unfair and unjust.

Dad used to say that the ground in front of the Bench is level, with equal access to all. A worthy goal if not a reality in the press of the modern work-a-day world of doing justice.

We have a fundamentally sound legal system, but not a perfect one. I think it is good to ponder the meaning of justice, to not be naive about the realities surrounding us, or the motivation behind specific laws.

I was traveling in New Mexico ten years after I retired when I went to my first Quaker Meeting. I felt like the Ugly Duckling who had finally landed in a pond with other swans. I realize I've always been a Quaker, I just didn't know it. Quakers are impossible to pigeon-hole but these words written in 1667 by Isaac Pennington while in Aylebury Prison under the most dire conditions because of his religious beliefs, represent something of the moral standard that Quakers strive for: "Our life is love, and peace, and tenderness; and bearing one with another, and forgiving one another, and not laying accusations one against another; but praying one for another and helping one another up with a tender hand." I have a limited amount of time and energy in this one life that I've been given; today I choose to focus on love, peace, and tenderness rather than being in charge of punishing people or imposing rigid rules onto their lives.

William Penn, the founder of the Commonwealth of Pennsylvania and early champion of democracy and religious freedom, became a Quaker at the age of 22, much to the horror of his aristocratic father, Admiral Sir William Penn. There is a widely told parable that is instructive of Penn's Quaker beliefs of pacifism. As a young man, Penn, like his father, wore expensive clothes and a sword at his side. After Penn joined the Quakers, he was a frequent companion of George Fox (founder of the Quaker movement); Penn asked Fox about continuing to wear the sword, which was not in keeping with Quaker beliefs. Fox responded, "Wear it as long as thou canst." The legend continues that when Penn later met Fox, without his sword, Penn explained, "I took thy advice; I wore it as long as I could."

A judge is in the business of forcing people to do what the

Legislators dictate. There is a limited place for coercion of those who are socially, emotionally, or mentally immature, but it's no longer my place. I wore my robe as long and as well as I could. My place, today, is in a beautiful world of diverse nature, adventure, kind strangers, beautiful children of all sizes and shapes; my business includes playing with my own grandchildren, helping people in various ways, and, of course, traveling.

After 600 jumps, I gave up skydiving because of a health issue, and I bought my first motorcycle at the age of 59. With both sports, your life depends upon remaining focused, in the moment, as you respond physically to ever-changing stimuli. For me, the bike is deeply satisfying; riding is something like skydiving except I can ride alone in the rain and I don't have to pay for a jump plane. There is something intrinsic about being on a bike out in the elements; you can smell the plowed field before you round the corner to see the tractor pulling a disk; you can smell a grill getting hot and sometimes even figure out what's cooking; you feel the temperature drop as the road dips into a hollow by the creek; you're conscious of your direction of travel because on how the sun shines in your face; you lean into the wind as needed when it begins to blow perpendicular to the bike; you watch the sky for changes in the weather and when on-coming traffic has headlights on, you consider stopping to put on rain gear. I love making long-distance bike trips because then I get to string together days and days of experiencing this country, without being caged inside a sound-proof, heated/air conditioned box.

I'd never managed to stay gone on the bike long enough to want the trip to end. So at the age of 64, I thought I'd take a very long trip while my body was still cooperating with my adventurous spirit. I decided to ride around the four geographic corners of the country–from Milton, Florida, west to San Isidro, California; then north to Blaine, Washington; turn east to Madawaska, Maine; head south to Key West,

Florida, and then northwest back to Milton. And while I was vicinity, I might as well go up into Canada because I'd never ridden up there and then over to Nova Scotia to watch the tide change at Fundy. I knew I'd have fun but perhaps I could also put a smile on a kid's face. So I made it an awareness/fund-raising ride for four child-focused charities (Shriners' Hospital, Ronald McDonald House, Habitat for Humanity, and the Child Advocacy Centers), and dubbed it 4 Corners 4 Kids. I set up a blog site, GypsyJudge.com, a Face Book page, "4 Corners 4 Kids," and had post cards printed explaining my trip with links to my blog and the four charities. I didn't collect donations but directed people to the charities to give their time or money. I bought a Goldwing (900-plus pounds of Tupperware and farkels balanced on two wheels), packed a tent and other essentials and took off alone. I scheduled stops at each of the charities, tent-camped some, stayed in motels when I wanted, and visited with friends and friends of friends. I was also able to attend several Quaker Meetings around the country. Seven weeks and 12,000 miles later, I returned to Milton. I rode for six weeks and sat down for one–a day or two here or there, waiting for my appointment at the next media event scheduled by a charity or simply resting. Seven weeks after leaving, I was disappointed when I pulled into the driveway for I was not ready for the trip to be over.

The downside to that much time alone on a bike, to realizing I could do things I'd never imagined–tent camping across the country, riding in every kind of weather, handling the bike in situations I might never have encountered. The downside to focusing on children's charities–spending time with children who were crippled, missing limbs, horrifically burned, or terminally ill, watching them smile and realizing that all they want is the chance to be kids. Talking with the grownups whose passion it is to help these children and their families, without pitying them; sharing the camaraderie of the volunteers who delight in building houses for low-income families and their children; talking with those willing to do the hard work required to be the voice of child victims. Well, the downside was that I came back feral—unable to politely engage in cocktail talk, indulge mean-spiritedness, or ignore malicious conversations. So I felt even more separated from the social world, and that was just fine by me.

The first morning back, I rode the Goldwing to the Milton cemetery. With a big smile on my face, I stood at my parents' double headstone, and we talked. I told them about my adventures—the date trees growing in the deserts of Arizona, the snow in the Washington Cascades, some of the kind strangers I met. I laughed as I told Mom I took her good-looking eyes with me and that the tide change at Fundy in Nova Scotia was more magnificent than the pictures in her National Geographic. Soon, it was time for me to leave again. I walked around to the back side of their tombstone—the one that marks the place where neither of my parents are buried—and I read

"For all that has been, Thanks. For all that will be, Yes."
Dag Hammarskjold

CPSIA information can be obtained at www.ICGtesting.com
Printed in the USA
LVOW13s0329211013

357763LV00002B/6/P